STUDY GUIDE
VOLUME 1, CHAPTERS 1-14
INTERMEDIATE ACCOUNTING
13e

K. Fred Skousen, PhD, CPA
Brigham Young University

Earl K. Stice, PhD
Hong Kong University of Science & Technology

James D. Stice, PhD
Brigham Young University

Prepared by
Sara York Kenny
College of Saint Mary

SOUTH-WESTERN College Publishing

An International Thomson Publishing Company

Accounting Team Director: Richard Lindgren
Senior Acquisitions Editor: David L. Shaut
Senior Marketing Manager: Sharon Oblinger
Developmental Editor: Leslie Kauffman
Production Editor: Rebecca Glaab/Mark Sears
Production House: Laurie Merz

Copyright © 1998
by South-Western College Publishing
Cincinnati, Ohio

International Thomson Publishing
South-Western is an ITP Company. The ITP trademark is used under license.

ALL RIGHTS RESERVED
The text of this publication, or any part thereof, may not be reproduced or transmitted in any form or by any means, electronic or mechanical, including photocopying, recording, storage in an information retrieval system, or otherwise, without prior written permission of the publisher.

Material from Uniform CPA Examination Questions and Unofficial Answers, Copyright 1980, 1983, 1985, 1986, 1987, 1988, 1989, 1990, 1991, 1992, 1993, 1994, and 1995 by the American Institute of Certified Public Accountants, Inc., is reprinted or adapted with permission.

ISBN: 0-538-86725-6

1 2 3 4 5 6 7   PN   3 2 1 0 9 8 7

Printed in the United States of America

Contents

1. FINANCIAL REPORTING 1
2. A REVIEW OF THE ACCOUNTING CYCLE 13
3. THE BALANCE SHEET AND NOTES TO THE FINANCIAL STATEMENTS 27
4. THE INCOME STATEMENT 41
5. THE STATEMENT OF CASH FLOWS 59
6. THE REVENUE/RECEIVABLES/CASH CYCLE 79
7. COMPLEXITIES OF REVENUE RECOGNITION 103
8. COST OF GOODS SOLD AND INVENTORY—IDENTIFICATION AND VALUATION 125
9. COST OF GOODS SOLD AND INVENTORY—ESTIMATION AND NONCOST VALUATION 147
10. DEBT FINANCING 165
11. EQUITY FINANCING 187
12. INVESTMENTS IN NONCURRENT OPERATING ASSETS—ACQUISITION 205
13. INVESTMENTS IN NONCURRENT OPERATING ASSETS—UTILIZATION AND RETIREMENT 219
14. INVESTMENTS IN DEBT AND EQUITY SECURITIES 233

CHAPTER 1

FINANCIAL REPORTING

KEY POINTS

I. Purpose of Financial Reporting and Primary Financial Statements
   A. Provide information useful in decision making.
   B. Who are the decision makers?
      1. *Stakeholders*:
         a. Internal: people who work for the company, including management and employees.
         b. External: people who invest in the company or are affected by its activities, such as shareholders, creditors, customers, vendors, government agencies and the general public.
   C. Primary financial statements provide information to decision makers:
      1. *Balance Sheet*: listing at a given point in time of the company's assets, liabilities, and shareholders' equity.
      2. *Income Statement*: report of the company's earnings during the period.
      3. *Statement of Cash Flows*: detailing of cash receipts and disbursements during the period.
      4. *Notes to Financial Statements*: supplemental information presented that outlines accounting assumptions and estimates and provides supplemental information to the financial statements.
   D. Auditor: external professional who provides opinions regarding the fairness of presentation of the information in the primary financial statements.
      1. Auditor issues opinions summarizing her findings:
         a. Unqualified (financial statements are fairly presented)
         b. Unqualified with Explanatory Language (financial statements are unqualified but there is an issue in them which needs further discussion or clarification)
         c. Qualified (auditor disagrees with accounting treatment the firm used for some item in the financial statements)
         d. No Opinion (auditor refuses to express an opinion)
         e. Adverse (auditor believes the financial statements are not in accordance with generally accepted accounting principles)

II. Function of Accounting Standards and How Standards are set in the United States
   A. Function: codify consistent and comparable techniques for measuring and recording certain types of economic events.
   B. Standards setting hierarchy:
      1. After Great Depression, SEC was created to oversee public trading of securities.
      2. SEC is responsible for establishing accounting standards.
      3. SEC generally allows professional standards setting bodies, such as the FASB, to perform this function.
   C. Standards setting is a sequential process:
      1. Item is first placed on FASB's agenda.
      2. FASB studies the item and issues *Discussion Memorandum (DM)*.
      3. Public commentary on the DM is encouraged.
      4. FASB studies public commentary and issues *Exposure Draft (ED)*, which is a proposed standard.
      5. More public commentary and FASB deliberation.
      6. *Statement of Financial Accounting Standard (SFAS)* issued.
   D. Standards setting process is lengthy.
      1. Emerging Issues Task Force (EITF) established to quickly address urgent issues.

III. Standards Setting Organizations
   A. U.S. organizations:
      1. FASB (current professional standards setting body in the U.S., responsible for accounting standards for for-profit entities)
      2. APB (predecessor to the FASB)
      3. CAP (predecessor to the APB)

4. GASB (current professional standards setting body in the U.S., responsible for accounting standards for governmental entities)
5. FAF (Financial Accounting Foundation, the oversight organization for the FASB and the GASB)
6. AAA (professional organization of accounting academics and practitioners that advises and comments to the FASB)
7. AICPA (American Institute of Certified Public Accountants, the professional organization for CPA's)
B. International Accounting Standards Committee (IASC)
1. International professional body charged with the development of a set of worldwide or "harmonized" accounting standards.
C. GAAP Hierarchy
1. Review Exhibit 1-5 carefully.

IV. Conceptual Framework of Accounting
A. Definition: underlying theoretical premises on which accounting standards and practices rest.
B. FASB articulated six statements of financial accounting concepts dealing with four major issues:
1. *Objectives*: purposes of financial reporting.
2. *Qualitative Characteristics*: characteristics accounting information must possess to meet objectives.
3. *Elements:* definitions of the items measured in financial accounting.
4. *Recognition, Measurement, and Reporting*: how to impound financial ramifications of economic events into the financial statements, i.e., when and how to write the journal entry.
C. *Objectives* of financial reporting: *who* needs *what* information and *why*.
1. Overall objective: provide information useful for decision making.
2. Key financial reporting objectives:
a. Usefulness.
b. Understandability.
c. Target audience: investors and creditors.
d. Assessing future cash flows.
e. Evaluating economic resources.
f. Primary focus on earnings.
D. *Qualitative Characteristics* of Accounting Information (Review Exhibit 1-6 in the text)
1. Overriding quality: *Decision Usefulness*
a. Information must be useful.
b. All other qualitative characteristics are evaluated in terms of their enhancement to decision usefulness.
2. Primary qualities:
a. Benefits greater than cost.
b. *Relevance*: the capacity to make a difference. Relevance is measured in terms of the users' perspectives.
1) Feedback value: confirms or alters expectations.
2) Predictive value: reduce uncertainty about the future.
3) Timeliness: received quickly enough to make a difference.
c. *Reliability*: freedom from error or intentional bias.
1) Verifiability: can be confirmed, and is thus, objective.
2) Representational faithfulness: measures what it reports to measure.
3) Neutrality: without bias, does not favor one user over another.
3. Secondary qualities
a. *Comparability*: relates to a known benchmark, such as other time periods or other companies.
b. *Consistency*: use the same accounting principles from one period to another and in similar situations.
4. Constraints
a. *Materiality*: significance, in terms of either net income or total assets.
E. *Elements* of Financial Statements
(Hint: be sure you study Exhibit 1-7 in the text carefully)
1. *Assets*: resources owned or controlled by the entity which will produce future economic benefits.
2. *Liabilities*: obligations that will require sacrifices of economic resources in the future.
3. *Equity*: also called "net assets," equity is the residual interest: Assets minus liabilities = equity.
4. *Investments by owners*: equity increases as a result of the receipt of resources from owners.
5. *Distributions to owners*: equity decreases as a result of payment or distribution of resources to owners.

6. *Comprehensive income*: change in equity during the period resulting from transactions and events not associated with owners' activities.
7. *Revenue*: inflows of resources from ongoing operating activities.
8. *Expenses*: outflows of resources from ongoing operating activities.
9. *Gains*: net inflows from peripheral activities.
10. *Losses*: net outflows from peripheral activities.

F. *Recognition, Measurement, and Reporting*: *what* to include in financial statements, *when* to include, and *how* to record the amount.
   1. *Recognize* if: item meets definition of one of the elements of financial statement.
   2. *Measure* using: historical cost or exchange price generally; however, other bases of measurement will be used for certain elements.
      a. Other bases of measurement include:
         Current replacement cost
         Current market value
         Net realizable value
         Present value
   3. *Reporting* includes: financial statements indicating all of the following items:
      a. Financial position at the end of the period.
      b. Earnings for the period.
      c. Cash flows for the period.
      d. Investments by and distributions to owners during the period.
      e. Comprehensive income.

V. Careers in Financial Accounting
   A. Public accounting
      1. Serves a variety of businesses and individuals.
      2. Traditionally the focus of public accountants has been auditing.
      3. Now, however, consulting services represent a major segment of the public accountants' activities and services.
      4. Public accountants are usually CPA's (*C*ertified *P*ublic *A*ccountant).
      5. Requirements to become a CPA:
         a. Pass the CPA exam;
         b. Satisfy educational and work experience requirements (these vary from state to state).
   B. Company accounting
      1. Accountants employed by one company to fulfill a variety of firm specific accounting activities, such as external and internal financial reporting, tax accounting, and internal auditing.
   C. User of accounting information
      1. Professionals in other business areas, such as banking, analysis, or consulting, who use accounting information, but who generally do not prepare it.

TEST YOUR UNDERSTANDING

Fill-in-the-Blanks

Required: Fill in the blanks to complete the following sentences.

1. _____ includes _____ and _____ issued by the FASB and those pronouncements issued by previous standards setting bodies that have not been suspended or superceded.

2. One major purpose of the conceptual framework is to provide broad definitions of the _____, _____ _____, and _____ _____ underlying accounting standards and practices.

3. The overall objective of financial reporting is to provide information that is useful for _____ _____ by present and potential creditors and investors.

4. The overriding quality or characteristic of accounting information is _____ _____.

Chapter 1

5. Relevant information normally provides _____ _____, _____ _____, and _____.

6. _____ _____ helps to confirm or change a decision maker's beliefs based on whether the information matches what is expected.

7. The three key ingredients of reliability are _____, _____, and _____.

8. The _____ _____ _____ _____ is an international group, based in London and representing accounting bodies in over 80 countries. It is charged with the goal of developing a set of _____ international accounting standards that can be applied worldwide.

9. The _____ _____ is a report about the fairness of a company's financial statements, issued by an _____ after reviewing the company's financial records.

10. An _____ opinion indicates that the financial statements are not in accordance with GAAP.

11. An _____ opinion indicates that the financial statements are in compliance with GAAP.

12. _____ is the process of formally recording an item in the accounting records and eventually reporting it in the financial statements.

13. _____ _____ is the change in equity of a business enterprise during a period from transactions and other events and circumstances from nonowner sources.

14. The cash equivalent price that would be paid currently to replace goods or services is called the _____ _____ _____.

15. The amount of cash expected to be received from conversion of assets in the normal course of business is the _____ _____ _____.

Multiple Choice

Required: Circle the best answer.

1. The purpose of accounting is to provide:
    A. useful information.
    B. quantitative information.
    C. useful quantitative information for decision makers.
    D. information about economic events.

2. The FASB issues all of the following types of documents except:
    A. Exposure Drafts.
    B. Statements of Position.
    C. Discussion Memorandum.
    D. Statements of Financial Accounting Standards.

3. The FASB's due process generally proceeds in what order?
    A. Discussion memorandum, statement of position, standard
    B. Exposure draft, discussion memorandum, standard
    C. Statement of position, exposure draft, standard
    D. Discussion memorandum, exposure draft, standard

Name: Chapter 1

4. The responsibility of the auditor in performing an independent audit is to examine:
   A. the company's financial statements and make sure they are correct.
   B. the company's books and records to make sure no fraud has occurred.
   C. the company's financial statements and express an opinion regarding the company's adherence to generally accepted accounting principles.
   D. each transaction recorded by the company to ensure that each transaction was recorded in accordance with generally accepted accounting principles.

5. Who is responsible for the preparation of a company's financial statements?
   A. The independent auditors
   B. The Board of Directors
   C. Company management
   D. All of the above

6. Prior to establishment of the FASB, accounting principles in the U.S. were established by:
   A. the IASC.
   B. the AICPA.
   C. the APB.
   D. the SEC.

7. The International Accounting Standards Committee is:
   A. a committee of the FASB that exists to recommend accounting principles to other countries.
   B. a committee of the FASB that exists to recommend accounting principles to U.S. multinational companies.
   C. an international organization that exists to develop worldwide accounting standards.
   D. an international organization that exists to coordinate accounting standards used on foreign stock exchanges.

8. The SEC was created by Congress to:
   A. ensure that investors received reliable and relevant information about publicly traded companies.
   B. oversee financial reporting by all U.S. companies.
   C. replace the APB.
   D. regulate the technical content of accounting principles established by the FASB.

9. The CPA exam is administered by:
   A. colleges and universities and is given to graduating accounting majors to test their technical proficiency in accounting.
   B. the AICPA and is given to candidates who meet various educational requirements.
   C. the AICPA to test technical proficiency and writing skills of candidates who wish to be CPAs.
   D. the AICPA and various colleges and universities to test the candidate's skill in auditing, governmental, tax and financial accounting.

10. The independent auditor is employed by:
    A. the Board of Directors.
    B. the creditors.
    C. the SEC.
    D. the shareholders.

11. The business enterprise viewed as separate and distinct from its owners and from other business enterprises is the accounting concept of:
    A. economic entity.
    B. going concern.
    C. accounting periods.
    D. decision usefulness.

Chapter 1

12. The preparation of financial statements at arbitrary points in time during a company's lifetime illustrates the accounting concept of:
    A. relevance.
    B. timeliness.
    C. accounting periods.
    D. decision usefulness.

13. The assumption that the entity will continue in business at least long enough to meet its current obligations is the accounting concept of:
    A. economic entity.
    B. going concern.
    C. predictive value.
    D. materiality.

14. There are two basic accounting methods to recognize revenue during construction on long-term contracts, the percentage-of-completion method and the completed-contracts method. Sayers Company uses the percentage-of-completion method for all of its long-term contracts. In July, 1997, Sayers entered into a long-term contract and adopted the completed-contracts method for recognizing revenue on this particular contract. Which qualitative characteristic of accounting is Sayers Company violating?
    A. Conservatism
    B. Consistency
    C. Materiality
    D. Timeliness

15. Small tools used by a large manufacturing company are recorded as expenses when purchased. This is an example of what accounting concept?
    A. Relevance
    B. Reliability
    C. Consistency
    D. Materiality

16. Accounts receivable are reported on the company's balance sheet at the gross amount of the receivables less the company's estimate for uncollectible accounts. This is an example of what measurement convention?
    A. Historical cost
    B. Current market value
    C. Net realizable value
    D. Current replacement cost

17. The company purchased land in Washington twenty years ago at a cost of $1,000 per acre. Today similar land is selling for $6,000 per acre. However, the company maintains the land in its financial statements at the acquisition cost of $1,000 per acre. This is an example of what accounting concept?
    A. Conservatism
    B. Materiality
    C. Relevance
    D. Historical cost

18. Joe has a horse to sell, and Ed is interested in buying it. Ed offers to pay $2,500 for the horse, but Joe says he'd like to receive $4,000. Eventually, Ed buys the horse from Joe for $3,200. This is an example of what accounting concept?
    A. Historical cost
    B. Arms-length transaction
    C. Net realizable value
    D. Going concern

19. The overriding qualitative characteristic of accounting information is:
    A. stewardship.
    B. relevance.
    C. reliability.
    D. decision usefulness.

20. Recording inventories on the balance sheet at the lower of cost or market value is an example of what accounting concept?
    A. Historical cost
    B. Current market value
    C. Conservatism
    D. Cost effectiveness

21. The six Concepts Statements address four major areas, which are:
    A. Objectives, Qualitative Characteristics, Elements, and Recognition/Measurement/Reporting.
    B. Financial Accounting Standards, Interpretations, Technical Bulletins, and Statements of Position.
    C. Balance Sheet, Income Statement, Cash Flow Statement, and Statement of Retained Earnings.
    D. Materiality, Relevance, Reliability, and Consistency.

22. Accounts Receivable are normally reported at:
    A. cost.
    B. current market value.
    C. present or discounted value.
    D. net realizable value.

23. Which of the following fall within the scope of recognition and measurement? (Hint: refer to Exhibit 1-8).
    A. Financial statements only.
    B. Financial statements, and notes to financial statements.
    C. Financial statements, notes to financial statements, and supplemental disclosures.
    D. Financial statements, notes to financial statements, supplemental disclosures, management discussion and analysis, and letter to shareholders.

24. According to the FASB conceptual framework, the objectives of financial reporting for business enterprises are based on:
    A. generally accepted accounting principles.
    B. reporting on management's stewardship.
    C. the need for conservatism.
    D. the needs of users of the information.   (AICPA adapted)

25. According to the FASB conceptual framework, the usefulness of providing information in financial statements is subject to the constraint of:
    A. consistency.
    B. cost-benefit.
    C. reliability.
    D. representational faithfulness.   (AICPA adapted)

26. Which is the underlying concept governing the generally accepted accounting principles pertaining to recording gain contingencies?
    A. Conservatism
    B. Relevance
    C. Consistency
    D. Reliability   (AICPA adapted)

27. According to the FASB conceptual framework, which of the following attributes would *not* be used to measure inventory?
    A. Historical cost
    B. Replacement cost
    C. Net realizable value
    D. Present value of future cash flows (AICPA adapted)

28. Conceptually, interim financial statements can be described as emphasizing:
    A. timeliness over reliability.
    B. reliability over relevance.
    C. relevance over comparability.
    D. comparability over neutrality. (AICPA adapted)

29. What are the Statements of Financial Accounting Concepts intended to establish?
    A. Generally accepted accounting principles in financial reporting by business enterprises.
    B. The meaning of "present fairly in accordance with generally accepted accounting principles."
    C. The objectives and concepts for use in developing standards of financial accounting and reporting.
    D. The hierarchy of sources of generally accepted accounting principles. (AICPA adapted)

30. According to the FASB conceptual framework, which of the following situations violates the concept of reliability?
    A. Financial statements were issued nine months late.
    B. Report data on segments having the same expected risks and growth rates to analysts estimating future profits.
    C. Financial statements included property with a carrying amount increased to management's estimate of market value.
    D. Management reports to stockholders regularly refer to new projects undertaken, but the financial statements never report projected results. (AICPA adapted)

31. Holmes Company presents 3 years' balance sheets, income statements, and statements of cash flows in its annual report. Holmes Company's presentation is an example of what accounting characteristic?
    A. Conservatism
    B. Materiality
    C. Full disclosure
    D. Comparability

32. According to the FASB conceptual framework, an entity's revenue may result from:
    A. a decrease in an asset from primary operations.
    B. an increase in an asset from incidental transactions.
    C. an increase in a liability from incidental transactions.
    D. a decrease in a liability from primary operations. (AICPA adapted)

33. According the FASB's conceptual framework, asset valuation accounts are:
    A. assets.
    B. neither assets nor liabilities.
    C. part of stockholders' equity.
    D. liabilities.

Name: _____ Chapter 1   9

Exercises and Problems

1. Acronyms
   Required: (1)   For each of the following acronyms, present the full and correct name/title.
               (2)   For each of the following acronyms, write a brief definition.

1.	APB	7.	EITF
2.	ARBs	8.	FASB
3.	AAA	9.	FAF
4.	AICPA	10.	GAAP
5.	CPA	11.	GASB
6.	CAP	12.	SEC

2. Matching
   Required: Match the statements below with the letter of the correct term. An answer (letter) may be used more than once, and some terms may require more than one answer (letter).

A.	Decision usefulness	I.	Neutrality
B.	Relevance	J.	Representational faithfulness
C.	Reliability	K.	Comparability
D.	Predictive value	L.	Consistency
E.	Understandability	M.	Cost effectiveness
F.	Feedback value	N.	Conservatism
G.	Timeliness	O.	Materiality
H.	Verifiability		

   _____ 1. Although dependent upon characteristics of users, implies clarity and comprehensibility.
   _____ 2. Value of possessing exceeds amount paid to acquire.
   _____ 3. Received quickly enough to make a difference.
   _____ 4. Free of bias and intentional error.
   _____ 5. Objective and gained through consensus.
   _____ 6. Similarity in application.
   _____ 7. Makes a difference.
   _____ 8. Continuity of application.
   _____ 9. Not supporting either side without bias.
   _____ 10. Overriding quality of accounting information.
   _____ 11. Confirms or changes users' expectations.
   _____ 12. Information today reduces uncertainty about future outcomes.
   _____ 13. Level of significance that could change expectations or decisions.
   _____ 14. Healthy skepticism.
   _____ 15. Measures what is purported to be measured.
   _____ 16. Quality that distinguishes better information from inferior information.
   _____ 17. Constraints upon informational qualities of accounting data.
   _____ 18. Threshold for recognition.
   _____ 19. Agreement between information reported and actual results of an economic activity.

Chapter 1

3. Matching
   Required: Match the statements on the left with the letter of the terms on the right. An answer (letter) may be used more than once, and some terms may require more than one answer (letter).

   A. Assets
   B. Liabilities
   C. Equity
   D. Investments by owners
   E. Distributions to owners
   F. Comprehensive income
   G. Revenues
   H. Expenses
   I. Gains
   J. Losses

   _____ 1. Increases in equity resulting from peripheral activities.
   _____ 2. Probable future economic benefits.
   _____ 3. Inflows resulting from ongoing operating activities.
   _____ 4. Change in equity during a specific period, excluding owner-related transactions.
   _____ 5. Outflows resulting from ongoing operating activities.
   _____ 6. Probable future economic sacrifices.
   _____ 7. Decreases in equity resulting from transfers to owners.
   _____ 8. Residual interest.
   _____ 9. Decreases in equity resulting from peripheral activities.
   _____ 10. Increases in equity resulting from owners' activities.
   _____ 11. Promises to pay.
   _____ 12. Rights to receive money or other items of value.
   _____ 13. Compilation of all earnings and cost activities during the period.
   _____ 14. Cash on hand.
   _____ 15. Cost of paying employees this period.
   _____ 16. Common stock issued and outstanding.
   _____ 17. Dividends.
   _____ 18. Accounts payable.
   _____ 19. Subscription fees received prior to delivery of magazines.
   _____ 20. Decline in market value of marketable securities, classified as trading securities.

SOLUTIONS TO TEST YOUR UNDERSTANDING

Fill-in-the-Blanks

1. GAAP; standards; interpretations
2. objectives; fundamental concepts; implementation guidelines
3. decision making
4. decision usefulness
5. feedback value; predictive value; timeliness
6. Feedback value
7. verifiability; neutrality; representational faithfulness
8. International Accounting Standards Committee; harmonized
9. audit opinion; auditor
10. adverse
11. unqualified
12. Recognition
13. Comprehensive income
14. current replacement cost
15. net realizable value

Name: _____   Chapter 1   11

Multiple Choice

1.	C	10.	A	18.	B	26.	A
2.	B	11.	A	19.	D	27.	D
3.	D	12.	C	20.	C	28.	A
4.	C	13.	B	21.	A	29.	C
5.	C	14.	B	22.	D	30.	C
6.	C	15.	D	23.	A	31.	D
7.	C	16.	C	24.	D	32.	D
8.	A	17.	A (D)	25.	B	33.	B
9.	C						

Exercises and Problems

1. Acronyms
    1. APB   **Accounting Principles Board**
       A board of the AICPA that issued opinions establishing accounting principles between 1959 and 1973; the APB was the predecessor of the FASB.
    2. ARBs   **Accounting Research Bulletins**
       The publications of the Committees on Accounting Procedure that established accounting standards between 1939 and 1959.
    3. AAA   **American Accounting Association**
       An organization for accounting academicians. The AAA is involved in standards setting by assisting the FASB in research projects.
    4. AICPA   **American Institute of Certified Public Accountants**
       A professional organization for CPAs. Membership in the AICPA is voluntary. The AICPA publishes the Journal of Accountancy.
    5. CPA   **Certified Public Accountant**
       Accountants who have met specified professional and educational guidelines.
    6. CAP   **Committee on Accounting Procedure**
       A committee of the AICPA that issued ARBs (accounting standards) between 1939 and 1959.
    7. EITF   **Emerging Issues Task Force**
       Task force created by the FASB whose members represent industry and the accounting profession. The EITF was established to quickly identify, study and recommend accounting procedures to deal with timely accounting issues.
    8. FASB   **Financial Accounting Standards Board**
       An independent private organization responsible for establishing accounting standards in the U.S. The FASB has seven full-time members and employs a staff to study accounting issues and develop appropriate accounting standards.
    9. FAF   **Financial Accounting Foundation**
       Organization responsible for selecting members to the FASB, GASB and their Advisory Councils. It is also responsible for funding the FASB and the GASB.
    10. GAAP   **Generally Accepted Accounting Principles**
        Accounting standards recognized by the accounting profession as required in the preparation of financial statements for external users.
    11. GASB   **Governmental Accounting Standards Board**
        Independent private organization responsible for establishing standards in the governmental area. Members to the GASB are appointed by the Financial Accounting Foundation.
    12. SEC   **Securities and Exchange Commission**
        Governmental agency created to regulate the issuance and trading of securities offered by corporations to the general public. SEC has the authority to establish accounting standards, but has abdicated that responsibility to the FASB; the SEC maintains oversight responsibility, however.

Chapter 1

2. Matching

   1. E
   2. M
   3. G
   4. C
   5. H
   6. K
   7. B, A
   8. L
   9. I
   10. A
   11. F
   12. D
   13. O
   14. N
   15. J
   16. A
   17. M, N, O
   18. O
   19. J

3. Matching

   1. I
   2. A
   3. G
   4. F
   5. H
   6. B
   7. E
   8. C
   9. J
   10. D
   11. B
   12. A
   13. F
   14. A
   15. H
   16. D
   17. E
   18. B
   19. B
   20. J

CHAPTER 2

A REVIEW OF THE ACCOUNTING CYCLE

KEY POINTS

I. Basic Steps in the Accounting Cycle
  A. Recording Phase
  B. Reporting Phase

II. Recording Phase
  A. Occurs daily as the business transacts business activities.
  B. Steps include:
    1. *Analyze business documents:* from source documents, determine which events should be recorded in the financial statements.
      (Hint: remember the concepts we studied in Chapter 1, such as recognition, measurement, and reporting? Use these concepts to decide which events should be recorded.)
    2. *Journalize:* write the journal entry, that is, record the debits and the credits associated with the transaction in a "journal."
    3. *Post:* transfer the debits and credits from the journal entries to the proper ledger accounts. (The accounts correspond to the elements we studied in Chapter 1, such as assets, liabilities, etc. In the general ledger, each element is represented by several accounts. For example, "assets" includes accounts such as "Cash," "Accounts Receivable." "Inventory," "Land," "Investments," etc.)

III. Reporting Phase
  A. Occurs occasionally, such as monthly, quarterly, or annually.
  B. Steps include:
    1. *Prepare a trial balance*: list of balances in all general ledger accounts.
    2. *Prepare adjusting entries*: updating the ledger with continuous transactions and events for which no exchange has occurred during the period. Usually these entries occur because time has passed, and thus, economic situations have changed.
    Examples:
    a. Asset depreciation: systematic allocation of cost of asset to expense and reduction in the carrying value of the asset during the periods in which the asset is used by the company.
    b. Doubtful accounts: estimated amount of uncollectible accounts receivable, charged to current period expense and results in a reduction in the net realizable value of accounts receivable.
    c. Accrued expenses: expenses incurred but for which no cash has changed hands yet.
    d. Accrued revenues: revenues earned but not billed or collected during this period.
    e. Prepaid expenses: recorded cash payments for benefits not received yet or for benefits only partially received.
    f. Deferred revenues: recorded cash receipts for services to be rendered in the future, or for services only partially rendered during the current period.
    g. Inventory adjustments
      1) If a periodic inventory system is used, then all purchases of inventory have been charged to an expense account (Purchases), which must be closed. Ending inventory, which will be the amount shown on the balance sheet, is recorded to reflect the amount of inventory still on hand at the end of the period.
      2) If a perpetual inventory system is used, all purchases of inventory have been charged to the asset account, "Inventory," so an adjustment to ending inventory is not necessary. Costs associated with sold inventory under the perpetual system have been recorded to the expense account, Cost of Goods Sold.
      3) Most companies periodically analyze inventory for obsolescence and shrinkage, the impact which is measured and recorded at this time.

3. *Prepare financial statements*: (Study question: what are the four financial statements to be prepared at this time? Yes, that's right: balance sheet, income statement, statement of cash flows, and retained earnings statement—good job!)
4. *Close nominal accounts:* Nominal accounts are also called temporary accounts, and they are the accounts whose balances are brought to zero at the end of each fiscal year. Generally, nominal accounts are those included on the income statement. Sometimes, however, there are some owner-related accounts, such as "Dividends" which are also closed at this time.
   Important: Close only nominal accounts—don't close asset, liability, or most equity accounts.
5. *Prepare a post-closing trial balance*: a list of all general ledger accounts and their balances. (Study question: What should be the balance in all the revenue and expense accounts? Zero, right! In fact, that's the main reason for preparing a post-closing trial balance—to make sure you closed all the nominal accounts).

IV. Accrual Versus Cash-Basis Accounting
   A. Accrual defined:
      System in which revenues are recorded when earned and expenses are recorded when incurred, not necessarily when the cash changes hands.
   B. Recall in Chapter 1, we read that the FASB favors accrual accounting (see Concepts Statement No. 1, for reference).
   C. Many small businesses and government entities use cash-basis accounting.
      1. Why?
         a. Cash flows are relatively easy to track, which facilitates accounting for small business.
         b. Magnitude of transactions for small businesses is not great, so accruals don't have the material impact on a small business that they do on large companies.
      2. For an example of a cash-basis system, refer to Paskett Concessions, the Demonstration Problem in this chapter.

V. Computers and Accounting
   A. Illustrations in this chapter in the text reflect activities associated with a manual accounting system.
   B. All of these activities can be readily performed by a computer, except the analysis of economic events.
   C. Computerized accounting systems facilitate recording, posting, and financial statement preparation.

VI. Special Journals and Subsidiary Ledgers (Expanded Material)
   A. Special journals eliminate much of the repetitive work involved in recording routine transactions, such as cash receipts or cash disbursements.
   B. Special journals allow accounting tasks to be divided among several accounting personnel.
      1. The division of responsibilities increases internal control.
      2. It also increases accuracy.
   C. Subsidiary ledgers provide detailed information about individual items in the general ledger account.
      1. Subsidiary ledgers are often used for accounts receivable, account payable and fixed assets.
      2. Total of subsidiary ledger should equal the balance in the general ledger account (which is sometimes called the "control account").

DEMONSTRATION PROBLEM

Paskett Concessions

Kelly and Tom Paskett operate a seasonal business selling snow cones, cotton candy, and other confections at county fairs and rodeos. They operate their business out of a self-contained trailer which they pull to each location with their personal vehicle. They have owned the trailer for about five years, and they paid $3,000 for it. They spent another $2,500 outfitting it. They borrowed the money to buy the trailer and fixtures from Kelly's uncle. They pay him $500 per month during the months they operate their business (June, July, and August) and nothing the other months. The following transactions relate to their business during the month of June, 1997:

| Name: | | Chapter 2   15 |

May 15   Kelly made arrangements to supply snow cones, cotton candy, and other confections at the following county fairs and celebrations during June:
- June 3-5: Johnson County Fair
- June 10-12: Sweetwater County Fair
- June 17-19: Douglas County Fair

She also arranged to supply concessions at the King County Fair, Rodeo, and 4th of July celebration over the 4th of July weekend.

She arranged similar schedules for each weekend during July and August as well.

June 1   Took the trailer in for service and cleaning: cost $200.

1   Called the insurance agent to buy a 3-month insurance policy on the trailer and contents: cost $300.

1   Purchased a 1997 business license: cost $100.

2   Preparations for county fair: purchased materials, such as sugar, ice, flavored syrup, cups, etc.: cost $500. Kelly estimates these supplies will last through the 3-day county fair they are attending this weekend.

3   Kelly got the cash box ready for the trip by going to the bank and withdrawing $70 in change and small bills.

3-5   Attended a county fair: gross receipts $4,000. Paid Kelly's son $100 for working during the weekend. Paid the county fair committee a vendor's fee of $100.

6   Took an inventory of materials and supplies. Although nearly 100 pounds of sugar remained, someone spilled syrup into it, so Kelly had to throw it away. About 100 cups and paper cones remained.

6   Paid Kelly's son $20 to clean the trailer. He spent $10 on cleaning supplies and Kelly reimbursed him for the costs.

9   Purchased supplies for the next county fair: cost $600.

10-12   Attended another county fair: gross receipts $5,500. Paid Kelly's son $100 for working. Because they were so busy, Kelly hired another worker and paid him $100 also. Paid the vendor's fee of $100.

12   On the way home, the trailer got a flat tire. Tom didn't have a spare so he had to buy a new tire: cost $100. Tom changed the tire himself. While they were stranded by the side of the road waiting for Tom to go to town, buy the tire, and change it, Kelly set up business. She sold $400 worth of snow cones before a highway patrol officer stopped by and told her she was breaking the law. He gave her a ticket for operating a roadside business without the proper permit: cost $100.

13   Paid Kelly's son $20 to clean the trailer. He spent $10 on cleaning supplies, and Kelly reimbursed him for the cost.

14   Kelly decided the other three tires on the trailer were in bad shape and feared another blowout, so she bought 3 new tires for the trailer: cost $70 each. Kelly paid her son $25 to install the new tires on the trailer.

15   Kelly sold the old tires for $10.

15   Gasoline bill of $300 arrived, and Kelly paid it. Kelly estimates that all of it relates to the business. To be sure for future bills, Kelly calls the oil company and gets a credit card just for the business.

15   Took inventory of remaining supplies and made a list of needed supplies.

16   Purchased supplies for next county fair: cost $700.

17-19   Attended another county fair: gross receipts $6,000. Paid Kelly's son $100 for working. Kelly hired another temporary worker and paid her $50. Paid the vendor's fee of $120.

20   Paid Kelly's son $20 to clean the trailer. He didn't buy anymore cleaning supplies as he had plenty on hand.

23   Purchased supplies for the next county fair: cost $700.

23-25   Attended the county fair. The weather was unpleasant, with rain, sleet and high winds. Since it was too cold for people to eat snow cones, Kelly rushed to the local grocery store and purchased supplies for coffee and hot chocolate at a cost of $300. She also purchased bottled water at a cost of $100. Gross receipts: $820. Kelly asked her son if he'd forego being paid since gross receipts were so low. Her son agreed but asked if he could earn a bonus at the end of the season if the season overall was good. Kelly agreed.

June	25	On the way home from the county fair, the Pasketts were involved in a traffic accident. Although no one was hurt, and the trailer was not seriously damaged, the force of the accident wreaked havoc inside the trailer. The snow cone machine was destroyed, the cotton candy machine was broken, and all the glass bottles of syrup broke splattering syrup everywhere.
	26	The insurance adjuster came out to survey the damage to the trailer and the contents. He agreed that it was a mess and said the insurance company would pay $1,000 for the damage to the contents. The damage to the trailer was estimated at $200, which was less than the deductible amount on the insurance policy, so the insurance company didn't pay anymore for that.
	27	Kelly's son began cleaning the trailer.
	27	Kelly received $1,000 from the insurance company.
	28	Kelly received a notice from the insurance company that the insurance was being cancelled effective July 1. Included in the notice was a refund check from the insurance company for unused coverage in the amount of $100.
	28	Kelly bought another insurance policy covering July and August: cost $300.
	28	Kelly's son continued to clean the trailer. He purchased $50 worth of cleaning supplies.
	29	Kelly purchased a new snow cone machine for $500, a new cotton candy machine for $700, and a new coffee pot for $75. Although they had never sold popcorn before, the vendor talked Kelly into buying a popcorn machine as well at a cost of $600.
	29	Kelly's son completed the cleaning of the trailer. He also installed the new snow cone machine, the popcorn machine, and the cotton candy maker. Kelly paid him $60.
	30	Knowing that a long holiday weekend was coming up, Kelly purchased more supplies than usual: cost $1,000. She also replaced all the lost incidental supplies (such as sugar and creamer packets and stir sticks for the coffee) at a cost of $100. She decided that since the weekend was going to be quite long she would also buy supplies for the family to use while at the 4th of July celebration. She bought a new tent, some miscellaneous camping gear, and food at a total cost of $1,200.
	30	Kelly arrived home from her shopping trip to find her husband excitedly counting the cash in the concession business cash box. "Great!" he exclaimed, "There's enough here for what I need." "What's that, dear?" Kelly asked. "Why, another horse, of course," said Tom as he rolled up a wad of bills and stuffed it into his pocket. "How much are you taking?" Kelly asked as Tom walked out the door. "About $4,000," he replied as the door closed.

Required: Set up an accounting system for Paskett Concessions, record June's transactions, and prepare a balance sheet and income statement for the month of June.

Solution to Demonstration Problem

Paskett Concessions is a case illustrating the differences between accrual- and cash-basis accounting. As we go through the solution, the differences between cash and accrual accounting will be pointed out. Recall that many small businesses use cash-basis accounting, and Paskett Concessions is no exception. In fact, as you read the case, it appears that the Pasketts run their concession business out of the cash box.

Before you begin working on the case, be sure to read through the entire case. As you do you will better understand the nature of the business. Understanding the nature of the business is very important and greatly assists the accounting effort.

First, let's review the introductory paragraph. Notice that the Pasketts borrowed the money for the trailer and fixtures from Kelly's uncle, and he asks them to pay on the debt only during the months when they are operating the business. Do you think this type of financing arrangement is unusual? Actually, it's not usual, but is common in seasonal industries. For example, in the northern states in which construction businesses are most active during the summer, many construction companies pay more on their bank debts during the summer months and pay relatively little during the winter when activity is slow.

If the Pasketts use a cash-basis system, will you write a journal entry for the trailer and fixtures at this time? No. Neither will you write a journal entry to record the debt at this time. Both transactions occurred in past accounting periods and should have been recorded then, regardless of the type of accounting system employed.

Will you write journal entries for Kelly's activities during May? No, because no exchange took place. Do Kelly's activities in May have an economic impact on Paskett Concessions? Certainly. Had Kelly not taken those actions, Paskett Concessions would not be set up to do business during the summer.

Let's analyze each day's activities:

June 1   Cost of cleaning and servicing the trailer is an expense, and it appears that Kelly paid cash for this; hence, the journal entry would be:
         Cleaning Expense   200
            Cash   200

1   Kelly purchased insurance. There are two ways we could record this transaction. If we use a cash basis system, the journal entry would be:
         Insurance Expense   300
            Cash   300
What if we used an accrual system? Then the insurance policy becomes an asset as it gives Paskett Concessions future economic benefit, so the journal entry would be:
         Prepaid Insurance   300
            Cash   300
If an accrual system is used, we would charge to expense 1/3 of the cost each month as an adjusting entry, thusly:
         Insurance Expense   100
            Prepaid Insurance   100
Let's assume the Pasketts prefer the cash-basis system, however.

1   Operating Expense   100
            Cash   100

Ok, timeout. The Pasketts have just spent $600. Where did they get the cash? We don't really have the information in this case to determine exactly where the cash originated. It could be that Paskett Concessions has a bank account from last year and that's where the cash is. Or, perhaps the Pasketts used their personal funds at this point. How would the journal entries look under each assumption?

If we assume the company has an account and thus its own cash, we don't need to make an entry at this point. However, if the Pasketts used their personal funds, then they've invested in the business:
         Cash   600
            Owners' Equity   600
(This dilemma will happen again on June 2 when Kelly buys supplies for the first county fair on June 2).

2   Supplies (expense)   500
            Cash   500
Let's assume the Pasketts use their own funds for start-up each year; thus, the entry for all the start-up expenses would be (cleaning $200, insurance $300, inventory $500):
         Cash   1,100
            Owners' Equity   1,100

3   Kelly goes to the bank and withdraws money to make change. If she withdraws money from Paskett Concessions' account, there is no entry to make as cash is fungible. Some companies will distinguish between cash in the bank (usually recorded in the ledger account called Cash) and cash on hand (often called Petty Cash). However, if Kelly withdraws money from her own personal account, we would make the following entry:

18 Chapter 2

	Cash	70	
	Owners' Equity		70
June 5	Cash	4,000	
	Sales		4,000
	Wages	100	
	Cash		100
	Operating Expense	100	
	Cash		100
6	What happened? It appears that inventory was leftover after the fair and could have been used in the future, but the accident effectively destroyed it. But notice that in a cash-basis system we have expensed the inventory when we purchased it (see the journal entry on June 2), so we don't need another entry at this time.		
6	Cleaning Expense	10	
	Wages	20	
	Cash		30
9	Supplies (expense)	600	
	Cash		600
12	Cash	5,500	
	Sales		5,500
	Wages	200	
	Cash		200
	Operating Expenses	100	
	Cash		100
12	Repairs	100	
	Cash		100
	Cash	400	
	Sales		400
	Operating Expense	100	
	Cash		100
13	Cleaning Expense	10	
	Wages	20	
	Cash		30
14	Repairs	210	
	Cash		210
	Repairs	25	
	Cash		25
15	Cash	10	
	Repairs		10

Ok, now why did we charge the entire cost of the tires to expense? In an accrual system, the cost of the tires might have been capitalized to the cost of the trailer, and the sale of the old tires would have been credited to the cost of the trailer. Then, as the trailer was depreciated, the basis for depreciation would have increased. In a cash system, however, the cost of the tires is "cash out" so the entire cost is expensed currently.

15	Operating Expense	300	
	Cash		300
15	No entry, because we don't have the information to measure the cost of the remaining supplies. In a cash-basis system, we have charged the cost of the inventory to expense when we purchased it.		
16	Supplies (expense)	700	
	Cash		700
19	Cash	6,000	
	Sale		6,000
	Wages	150	
	Cash		150
	Operating Expenses	120	
	Cash		120

20	Cleaning Expense	20	
	Cash		20
23	Supplies (expense)	700	
	Cash		700
25	Supplies (expense)	400	
	Cash		400
	Cash	820	
	Sales		820

Whoa, Kelly's son worked at the fair, but was not paid. Since no cash was transferred, in a cash-basis system, there is no journal entry for the son's work efforts. In an accrual system, however, we would need to accrue the wages, even though none had been paid.

How do we record the loss of the cotton candy and snow cone machines? In an accrual system, we would record the loss of the equipment as the amount of the book value of the equipment lost. Assuming the following entry was written when the assets were purchased, the entry to record the loss would be:

Equipment	2,500	
Cash		2,500
Owners' Equity	2,500	
Equipment		2,500

What about the cash basis? Well, no cash has changed hands at this point, right? So, under a strict cash-basis system there would be no entry at this time. However, most companies, even those on a cash basis, realize that a real economic loss has occurred, so we might expect an entry to recognize the loss. Generally, the entry would be made at the time the insurance proceeds are received (refer to June 27).

26	No entry.		
27	No entry for the cleaning.		
28	Cash	1,000	
	Owners' Equity		1,000
28	Cash	100	
	Insurance Expense		100
28	Insurance Expense	300	
	Cash		300
28	Cleaning Expenses	60	
	Cash		60
29	Equipment	1,875	
	Cash		1,875
29	Wages	60	
	Cash		60
30	Supplies	1,100	
	Owners' Equity	1,200	
	Cash		2,300
30	Owners' Equity	2,000	
	Cash		2,000

Are there any other entries which, even on a cash basis, we should write? Probably. Most likely, the Pasketts need to pay the uncle $500 on the trailer and equipment loan, but we don't know that the cash has been transferred. Until it is, no entry is written.

After we set up a ledger and post the journal entries, we can prepare a balance sheet and income statement. Since we assumed the entity, Paskett Concessions, had no cash at the beginning of the season, the ledger account "Cash" can begin with a zero balance. If we do that, the ending cash balance will be $7,400.

How would the balance sheet and income statement differ if we had used an accrual system? Which system do you think better reflects the economic activity of Paskett Concessions for the month of June? Consider the following: (1) Supplies purchased on June 30 will be sold during July so the cost should be an asset, Inventory. Likewise, the cost of all supplies purchased would first be debited to the inventory account, and the cost of goods sold would be calculated based upon supplies used (or remaining if a periodic inventory system is used). (2) Payroll and income taxes will have to be paid, and in an accrual system, these will be accrued monthly, even if they are remitted to the taxing authority only quarterly. (3) In this case we have assumed sales tax is not a problem, because the vendor's license, in essence, takes care of that requirement. (4) Expenses for earned but unpaid wages would be accrued at the end of the month. What other items can you think of which are treated differently in an accrual system? (Hint: acquisition, depreciation, and loss of machinery)

TEST YOUR UNDERSTANDING

Fill-in-the-Blanks

Required: Fill in the blanks to complete the following sentences.

1. The accounting process consists of the _____ phase and the _____ phase.

2. Assets, expenses, and dividends are _____ by debits and _____ by credits.

3. Liabilities, owners' equity, and revenues are _____ by debits and _____ by credits.

4. The original materials evidencing business transactions are called _____ _____.

5. Information recorded in the journals is transferred to appropriate accounts in the ledgers by a process referred to as _____.

6. The _____ _____ includes all accounts appearing in the financial statements, while _____ _____ provide additional detail in support of certain general ledger balances.

7. A reduction in the building account for depreciation is usually recorded by a credit to a _____ _____, Accumulated Depreciation.

8. Freight-In and Additional Paid-In Capital are examples of _____ _____.

9. _____ _____ include all income statement accounts plus the dividends or drawing accounts.

10. A _____ is an exchange of goods and services between entities or some other event having an economic impact on a business enterprise.

11. A list of all accounts and their balances is a _____ _____.

12. _____ _____ are required at the end of each accounting period to update the accounts as necessary to fully recognize, on an accrual basis, revenue and expense for the period.

Name: **Chapter 2** 21

Multiple Choice

Required: Circle the best answer.

1. Adjusting entries normally involve:
   A. real accounts only.
   B. nominal accounts only.
   C. real and nominal accounts.
   D. liability accounts only.

2. An accrued expense can be described as an amount:
   A. paid and matched with earnings for the current period.
   B. paid and not matched with earnings for the current period.
   C. not paid and not matched with earnings for the current period.
   D. not paid and matched with earnings for the current period.

3. In November and December, 1997, Bee Company, a newly organized newspaper publisher, received $72,000 for 1,000 three-year subscriptions at $24 per year, starting with the January 2, 1998 issue of the newspaper. How much should Bee report in its 1997 income statement for subscription revenue?
   A. $72,000
   B. $24,000
   C. $12,000
   D. $-0-

   (AICPA adapted)

4. Lawrence Freeman, M.D., keeps his accounting records on a cash basis. During 1997, Dr. Freeman collected $200,000 in fees from his patients. At December 31, 1996, Dr. Freeman had accounts receivable of $40,000. At December 31, 1997, Dr. Freeman had accounts receivable of $60,000 and unearned fees of $2,000. On an accrual basis, how much was Dr. Freeman's patient service revenue for 1997?
   A. $222,000
   B. $218,000
   C. $180,000
   D. $178,000

   (AICPA adapted)

5. Arkin Company sells $100,000 of stock to investors. The journal entry to record this transaction would be:
   A. Cash   100,000
         Revenue   100,000
   B. Cash   100,000
         Common Stock   100,000
   C. Cash   100,000
         Long-Term Debt   100,000
   D. Common Stock   100,000
         Cash   100,000

Chapter 2

6. The River Company purchases $100,000 of machinery with $10,000 down and a $90,000 long-term note. The journal entry to record the transaction would be:

    A. Cash   100,000
            Cash   10,000
            Long-Term Note   90,000
    B. Machinery   100,000
            Cash   10,000
            Long-Term Note   90,000
    C. Machinery   100,000
            Cash   10,000
            Retained Earnings   90,000
    D. Machinery   100,000
            Cash   100,000

Use the following information for questions 7 and 8:

Accounts Receivable balance, beginning	$ 40,000
Accounts Receivable balance, ending	60,000
Allowance for Doubtful Accounts balance, ending (before adjustment)	2,500

7. The company determines 8% of the ending accounts receivable will be uncollectible. The adjusting journal entry would be:

    A. Uncollectible Accounts Expense   2,300
            Allowance for Doubtful Accounts   2,300
    B. Uncollectible Accounts Expense   4,800
            Allowance for Doubtful Accounts   4,800
    C. Uncollectible Accounts Expense   7,300
            Allowance for Doubtful Accounts   7,300
    D. Uncollectible Accounts Expense   4,800
            Allowance for Doubtful Accounts   4,800

8. Despite numerous attempts to collect, the credit manager has determined that the account of Customer XYX is uncollectible. The account has a balance of $1,600. The journal entry to write off the account would be:

    A. Uncollectible Accounts Expense   1,600
            Accounts Receivable   1,600
    B. Allowance for Doubtful Accounts   1,600
            Accounts Receivable   1,600
    C. Allowance for Doubtful Accounts   1,600
            Uncollectible Accounts Expense   1,600
    D. Accounts Receivable   1,600
            Allowance for Doubtful Accounts   1,600

9. Companies often use special journals in addition to the general journal. Special journals are useful because they:
    A. eliminate much of the repetitive work involved in recording routine transactions.
    B. permit the recording function to be divided among several accounting personnel, thus increasing internal control.
    C. often provide useful information.
    D. All of the above.

Name: Chapter 2   23

10. Which of the following describes subsidiary ledgers?
    A. Subsidiary ledgers provide detail of individual accounts in support of control accounts in the general ledger.
    B. Subsidiary ledgers take the place of the general ledger.
    C. Subsidiary ledgers are used only if the company also has a voucher system.
    D. "Subsidiary ledger" is synonymous with "check register."

11. ABC Company sells widgets and uses a perpetual inventory system to account for its inventory of widgets. ABC purchased widgets from Iowa Widget Manufacturers at a cost of $19,500, payable at the time of delivery. The entry to record this transaction would be:

    A. Purchases   19,500
            Accounts Payable   19,500
    B. Inventory   19,500
            Accounts Payable   19,500
    C. Purchases   19,500
            Cash   19,500
    D. Inventory   19,500
            Accounts Payable   19,500

12. On February 1, 1995, Tory began a service proprietorship with an initial cash investment of $2,000. The proprietorship provided $5,000 of services during February and received full payment in March. The proprietorship incurred expenses of $3,000 in February, which were paid in April. During March, Tory drew $1,000 against the capital account. In the proprietorship's financial statements for the two months ended March 31,1995, prepared under the cash basis of accounting, what amount should be reported as capital?
    A. $1,000
    B. $3,000
    C. $6,000
    D. $7,000

Exercises and Problems

1. Recording transactions
   Required: Write the journal entries, in good form, for each of the following transactions:

   Sept. 1 Sold merchandise on account, $15,000. Cost of merchandise sold: $10,000 (company uses a perpetual inventory system).
          2 Received payment on account, $200.
          3 Purchased equipment with cash, $1,000.
          4 Received telephone bill, $75.
          5 Borrowed $10,000 from First National Bank. The loan will be repaid over a three-year term with a simple interest rate of 10%.
          6 Purchased a building for $50,000 in cash and a mortgage of $40,000.
          7 Warehouse flooded and $5,000 worth of inventory was destroyed. Insurance proceeds were $2,000.
          8 Purchased office supplies, $20.

2. Adjusting entries
   Required: Write the necessary adjusting entries, in good form, for each of the following events:

   (a) Interest of $2,000 is accrued on notes payable.
   (b) Four work days are remaining in the month, but payday will not occur until next month. Workers earn $200 per day. Accrue wages.

Chapter 2

(c) Accrue depreciation on equipment, $1,000.
(d) An analysis of accounts receivable indicates that $2,500 will be uncollectible. The company maintains an allowance for uncollectible accounts, and the balance in the account is zero.
(e) Analysis of accounts receivable indicates that $2,500 will be uncollectible. The company maintains an allowance for uncollectible accounts, and the credit balance in the account is $1,000.
(f) A customer declared bankruptcy and thus his account will not be collectible, $150. The company maintains an allowance for uncollectible accounts.

3. Analysis of journal entries
   Required: Write the explanation for each of the following journal entries:

   (a) Interest Receivable   100
           Interest Revenue   100
   (b) Accounts Receivable   200
           Sales   200
   (c) Retained Earnings   500
           Income Summary   500
   (d) Cost of Goods Sold   300
           Inventory   300
   (e) Allowance for Uncollectible Accounts   200
           Accounts Receivable   200
   (f) Accumulated Depreciation   300
       Cash   500
       Loss on Sale   200
           Equipment   1,000
   (g) Unearned Revenue   600
           Subscription Revenue   600
   (h) Retained Earnings   200
           Dividends   200
   (i) Cash   200
       Equipment   400
           Common Stock   100
           Paid in Capital in Excess of Par   500
   (j) Income Summary   1,000
           Wage Expense   200
           Cost of Goods Sold   400
           Miscellaneous Expense   200
           Tax Expense   200

4. Analysis of transactions and accounts
   Required: Using the information provided, determine the net income for Ratt Company:

Cash	$25,000	Accounts Payable	$12,000
Sales	50,000	Accounts Receivable	16,000
Dividends	3,000	Prepaid Rent	1,000
Inventory	7,500	Interest Receivable	200
Common Stock	50,000	Cost of Goods Sold	30,000
Dividends Payable	3,000	Selling Expenses	4,000
General Expense	4,000	Retained Earnings	19,500
Land	30,000	Wage Expense	10,000
Tax Expense	1,000	Taxes Payable	1,000
Interest Revenue	200	Other Assets	1,000

SOLUTIONS TO TEST YOUR UNDERSTANDING

Fill-in-the-Blanks

1. recording; reporting
2. increased; decreased
3. decreased; increased
4. source documents
5. posting
6. general ledger; subsidiary ledgers
7. contra account
8. adjunct accounts
9. nominal accounts
10. transaction
11. trial balance
12. Adjusting entries

Multiple Choice

1. C
2. D
3. D
4. B
5. B
6. B
7. A
8. B
9. D
10. A
11. D
12. C

Exercises and Problems

1. Recording transactions

Sept.				
1		Accounts Receivable	15,000	
		Sales		15,000
		Cost of Goods Sold	10,000	
		Inventory		10,000
	2	Cash	200	
		Accounts Receivable		200
	3	Equipment	1,000	
		Cash		1,000
	4	Utilities Expense	75	
		Accounts Payable		75
	5	Cash	10,000	
		Note Payable		10,000
	6	Building	90,000	
		Cash		50,000
		Mortgage Payable		40,000
	7	Cash	2,000	
		Flood Loss	3,000	
		Inventory		5,000
	8	Supplies Expense (or Supplies)	20	
		Cash		20

26   Chapter 2

2. Adjusting entries

(a)	Interest Expense	2,000	
	Interest Payable		2,000
(b)	Wage Expense	800	
	Wages Payable		800
(c)	Depreciation Expense	1,000	
	Accumulated Depreciation		1,000
(d)	Uncollectible Accounts Expense	2,500	
	Allowance for Uncollectible Accts.		2,500
(e)	Uncollectible Accounts Expense	1,500	
	Allowance for Uncollectible Accts.		1,500
(f)	Allowance for Uncollectible Accounts	150	
	Accounts Receivable		150

3. Analysis of journal entries

   (a) Accrued interest earned.
   (b) Sold merchandise on account.
   (c) Net loss of $500 was closed to Retained Earnings.
   (d) Inventory costing $300 was sold.
   (e) Uncollectible account was written off.
   (f) Sold equipment at a loss.
   (g) Subscription fees were received prior to delivery of the service; this adjusting entry recognizes the portion of the service which has been earned during this period.
   (h) Dividends were apparently declared earlier and are now being closed to Retained Earnings.
   (i) Cash and equipment (with a fair market value of $400) were received in exchange for common stock.
   (j) This journal entry is a closing entry in which the expense accounts are closed into Income Summary. Will there also be an entry to close the revenue accounts? (Yes, and Income Summary will be credited. Then the balance in Income Summary will be closed to Retained Earnings.)

4. Analysis of transactions and accounts

Sales		$50,000
Cost of goods sold		30,000
Gross profit		$20,000
Selling expense	$ 4,000	
Wages	10,000	
General expenses	4,000	
Tax expense	1,000	19,000
Operating income		$ 1,000
Interest revenue		200
Net income		$ 1,200

CHAPTER 3

THE BALANCE SHEET AND NOTES TO THE FINANCIAL STATEMENTS

KEY POINTS

I. Elements of the Balance Sheet
  A. *Assets*: resources owned and controlled by the entity.
  B. *Liabilities*: claims on resources.
  C. *Owners' Equity*: also called "residual interest," the difference between assets and liabilities. The owners' claims against assets.
  D. Classifications of the balance sheet
    1. Categorize according to common characteristics:
       <u>Assets</u>
       Current assets
       Noncurrent assets
         Investments
         Property, plant, and equipment
         Intangible assets
         Other noncurrent assets
       <u>Liabilities</u>
       Current liabilities
       Noncurrent liabilities
         Callable obligations
         Long-term debt
         Long-term lease obligations
         Deferred income tax liability
         Other noncurrent liabilities
         Contingent liabilities
       <u>Owners' Equity</u>
       Contributed capital
         Stock
         Paid-in capital in excess of par
       Retained earnings
  E. Definitions of the common classifications on the balance sheet
    1. *Current Assets:* cash, assets readily convertible to cash, and/or assets held for consumption within the normal operating cycle of the enterprise (usually one year or less).
       a. Examples: Cash, Accounts Receivable, Inventory, Trading Securities.
    2. *Noncurrent Assets*:
       a. *Investments*: assets held for long-term purposes such as regular income, appreciation, or ownership control.
          1) Examples: stocks; bonds; mortgage holdings; securities of affiliated companies; funds set aside for the redemption of bonds, replacement of buildings, or payment of pensions; land held for investment; cash surrender value of life insurance.
          2) Generally reported at historical cost, though modifications are occasionally recommended.
       b. *Property, Plant, and Equipment (PP&E):* (also called Land, Buildings, and Machinery) includes tangible real and permanent property.
          1) Examples: land, buildings, tools, machinery, furniture and fixtures, vehicles.
          2) Carried at historical cost, less accumulated depreciation.
       c. *Intangible Assets:* long-term rights and privileges that are not tangible.
          1) Examples: goodwill, patents, trademarks, franchises (note the franchise asset on the Celtics' balance sheet in the text), leaseholds, copyrights.
          2) Generally carried at historical cost, less accumulated amortization.

d. *Other Noncurrent Assets*: long-term assets that don't fit into the other categories.
   1) Examples: long-term assets to officers, long-term receivables, deposits made with utility companies or government agencies, and deferred income tax assets.
3. *Current Liabilities:* obligations to be paid within one operating cycle (usually one year or less); generally paid with current assets.
   a. Examples: accounts payable, short-term borrowings, accrued expenses, current portion of long-term debt, callable obligations (if the borrower is in violation of certain provisions of the debt instrument).
4. *Noncurrent Liabilities*:
   a. *Callable Obligations:* debt that is payable on demand or has a specified due date which may be accelerated to "on demand" if certain conditions in the loan agreement are violated by the borrower.
   b. *Long-Term Debt:* debt whose term exceeds the current period.
      1) Examples: long-term notes, bonds, mortgages.
      2) Generally carried at the maturity amount less the discount (if the debt was issued at a discount) or plus the premium (if the debt was issued at a premium).
   c. *Long-Term Lease Obligations*: capital leases, which are leases that are, in economic substance, purchases.
      1) Generally recorded at the present value of the future minimum lease payments.
   d. *Deferred Income Tax Liability:* the difference between the cumulative calculation of the marginal tax rate times book net income and the amount of income tax actually paid. Generally, the account has a credit balance (and thus, it represents a liability) because taxable income is generally less than reported or book income. The account implies that sometime in the future the company will have to pay this amount of tax, but because the actual timing of that payment is not known (and it's actual payment as well), the account is recorded as a noncurrent liability.
   e. *Other Noncurrent Liabilities:* long-term obligations that don't fit into the other categories defined.
      1) Examples: long-term obligations to company officers; matured but unclaimed bond principal and interest obligations; long-term liabilities under pension plans; unearned revenues.
   f. *Contingent Liabilities*: potential liabilities, that is liabilities that might exist if certain future events occur or fail to occur.
      1) Generally contingent liabilities are recognized on the balance sheet only when both the amount and likelihood of occurrence are reasonably certain. (See, for more reference FASB Statement No. 5)
      2) Examples: co-signor on a loan (generally this contingent liability is not recognized on the co-signor's balance sheet); warranty claims (generally the amount and likelihood of occurrence can be reasonably estimated so these are usually recognized on the balance sheet).
5. *Owners' Equity*
   a. Description of owners' equity varies with type of business organization:
      1) Proprietorships = Owner's capital account.
      2) Partnerships = Capital account for each owner.
      3) Corporations = Owners' equity, shareholders' equity or capital.
         a) Divided into contributed capital and earned surplus (i.e., retained earnings).
   b. Corporations
      1) *Contributed Capital*
         a) Capital stock: Number of shares issued multiplied by the par value per share.
         b) Additional paid-in capital: amount received by the corporation when stock is issued less the par value of the stock = paid-in capital in excess of par.
         c) Treasury stock: previously issued capital stock that the company has repurchased for some specific purpose.
      2) *Retained Earnings:* amount of accumulated undistributed earnings of past periods.

II. Form of the Balance Sheet
   A. Two basic formats:
      1. Account Form: assets reported on the left; liabilities and owners' equity reported on the right.
         a. This format is most common.
      2. Report Form: assets, liabilities, and owners' equity sections appearing in vertical arrangement.

B. Generally, assets and liabilities are presented in order of liquidity to facilitate calculation and assessment of working capital.

III. Balance Sheet Analysis
  A. Analyze balance sheet in two ways (both use ratios):
    1. Relationships between balance sheet amounts.
    2. Relationships between balance sheet and income statement amounts.
  B. Relationships between balance sheet amounts
    1. Assess liquidity (ability of the firm to meet its short-term obligations).
      a. Common ratios and calculations:
        1) Current ratio = $\dfrac{\text{Current assets}}{\text{Current liabilities}}$
          a) Measures the proportion of current assets to current liabilities.
          b) Measures the compounded effect of changes in current assets and current liabilities.
        2) Quick ratio = $\dfrac{\text{Quick assets}}{\text{Current liabilities}}$
          a) Quick assets are those which are either cash or readily convertible to cash, such as accounts receivable, marketable securities, and cash.
          b) More conservative measure of liquidity than the current ratio because it excludes inventory (which is generally converted to accounts receivable and then to cash, and thus, takes longer to convert to cash than is often required for fulfilling current obligations).
    2. Assess leverage (degree to which company relies upon debt financing).
      a. Common ratio used:
        1) Debt ratio = $\dfrac{\text{Total liabilities}}{\text{Total assets}}$
    3. Asset mix (proportions of assets in each category)
      a. Common ratios used:
        1) Any specific asset category divided by total assets; e.g., $\dfrac{\text{Current assets}}{\text{Total assets}}$.
  C. Relationships between balance sheet and income statement
    1. Assess efficiency (effectiveness of using resources to increase wealth)
      a. Common ratios used:
        1) Asset turnover = $\dfrac{\text{Sales}}{\text{Total assets}}$
    2. Assess overall profitability
      a. Common ratios used:
        1) Return on assets [ROA] = $\dfrac{\text{Net income}}{\text{Total assets}}$
        2) Return on equity [ROE] = $\dfrac{\text{Net income}}{\text{Total equity}}$
  D. How to interpret ratios
    1. Ratios are more useful as trends; therefore, analysts calculate ratios for several periods.
    2. Ratios are more useful if compared to ratios of other companies in the same industry or of the same size.
    3. Generally, there is not necessarily a target number for each ratio to be; rather, analysts use ratios to **detect** deviations from the norm of the industry.

IV. Notes to the Financial Statements
  A. Supplemental information given to explain or expand the data presented in the financial statements.
    1. Notes to financial statements.
      a. Must include a footnote detailing significant accounting policies.

Chapter 3

  b. Generally includes footnotes describing and summarizing transactions in the financial statements.
  c. Generally includes footnotes about items not in the financial statements, such as contingencies.
  d. Generally includes footnotes about subsequent events:
     1) Subsequent events are events that occur after the balance sheet date but prior to the issuance of the financial statements which have a significant impact on the business.
        a) Type I subsequent event: confirms event which was set in place prior to the balance sheet date, so this event requires restatement of year-end financial statements and a footnote disclosure describing the event.
        b) Type II subsequent event: significant but does not change the relationships of items on the financial statements at year-end and thus, requires no restatement but rather just footnote disclosure.
  2. Separate supplemental schedules
     a. Used to supplement footnotes and to clarify data in footnotes and financial statements.

V. Limitations of the Balance Sheet
   A. Most balances reported at historical cost, which may not approximate current market value; thus, balance sheet cannot be a statement of valuation.
   B. If the purchasing power of the dollar changes, then assets which the company has owned for a long time are mixed with new assets, even though the measuring unit is dissimilar.
   C. While there are some general rules for recording of transactions, companies can choose from among several alternative techniques; this choice leads to a lack of comparability between companies.

TEST YOUR UNDERSTANDING

Fill-in-the-Blanks

Required: Fill in the blanks to complete the following sentences.

1. In a corporation, the difference between _____ _____ _____ and _____ _____ _____ is called working capital.

2. A debit balance in retained earnings is properly referred to as a *deficit*.

3. The _____ _____ _____ of the dollar is regarded as a limitation of the balance sheet.

4. Current assets are normally listed on the balance sheet in the order of their _____.

5. _____ _____ is stock that has been issued but subsequently reacquired by the corporation and is being held for possible future reissuance or retirement.

6. Treasury stock is normally reported in the _____ section of the balance sheet.

7. Events that take place during the _____ _____ period may have an impact on the balance sheet and the other basic financial statements for the preceding year.

8. Owners' equity is sometimes referred to as _____ _____.

9. _____ _____ represents the total amount of undistributed earnings of prior periods.

10. Debt and equity securities that are purchased with the intent of selling them in the near future are classified as _____ _____. These securities are reported in the _____ _____ section of the balance sheet and are reported at _____ _____ _____.

11. An expected future benefit from the tax deductions that have been recognized as expense in the income statement but have not yet been deducted for tax purposes are called _____ _____ _____. They are reported on the balance sheet in the _____ _____ _____ section.

12. A callable obligation is a debt instrument that is (1) _____ _____ _____, or (2) has a specified due date but is callable if the debtor _____ on the provisions of the loan agreement.

13. A _____ is a business entity owned by one person. A _____ is a business entity owned and operated by two or more persons.

14. _____ _____ is the part of the equity section that represents investments by shareholders. It includes _____ _____, _____ _____, and _____ _____-_____-_____.

15. The ability of a company to pay its short term obligations is called _____.

Multiple Choice

Required: Circle the best answer.

1. The accounts and balances below relate to Looms, Inc as of December 31, 1997 (note: all account balances are normal):

Cash	$ 25,600
Mortgage Payable	251,600
Goodwill	96,800
Prepaid Insurance	2,600
Salaries Payable	12,900
Inventory	22,400
Marketable Securities	6,300
Accounts Payable	18,500
Investment in Subsidiary	88,600
Common Stock	100,000

    Working capital for Looms, Inc is:
    A. $56,900.
    B. 1.81.
    C. $25,500.
    D. -$5,800.

2. The form of the balance sheet which lists assets, liabilities, and owners' equity sequentially and vertically is called the:
    A. British form.
    B. report form.
    C. account form.
    D. vertical form.

3. Which of the following describes the characteristics of current assets?
    A. Monetary in nature
    B. Liquid
    C. Converted to cash or consumed within an operating cycle
    D. Arising from current liabilities

Chapter 3

4. Which of the following would *not* appear in the current liability section of a balance sheet?
   A. Accruals for vacation pay for employees
   B. Advances to sales personnel
   C. Property tax assessments
   D. Payments due to utility companies

5. A subsequent event occurs:
   A. after the balance sheet date and after the financial statements are issued.
   B. after the balance sheet date.
   C. before the balance sheet date but is not known until after the books have been closed.
   D. after the balance sheet date but prior to the issuance of the financial statements.

6. Which of the following items would generally *not* be listed in the stockholders' equity section of the balance sheet?
   A. Unrealized gain (loss) on available-for-sale securities
   B. Treasury stock
   C. Foreign currency translation adjustment
   D. All of the above items *would* be listed in the stockholders' equity section of the balance sheet.

7. Venus Mousetraps Company calculated its 1997 working capital as $42,000. Included in the calculation were the following items:

Cash	$10,000
Accounts receivable	15,000
Inventory	25,000
Idle Machinery	12,000
Cash Surrender Value of Life Insurance on Company President	10,000
Treasury Stock	13,000
Accounts Payable	15,000
Accrued Liabilities	6,000
Pension Liabilities	22,000

   The working capital for Venus Mousetraps Company should be:
   A. $42,000.
   B. $7,000.
   C. $41,000.
   D. $29,000.

8. As of January 1, 1997, the balance sheet of Lea Company reported retained earnings of $25,000, common stock of $30,000, additional paid-in capital of $10,000, treasury stock of $5,000 and total debt of $60,000. During 1997, the company earned net income of $12,000, paid dividends of $6,000, borrowed $15,000 and settled current liabilities of $4,000. Total assets as of December 31, 1997 are:
   A. $120,000.
   B. $130,000.
   C. $137,000.
   D. $145,000.

9. Dream Weavers Inc. closed its books as of December 31, 1997. Its financial statements are generally issued on March 15. The following events occurred after December 31 but prior to March 15.
   - The company president died; the company collected $1,000,000 in life insurance.
   - A lawsuit was settled and the company was ordered to pay the plaintiff $400,000. The company plans to pay in June. The lawsuit had been filed several years ago, and the company had prepared a footnote disclosure about it each year since, although no estimated costs had been recognized in the financial statements.
   - The company released a new product line.

How should each of the above mentioned subsequent events be reported on the 1997 financial statements?
- A. None of the events should be reported on the 1997 financial statements.
- B. Each of the three events should be reported via footnote disclosure on the 1997 financial statements.
- C. The company should restate the 1997 financial statements to reflect the verdict and judgement in the lawsuit and should disclose the other two events via footnotes.
- D. The company should restate the 1997 financial statements to reflect the verdict and judgement in the lawsuit. It should also disclose the death of the president in a footnote, but it need not report the new product line in the 1997 financial statements at all.

10. Which of the following is generally considered a limitation of the balance sheet?
- A. Most items are reflected at historical cost, which may not represent current value.
- B. Most items are reflected at historical cost, which may not impound the effects of the dollar's changing purchasing power.
- C. Not all of the company's resources and obligations are reported on the balance sheet.
- D. All of the above are limitations of the balance sheet.

11. Balance sheet analysis is useful in assessing a firm's liquidity, which is the ability to:
- A. satisfy short-term obligations.
- B. meet obligations as they come due.
- C. maintain past levels of preferred and common dividends.
- D. borrow money at a preferred rate.

(Note: Use the following information to respond to questions 12,13,14 and 15):
The accounts and balances shown below were gathered from Vernie Corporation's trial balance on December 31, 1997. All adjusting entries have been made, and all account balances are normal.

Sales	$235,000
Wages Payable	25,600
Cash	17,700
Mortgage Payable	151,600
Dividends Payable	14,000
Prepaid Rent	13,600
Inventory	81,800
Intangible Assets	52,400
Short-Term Available-for-Sale Securities	15,200
Premium on Bonds payable	4,600
Investment in Subsidiary	102,400
Taxes Payable	22,800
Accounts Payable	24,800
Accounts Receivable	36,600

Additional information:
Net income for 1997   26,500

12. The amount that should be reported as current assets on Vernie Corporation's balance sheet is:
- A. $151,300.
- B. $164,900.
- C. $217,300.
- D. $267,300.

34   **Chapter 3**

13. The amount that should be reported as current liabilities on Vernie Corporation's balance sheet is:
    A. $87,200.
    B. $91,800.
    C. $73,200.
    D. $238,800.

14. Total asset turnover for Vernie Corporation for 1997 is: (Note: assume ending total assets is also average total assets.)
    A. 1.36.
    B. .08.
    C. .88.
    D. .74.

15. Return on assets for Vernie Corporation for 1997 is: (Note: assume ending total assets is also average total assets.)
    A. 136%.
    B. 8%.
    C. 88%.
    D. 74%.

16. The December 31, 1996 balance sheet of M Company reported total assets of $1,050,000 and total liabilities of $680,000. Additional information about M Company:
    - M Company issued an additional 5,000 shares of common stock at $25 per share on July 1, 1997.
    - M Company paid dividends during 1997 of $80,000.
    - Net income for the year was $110,000.
    - No other changes occurred in the stockholders' equity during 1997.

    The stockholders' equity section of the December 31, 1997 balance sheet of M Company would report a balance of:
    A. $400,000.
    B. $525,000.
    C. $685,000.
    D. $835,000.

17. The form of the balance sheet that lists assets on the left side of the statements with liabilities and owners' equity on the right side is referred to as the:
    A. account form.
    B. report form.
    C. comparative form.
    D. double-entry form.

18. Pending litigation would generally be considered a:
    A. nonmonetary liability.
    B. contingent liability.
    C. long-term liablity.
    D. callable obligation.

19. Nest Co. issued 100,000 shares of common stock. Of these, 5,000 were held as treasury stock at December 31, 1997. During 1998, transactions involving Nest's common stock were as follows:
    May 3:   1,000 shares of treasury stock were sold.
    August 6:   10,000 shares of previously unissued stock were sold.
    November 18:   A 2-for-1 stock split took effect.

Laws in Nest's state of incorporation protect treasury stock from dilution. At December 31, 1998, how many shares of Nest's common stock were issued and outstanding?

	SHARES	
	Issued	Outstanding
A.	220,000	212,000
B.	220,000	216,000
C.	222,000	214,000
D.	222,000	218,000

(AICPA adapted)

20. Barr Co. has total debt of $420,000 and stockholders' equity of $700,000. Barr is seeking capital to fund an expansion. Barr is planning to issue an additional $300,000 in common stock, and is negotiating with a bank to borrow additional funds. The bank allows a debt-to-assets ratio of .40. What is the maximum additional amount Barr will be able to borrow?
   A. $250,000
   B. $330,000
   C. $525,000
   D. $200,000

(AICPA adapted)

21. What effect would the sale of a company's trading securities at their carrying amounts for cash have on each of the following ratios?

	Current ratio	Quick ratio
A.	No effect	No effect
B.	Increase	Increase
C.	No effect	Increase
D.	Increase	No effect

(AICPA adapted)

22. The following data pertain to Cowl, Inc., for the year ended December 31, 1997:

Net Sales	$ 600,000
Net Income	150,000
Total assets, (average)	2,500,000

What was Cowl's rate of return on assets for 1997?
   A. 5%
   B. 6%
   C. 20%
   D. 24%

(AICPA adapted)

Use the following information for questions 23, 24, and 25 (Note: all three problems are AICPA adapted)
The following trial balance of Mint Corp. at December 31, 1997 has been adjusted except for income tax expense.

	Dr.	Cr.
Cash	$ 600,000	
Accounts receivable, net	3,500,000	
Inventory	900,000	
Prepaid taxes	450,000	
Property, plant & equipment, net	1,480,000	
Note payable, non-current		$ 1,620,000
Common stock		750,000
Additional paid-in capital		2,000,000
Retained earnings		1,060,000
Revenues		6,680,000
Cost and expenses	5,180,000	
	$12,110,000	$12,110,000

Other data for 1997:
   During 1997, estimated tax payments of $450,000 were made and were charged to prepaid taxes. Mint has not recorded income tax expense for 1997. There are no temporary and no permanent differences (relating to book-to-tax adjustments), and Mint's tax rate is 30%.

23. Total retained earnings?
   A. $1,950,000
   B. $2,110,000
   C. $2,400,000
   D. $2,560,000 (AICPA adapted)

24. Total noncurrent liabilities?
   A. $1,620,000
   B. $1,780,000
   C. $2,320,000
   D. $2,480,000 (AICPA adapted)

25. Total current assets?
   A. $5,000,000
   B. $5,450,000
   C. $5,700,000
   D. $6,150,000 (AICPA adapted)

26. Montana Inc. was incorporated on January 1, 1997 with proceeds from the issuance of $750,000 in stock and borrowed funds of $110,000. During the first year of operation, revenues from sales and consulting amounted to $82,000 and operating costs and expenses totaled $64,000. On December 15, Montana declared a $3,000 cash dividend payable to stockholders on January 15, 1998. No additional activities affected owners' equity in 1997. Montana's liabilities increased to $120,000 by December 31, 1997. On Montana's December 31, 1997 balance sheet, total assets should be reported at:
   A. $885,000.
   B. $882,000.
   C. $878,000.
   D. $875,000. (AICPA adapted)

27. The following changes in Vel Corp.'s account balances occurred during 1997:

	Increase
Assets	$89,000
Liabilities	27,000
Capital Stock	60,000
Additional paid-in capital	6,000

   Except for a $13,000 dividend payment and the year's earnings, there were no changes in retained earnings for 1997. What was Vel's net income for 1997?
   A. $ 4,000
   B. $ 9,000
   C. $13,000
   D. $17,000 (AICPA adapted)

28. What is the purpose of information presented in notes to the financial statements?
   A. To provide disclosures required by generally accepted accounting principles.
   B. To correct improper presentation in the financial statements.
   C. To provide recognition of amounts *not* included in the totals of the financial statements.
   D. To present management's responses to auditor comments. (AICPA adapted)

Exercises and Problems

1. Balance sheet classification
   Required: State how each of the following accounts would be classified on the balance sheet. If the account would not appear on the balance sheet, so state.

   (1) Cash
   (2) Plant Assets
   (3) Unearned Revenue
   (4) Cumulative Transaction Adjustment
   (5) Treasury Stock
   (6) Brand Name (developed internally)
   (7) Accumulated Depreciation
   (8) Prepaid Insurance
   (9) Pension Liabilities
   (10) Postage Stamps
   (11) Inventory
   (12) Accrued Income Taxes
   (13) Intangible Assets
   (14) Bonds Payable
   (15) Investment in Oil Wells (long-term)
   (16) Goodwill
   (17) Depreciation Expense
   (18) Allowance for Doubtful Accounts
   (19) Dividends Payable
   (20) Retained Earnings

2. Prepare a balance sheet
   Required: Using the following information, prepare, in good form, a classified balance sheet for Sandy Loom, Inc. as of December 31, 1997. In addition, calculate working capital, current ratio, and the debt-to-asset ratio.

Account	Amount
Accounts Payable	$ 66,000
Accounts Receivable	60,000
Accumulated Depreciation	48,000
Allowance for Doubtful Accounts	20,000
Cash	22,000
Certificates of Deposit	16,000
Common Stock (par)	100,000
Deferred Income Tax Liability	40,000
Looms (equipment)	220,000
Inventory	49,000
Investment in Massachusetts Loom Company (35% of the outstanding stock)	76,000
Investment in Reed Ready, Inc. (current investment securities classified as available-for-sale)	21,000
Notes Payable (current)	6,000
Notes Payable (due in 1999)	86,000
Paid-In Capital in Excess of Par	42,000
Prepaid Insurance	6,000
Rent Expense	37,000
Revenue Received in Advance (weaving class fees; classes meet over 6 months)	12,000
Research and Development Costs	72,000
Retained Earnings	98,000
Taxes Payable	10,000
Tools and Fixtures	52,000

Chapter 3

SOLUTIONS TO TEST YOUR UNDERSTANDING

Fill-in-the-Blanks

1. total current assets; total current liabilities
2. deficit
3. changing purchasing power
4. liquidity
5. Treasury stock
6. equity
7. subsequent events
8. net assets
9. Retained earnings
10. trading securities; current assets; current market value
11. deferred tax assets; noncurrent assets
12. payable on demand; defaults
13. proprietorship; partnership
14. Contributed capital; common stock, preferred stock, additional paid-in-capital
15. liquidity

Multiple Choice

1.	C		15.	B
2.	B		16.	B
3.	C		17.	A
4.	B		18.	B
5.	D		19.	A
6.	D		20.	A
7.	D		21.	A
8.	C		22.	B
9.	C or D		23.	B
10.	D		24.	A
11.	A		25.	A
12.	B		26.	A
13.	A		27.	B
14.	D		28.	A

Exercises and Problems

1. Balance sheet classification

   (1) Current Asset
   (2) Noncurrent Asset
   (3) Current Liability
   (4) Shareholders' Equity
   (5) Shareholders' Equity
   (6) Not on Balance Sheet
   (7) Noncurrent Asset
   (8) Current Asset
   (9) Noncurent Liability
   (10) Not on Balance Sheet
   (11) Current Asset
   (12) Current Liability
   (13) Noncurrent Asset
   (14) Noncurrent Liability
   (15) Noncurrent Asset
   (16) Noncurrent Asset
   (17) Not on Balance Sheet
   (18) Current Asset
   (19) Current Liability
   (20) Shareholders' Equity

2. Prepare a balance sheet

Sandy Loom, Inc.
Balance Sheet
As of December 31, 1997

Assets

Current assets:			
Cash		$22,000	
Certificates of deposit		16,000	
Investment securities (Reed Ready, Inc.)		21,000	
Accounts receivable	$ 60,000		
Less: Allowance for doubtful accounts	(20,000)	40,000	
Inventory		49,000	
Prepaid insurance		6,000	
Total current assets			$154,000
Noncurrent assets:			
Tools and fixtures	$ 52,000		
Looms	220,000		
Less: Accumulated depreciation	(48,000)		
Net equipment		$224,000	
Investment in Massachusetts Loom Company		76,000	
Total noncurrent assets			300,000
Total assets			$454,000

Liabilities and Shareholders' Equity

Current liabilities:			
Accounts payable		$66,000	
Notes payable (current)		6,000	
Revenue received in advance		12,000	
Taxes payable		10,000	
Total current liabilities			$ 94,000
Noncurrent liabilities:			
Notes payable		$86,000	
Deferred tax liability		40,000	
Total noncurrent liabilities			126,000
Total liabilities			$220,000
Shareholders' equity			
Contributed capital:			
Common stock (par)	$100,000		
Paid-in capital in excess of par	42,000		
Total contributed capital		$142,000	
Retained earnings		92,000	
Total shareholders' equity			234,000
Total liabilities and shareholders' equity			$454,000

CHAPTER 4

THE INCOME STATEMENT

KEY POINTS

I. Income—What It Isn't And What It Is
   A. General definition of income: return over and above investment.
   B. Two major concepts for measuring income:
      1. Capital maintenance.
      2. Transaction approach.
   C. Capital maintenance concepts:
      1. Amount the entity could return to its investors at the end of the period without decreasing the entity's net worth.
      2. *Financial capital maintenance*: income is the excess of net assets at the end of the accounting period over the net assets at the beginning of accounting period, excluding transactions with owners.
      3. *Physical capital maintenance*: income is the excess of the current cost of the physical productive capacity at the end of the accounting period over the current cost of the physical productive capacity at the beginning of the period, excluding the effects of transactions with owners.
      4. Both capital maintenance concepts considered by FASB, but financial capital concept adopted.

II. Why Is The Measure Of Income Important?
   A. Reporting income is a primary function of accounting.
   B. Measurement of income requires application of professional judgement.
      1. Because of the subjectivity involved in measuring income, there is also considerable opportunity for mis-reporting and fraud with respect to income determination.

III. How Is Income Measured?
   A. Transaction approach
      1. Income is the result of the effects of certain specifically defined events, including revenues, expenses, gains, and losses.
      2. Implies that income is the difference between resource inflows (revenues and gains) and resource outflows (expenses and losses).
      3. Also sometimes called the "matching concept."
      4. Transaction approach yields same net income number as financial capital maintenance and provides means of measuring cash flows as well.
   B. Revenue and gain recognition
      1. Revenues are inflows of assets from ongoing operations.
      2. *Realization* is the conversion of noncash items to cash.
      3. Revenues and gains are *realizable* when assets held or received in exchange can be readily converted into known amounts of cash in a reasonably estimatable amount of time.
      4. Revenue is *realizable* when the *earnings process is substantially complete.*
         a. Earnings process is substantially complete when the entity has completed its required activities and has no significant additional obligations to perform.
      5. Revenue that is *realizable* (i.e., the earnings process is substantially complete) can be *recognized* (that is, recorded in the books and records).
      6. When can revenue be recognized?
         a. Point-of-sale
            1) Most common.
            2) Title transfers at the point-of-sale, generally, and usually the title of transfer indicates that the seller's obligations have been completed.
            3) Example: Your local grocery store recognizes revenue when you buy groceries.

b. Prior to the point-of-sale
1) Applicable when the project takes a long time to complete, but there are identifiable milestones along the way to indicate that revenue is being earned.
2) Revenue is recognized throughout or at the completion of the project.
3) Used in construction, shipbuilding, agriculture, and airplane construction industries.
c. After the point-of-sale
1) Applicable when there is doubt about the amount and/or timing of the cash flows.
2) Revenue is recognized as cash is received.
3) Used in speculative real estate sales transactions.
C. Expense and loss recognition
1. *Direct matching*: expenses (actual and accrued) should be recognized in the same period as the related revenues.
a. Example: Wages incurred in 1994 should be matched to 1994 revenues.
2. *Systematic and rational allocation*: costs that benefit more than one period should be expensed over the periods benefited.
a. Example: A three-year insurance policy benefits three years, so its cost should be allocated over the revenues of the three years benefited, generally evenly.
3. *Immediate recognition*: costs that are necessary to sustain business but are not specifically identifiable to revenues should be expensed immediately.
a. Example: The cost of the independent audit should be expensed immediately.

IV. Form of the Income Statement
A. Income reported in the **income statement**.
1. Income statement is a **flow** statement.
a. Thus, title notes "for the period ending..."
b. Contrast with the balance sheet, which is an end-of-period snapshot, and title is "as of..."
B. Reporting of income from continuing operations:
1. Single-step form
a. All revenues and gains less all expenses and losses, with little detail provided.
2. Multiple-step form
a. Components of revenues, expenses, gains, and losses reported.
C. Comparative financial statements
1. Present several years' financial statements side by side.
D. Consolidated financial statements
1. Combine the financial results of the "parent company" (the owning company) with the results of all the companies the parent owns (the subsidiaries) into one consolidated entity.

V. Components of the Income Statement
A. Although format is flexible, income statement must report the following elements separately:
1. Income from continuing operations
2. Irregular and extraordinary items, including:
a. Discontinued operations
b. Extraordinary items
c. Cumulative effects of changes in accounting principles
3. Net income (loss)
4. Earnings per share
(Hint: Refer to the income statement for Techtronics Corporation on page 173 of your text as you study the rest of this section. As you study each definition, see if you can locate that item on Techtronics' income statement)
B. Income from continuing operations
1. **Revenue from net sales**
Total sales to customers less discounts and returns.

2. **Cost of goods sold**
     Beginning Inventory
    + Net Purchases
    + Freight-In
    + <u>Other Inventory Acquisition Costs</u>
    = Goods Available for Sale
    − <u>Ending Inventory</u>
    = <u>Cost of Goods Sold</u>
3. **Gross profit on sales**
   Net Sales less Cost of Goods Sold = Gross Profit.
4. **Gross profit percentage on sales**
   Gross Profit divided by Net Sales. (Usually not reported on the income statement.)
5. **Operating expenses**
   Selling Expenses + General and Administrative Expenses.
6. **Other revenues and gains**
   Includes items such as interest, dividends from other companies, and gains on the sale of operating assets.
7. **Other expenses and losses**
   Includes items such as interest paid and loss on the sale of assets.
8. **Income taxes on continuing operations**
   Marginal tax rate x [Net Sales − Cost of Goods Sold − Operating Expenses + Other Revenues + Gains − Other Expenses − Losses] = Income Tax on Continuing Operations.
   Note: calculate tax on continuing operations separately from irregular and extraordinary items: intraperiod tax allocation.

C. Discontinued Operations
  1. What is a discontinued operation?
     a. Cessation of a segment of the business.
  2. How to define a segment?
     a. Identifiable assets and revenues.
     b. Major product line, major customer line, or subsidiary.
  3. Report discontinued operations separately on income statement (refer to Techtronics Corporation Income Statement on page 173).
     a. Interim activities
     b. Disposal
  4. Measurement:
     a. Measurement date (date company decides to discontinue the operation).
     b. Disposal date (date when the segment is actually sold, spun-off, or abandoned).
     c. Generally, several months elapse between measurement date and disposal date.
     d. During the interim (the phase-out period), segment is operating and winding down:
        1) Report results of these operations net of tax and separately.
     e. If accounting period ends after measurement date but before disposal date, must estimate loss (or gain) on disposal of assets.
        1) If loss expected, report the entire amount, net of tax, and separately from interim activities.
        2) If gain expected, report only to the extent of the actual interim activity loss.

D. Extraordinary Items
  1. APB Opinion No. 30: **unusual in nature and infrequent in occurrence**.
     a. Definition is meant to be restrictive.
  2. Requires professional judgement to determine what is extraordinary and what is not.
  3. What is extraordinary for one company may not be extraordinary for another.
  4. Gain (or loss) on the early retirement of long-term bonds is always extraordinary.
  5. Report separately and net of tax on income statement.

E. Cumulative effect of changes in accounting principle
   1. When the FASB promulgates a new accounting standard which requires company to change the method of accounting it has been using for a particular event, the company must report the cumulative effect of the change.
   2. For example, refer to Techtronics Corporation Income Statement and to the Annual Report of Walt Disney Company (in the Appendix to your text).
F. Changes in estimates
   1. As new information becomes available or circumstances change, accountants have to revise estimates which are used to determine or allocate certain types of costs in the current accounting period.
      a. Such changes are all recognized in the current period.
      b. Example: revision of estimates regarding warranty claims or uncollectible accounts.
G. Effects of changing prices
   1. Recall (from Chapter 1) that a stable monetary unit is one of the underlying assumptions of modern accounting theory.
   2. If the monetary unit is not stable, the effects of that instability should likely be taken into account in the financial statements.
   3. However, U.S. GAAP does not presently require such adjustments, primarily due to the measurement difficulty associated with estimating the effects of changing prices on each aspect of the business.
H. Net income or loss
I. Earnings per share (EPS)
   1. ABP Opinion No. 15 requires converting certain income components to earnings per share (EPS).
   2. EPS must be reported separately for:
      a. Continuing operations
      b. Discontinued operations
      c. Extraordinary items
      d. Cumulative effect of change in accounting principle
      e. Net income (loss)
   3. Calculation:
      a. Income from continuing operations divided by weighted average number of shares of common stock outstanding for the reporting period.
      b. Repeat for each component of income statement.
   4. Price-earnings ratio (P/E ratio):
      a. Market value per share divided by EPS
      b. What does it mean?
         1) Measure of attractiveness of stock on stock market, with higher P/E indicating more attractiveness than low P/E.
J. Retained Earnings Statement (page 189)
   1. Net Income closes into Retained Earnings.
   2. Other activities impact Retained Earnings also:
      a. Dividends declared to shareholders.
      b. Certain prior-period adjustments.
   3. Retained Earnings Statement reconciles beginning balance in Retained Earnings to ending balance in Retained Earnings.

IV. Reporting Implications of the FASB's Conceptual Framework
   A. Comprehensive income concept
      1. Includes all revenue, expense, gain, and loss activities during the period.
   B. June, 1996 Exposure Draft from FASB
      1. Proposed standard would require separate financial statement disclosure of "comprehensive income."
      2. Proposed standard would allow companies two options for reporting comprehensive income:
         a. Report as an additional section of the income statement.
         b. Report in a separate financial statement.

Name: *Chapter 4*

DEMONSTRATION PROBLEM

(Note, this problem is AICPA adapted and has been modified slightly)

The following information relates to Arlon Company:

Arlon Company
Trial Balance
December 31, 1997

	Debit	Credit
Cash	$ 25,000	
Accounts receivable, net	75,000	
Inventory	125,000	
Property, plant & equipment	755,000	
Accumulated depreciation		$ 239,000
Accounts payable		70,000
Income tax payable		6,000
Rent revenue received in advance		5,000
Notes payable		55,000
Common stock, $.05 par		50,000
Additional paid-in-capital		305,000
Retained earnings, 1/1/97		150,000
Sales—regular		500,000
Sales—Mem Division		100,000
Proceeds from term life insurance policy		10,000
Cost of goods sold—regular	310,000	
Cost of goods sold—Mem Division	45,000	
Administrative expenses—regular	103,000	
Administrative expenses—Mem Division	15,000	
Interest expense—regular	10,500	
Interest expense—Mem division	7,000	
Loss on disposal of Mem Division	12,500	
Gain on acquisition of bonds payable		13,000
Income tax expense	20,000	
Totals	$1,503,000	$1,503,000

Other Information:

Income taxes:

Paid with Federal Tax Deposit Forms	$14,000
Accrued	6,000
Total expense in trial balance	$20,000

This amount must be adjusted, however, to comply with FASB Statement No. 109, which is a standard you have not studied yet. So, the result of all those adjustments has been made for you, and the amount you should use as income tax expense from continuing operations will be $16,830.

For other calculations, assume Arlon's marginal tax rate is 22%.

Discontinued operations:
On June 30, 1997, Arlon sold its Mem Division for $200,000. The carrying amount of this business segment was $212,500 at that date. The sale was considered as a disposal of a segment of a business for financial statement purposes. Since there was no phaseout period, the measurement date was June 30, 1997.

Liabilities:
On June 30, 1995, Arlon acquired $100,000 carrying amount of its long term bonds for $87,000. All other liabilities mature in 1998.

Capital Structure:

Common stock, $.05 par, traded over-the-counter; 1,000,000 shares issued and outstanding at 1/1/97 and at 12/31/97.

Required: Prepare, in good form, a multiple step income statement for Arlon for the year ended December 31, 1997.

Solution to Demonstration Problem

Where do we start with this problem? First, we need to plan how to approach it. We know that the problem asks for a multiple-step income statement. So, the first thing to do is to recall what the multiple-step income statement looks like. Go to page 173 and review the income statement for Techtronics Corporation; this is a multiple-step income statement.

Next, we need to figure out the components of the income statement we have in this problem. Do we have continuing operations? Yes. How about a discontinued operation? Yes, that is the Mem Division sale. How about an extraordinary item? Yes, the FASB formally defines gains and losses from the early retirement of long-term debt as extraordinary, so Arlon has an extraordinary item. Finally, is there an accounting change this year? No (whew!).

Let's begin with income from continuing operations. Go through the trial balance and highlight all those accounts that you think might be part of income from continuing operations. You should have highlighted the following:

	Debit	Credit
Sales—regular		$500,000
Proceeds from term life insurance policy		10,000
Cost of goods sold—regular	$310,000	
Administrative expenses—regular	103,000	
Interest expense—regular	10,500	
Income tax expense	20,000	

Did you try to include the rent revenue received in advance? Remember, that account represents money people have paid Arlon in advance, but the rent has not been earned yet, so Arlon cannot recognize it as revenue. Rather, it is a liability.

Also, the income tax expense account is picked up here, but remember, we have to make some adjustments to it, so the amount we will actually use for income tax expense for continuing operations will be different. And we will also have to allocate some income tax expense or benefit to the discontinued operations and the extraordinary item (this is the principle of intraperiod tax allocation).

Note, did you find any mention of depreciation expense? Doesn't it seem odd that there is no account for depreciation expense, yet there are fixed assets on the trial balance? Where could depreciation be? Probably it is included in the administrative expenses.

Let's construct the income from continuing operations section now:

Sales		$500,000
Cost of goods sold		310,000
Gross profit		$190,000
Administrative expenses		103,000
Operating income		$ 87,000
Other income and expense:		
Proceeds from term life insurance policy	$ 10,000	
Interest expense	(10,500)	(500)
Income from continuing operations before income taxes		$ 86,500
Income taxes on continuing operations		16,830
Income from continuing operations		$ 69,670

Do you understand how to compute this section? It's really important that you are able to construct an income statement, and the first part, income from continuing operations is the focal point of the income statement.

Ready to go on?

Next, let's take care of the discontinued operations. Go through the trial balance and highlight the accounts you think will relate to the discontinued operation. You should highlight the following accounts:

	Debit	Credit
Sales—Mem Division		$100,000
Cost of goods sold—Mem Division	$45,000	
Administrative expenses—Mem Division	15,000	
Interest expense—Mem Division	7,000	
Loss on disposal of Mem Division	12,500	

Recall that the section detailing discontinued operations has two sections: (1) income or loss from operations (that is, how much money did Mem Division make or lose *prior* to the date the company decided to sell and *during* the phase-out period, while it was being sold?); and (2) gain or loss from the sale of the division's assets.

In the case of Mem, there is no phase-out period as the company simply sold the entire division on June 30. Therefore, the only income or loss from its operations will be those incurred up until June 30. This amount will be:

Sales		$100,000
Cost of goods sold	$45,000	
Administrative expenses	15,000	
Interest expense	7,000	67,000
Income		$ 33,000
Income tax expense (22% x $33,000)		7,260
Net of income tax		$ 25,740

Next, we need to compute the gain or loss on the disposition of Mem's assets, which will be:

Loss on disposal of Mem Division	$(12,500)
Income tax savings (22% x 12,500)	2,750
Net of income tax	$ (9,750)

The amounts we computed for the discontinued operations will be included on the income statement, but we do have to present all the detail. Rather, we will just present the net income from operations (and the tax thereon) and the net loss from disposition (and the tax thereon).

Do you understand discontinued operations???????

Let's go on to the extraordinary item:

Gain on acquisition of bonds payable	$13,000
Income tax (22% x 13,000)	2,860
Net of income tax	$10,140

We are almost ready to put the entire income statement together. All we need now are the earnings per share computations for each section:

Income from continuing operations	$69,670	
Number of shares outstanding	1,000,000	
EPS	$.070	
Discontinued operations ($25,740 less $9,750)	$15,990	
Number of shares outstanding	1,000,000	
EPS	$.016	
Extraordinary item	$10,140	
Number of shares outstanding	1,000,000	
EPS	$.010	
Total EPS	$.096	

The last step, then is to put all this information together, in good form:

Arlon Company
Income Statement
For the Year Ended December 31, 1997

Sales		$500,000
Cost of goods sold		310,000
Gross profit		$190,000
Administrative expenses		103,000
Operating income		$ 87,000
Other income and expense:		
Proceeds from term life insurance policy	$ 10,000	
Interest expense	(10,500)	(500)
Income from continuing operations before income taxes		$ 86,500
Income taxes on continuing operations		16,830
Income from continuing operations		$ 69,670
Discontinued operations		
Income from discontinued Mem Division (less applicable income tax of $7,260)	$25,740	
Loss on disposal of Mem Division (less applicable income tax benefit of $2,750)	(9,750)	15,990
Income before extraordinary item		$ 85,660
Extraordinary item—gain on acquisition of bonds payable (less applicable income tax of $2,860)		10,140
Net income		$ 95,800
Earnings per share		
Income from continuing operations		$0.070
Discontinued operations		$0.016
Extraordinary item		$0.010
Net income		$0.096

TEST YOUR UNDERSTANDING

Fill-in-the-Blanks

Required: Fill in the blanks to complete the following sentences.

1. The **financial capital maintenance** concept of income determination assumes that an enterprise has income "only if the dollar amount of an enterprise's net assets at the end of the period exceeds the dollar amount of net assets at the beginning of the period after excluding the effects of transactions with owners."

2. **Losses** are decreases in equity from incidental transactions of an entity and from all other transactions and events affecting the entity except those that result from expenses and distributions to owners.

3. Under generally accepted accounting principles, revenue recognition normally occurs when the **earnings process** is **substantially complete** and revenue has been **earned**.

4. In current practice, the most common revenue recognition point is **point-of-sale**.

5. Extraordinary items are events and transactions that are both **unusual in nature** and **infrequent in occurrence**.

6. The FASB adopted the **transaction** approach to the determination of income.

7. Under the **physical capital maintenance** concept, income occurs only if the physical productive capacity of the enterprise at the end of the period is greater than it was at the beginning.

8. The format of the income statement that combines revenues and gains and expenses and losses is called the **single-step** format.

9. Financial statements reflecting data for two or more periods are called **comparative financial statements**.

10. Consolidated financial statements include the financial results of the **parent** and its **subsidiaries**.

11. **Income** from **continuing operations** includes all revenues and expenses and gains and losses arising from the ongoing operations of the firm.

12. The separation of income taxes into the different sections of the income statement is called **intraperiod income tax allocation**.

13. The disposal of a major segment of a business either through sale or abandonment is reported separately on the income statement under the heading, "**Discontinued operations**".

14. Income for the period reported on a per-share basis is called **earnings per share**.

15. The price-earnings ratio expresses the **market value** of common stock as a **multiple** of **earnings**.

Chapter 4

Multiple Choice

Required: Circle the best answer.

1. The FASB's concept of "earnings" excludes which of the following:
   A. Income from continuing operations
   B. Cumulative effect of accounting changes
   C. Extraordinary gain (loss)
   D. Gain (loss) from discontinued operations

2. The changes in account balances of Bear Gulch Company during 1997 are presented below:

	Increase
Assets	$100,000
Liabilities	60,000
Common Stock	10,000
Paid-in Capital	5,000

   Assuming dividends of $16,000 and no other changes in retained earnings except net income, what was the 1997 net income for Bear Gulch Company?
   A. $25,000
   B. $41,000
   C. $9,000
   D. $40,000

   (AICPA adapted)

3. The following information relates to the 1997 operations of Mock's Trading Post:

Credit card sales (net)	$200,000
Cash sales	100,000
Salespersons' salaries	50,000
Beginning inventory	60,000
Legal fees	2,000
Inventory purchases (net)	60,000
Miscellaneous expense	2,000
Ending inventory	50,000
Freight-in	500

   Cost of goods sold for 1997 is:
   A. $70,500.
   B. $70,000.
   C. $50,000.
   D. $69,500.

4. In contrast with the multiple-step income statement, the single-step income statement does not separately disclose:
   A. earnings per share.
   B. cost of goods sold.
   C. income taxes on continuing operations.
   D. gross profit.

5. A fast-food restaurant would normally recognize revenue when:
   A. the product is available for sale to the customer.
   B. goods are delivered to the customer.
   C. cash is received from the customer.
   D. the food is prepared and ready for the customer.

6. The ending inventory balance was overstated. If all other account balance are correct, cost of goods sold will be:
   A. overstated.
   B. understated.
   C. not affected.
   D. cannot determine the effect from the information given.

7. Cotton Candy Inc. experienced the following unusual events during 1998:
   - The company sold its entire "homespun cotton" division at a net gain of $50,000.
   - The company reported net losses in the foreign currency market of $10,000.
   - The company retired long-term debt at a net gain of $60,000.

   In its 1998 income statement, how much should Cotton Candy Inc. report as extraordinary?
   A. $60,000 gain
   B. $50,000 gain
   C. $10,000 loss
   D. $100,000 gain

8. Warranty costs are recognized according to which of the following expense recognition principles?
   A. Direct matching
   B. Immediate recognition
   C. Systematic and rational allocation
   D. Cash disbursement

9. On March 31, 1997, the management of Play Pals decided to liquidate one of its unprofitable business segments, Sof-Toys. Play Pals has a December 31 fiscal year-end, and estimated that Sof-Toys could be completely liquidated before year-end. From January 1 through March 31, Sof-Toys incurred a loss of $10,000. Between March 31 and the liquidation date (which was December 15), Sof-Toys incurred operating losses of $40,000. The assets of Sof-Toys were sold on December 15 at a gain of $15,000. Assuming a 30% tax rate, what amount will Play Pals report as discontinued operations on its 1997 income statement?
   A. $38,000 loss
   B. $26,000 loss
   C. $19,600 loss
   D. $28,000 loss

10. The cumulative effects of changes in accounting principles are generally reported on the income statement as:
    A. adjustments to income from operations.
    B. extraordinary items.
    C. adjustments to current period financial statements only.
    D. adjustments to prior period statements.

11. The following information is derived from the income statement for Ruth's Restaurant:
Sales	$500,000
Cost of Good Sold	300,000
Other operating expenses	150,000
Extraordinary loss (gross)	30,000
Tax rate	20%
Common stock outstanding	5,000 shares

    Earnings per share (EPS) from continuing operations is:
    A. $8.00 per share.
    B. $3.20 per share.
    C. $4.80 per share (loss).
    D. $4.80 per share.

12. Fresh Foods Inc. owns and operates a chain of natural food stores. On March 1, 1997, Fresh Foods decided to close its store in Plano, Texas. The store was closed by May 31, 1997. Between March 1 and May 31, the store lost $20,000. Costs associated with the closure and transfer of inventory and fixtures to other Fresh Foods stores were $40,000. The losses should be reported on Fresh Foods Inc.'s income statement as a(n):
    A. component of income after extraordinary items.
    B. component of income from continuing operations.
    C. component of income from discontinued operations.
    D. extraordinary item.

13. Fogg Co., a U.S. company contracted to purchase foreign goods. Payment in foreign currency was due one month after the goods were received at Fogg's warehouse. Between the receipt of the goods and time of payment, the exchange rates changed in Fogg's favor. The resulting gain should be included in Fogg's financial statements as a(n):
    A. component of income from continuing operations.
    B. extraordinary item.
    C. deferred credit.
    D. separate component of stockholders' equity. (AICPA adapted)

14. On April 30, 1997, Deer Corp. approved a plan to dispose of a segment of its business. For the period January 1 through April 30, 1997, the segment had revenues of $500,000 and expenses of $800,000. The assets of the segment were sold on October 15, 1997 at a loss which resulted in no tax benefit. In its income statement for the year ended December 31, 1997, how should Deer report the segment's operations from January 1 through April 30?
    A. $500,000 and $800,000 should be included with revenues and expenses respectively, as part of continuing operations.
    B. $300,000 should be reported as part of the loss on the disposal of the segment.
    C. $300,000 should be reported as an extraordinary loss.
    D. $300,000 should be reported as a loss from operations of a discontinued segment. (AICPA adapted)

15. During 1997 both Rain Co. and Cain Co. suffered losses due to the flooding of the Mississippi River. Rain is located two miles from the river and sustains losses of this nature every two or three years. Cain is located 50 miles from the river and in its 25 years at this location has never suffered a flood loss. How should both companies report the losses on their 1997 income statements?

Rain	Cain
A. Income from continuing operations	Extraordinary item
B. Income from continuing operations	Income from continuing operations
C. Extraordinary item	Income from continuing operations
D. Extraordinary item	Extraordinary item (AICPA adapted)

16. Lore Company changed from the cash basis of accounting to the accrual basis of accounting during 1997. The cumulative effect of the change should be reported in Lore's 1997 financial statements as:
    A. prior period adjustment resulting from the correction of an error.
    B. prior period adjustment resulting from the change in an accounting principle.
    C. extraordinary item.
    D. cumulative effect of change in accounting principle. (AICPA adapted)

17. Witt Company incurred the following infrequent losses during 1997:
    - $175,000 from a major strike by employees.
    - $150,000 from early extinguishment of debt.
    - $125,000 from the abandonment of equipment used in the business

    The amount Witt should report as an extraordinary item on its 1997 income statement is:
    A. $275,000.
    B. $150,000.
    C. $325,000.
    D. $450,000. (AICPA adapted)

18. Kent Company incurred the following infrequent losses during 1997:
    - $300,000 loss incurred in the disposal of one of four dissimilar factories.
    - A major currency devaluation caused a $120,000 exchange loss.
    - Inventory valued at $190,000 was made worthless by a competitor's unexpected introduction of a new product.

    In Kent's 1997 income statement, what amount should Kent report as loss that is *not* extraordinary?
    A. $610,000
    B. $490,000
    C. $420,000
    D. $310,000 (AICPA adapted)

19. A material loss should be presented separately as a component of income from continuing operations when it is:
    A. an extraordinary item.
    B. a cumulative effect-type change in accounting principle.
    C. infrequent in occurrence and unusual in nature.
    D. infrequent in occurrence but NOT unusual in nature. (AICPA adapted)

20. In open market transactions, Oak Company simultaneously sold its long-term investment in Maple Company bonds and purchased its own outstanding bonds. The broker remitted the net cash from the two transactions. Oak's gain on the purchase of its own bonds exceeded the loss on the sale of the Maple Company bonds. Oak should report the:
    A. net effect of the two transactions as an extraordinary item.
    B. net effect of the two transactions in income before extraordinary items.
    C. effect of its own bond transaction in income from continuing operations and the Maple bond transaction as an extraordinary item.
    D. effect of its own bond transaction as an extraordinary item and report the Maple bond transaction in income from continuing operations. (AICPA adapted)

21. On April 30, 1998, Carty Corporation approved a plan to dispose of a segment of its business. The estimated disposal loss is $480,000, including severance pay of $55,000 and employee relocation costs of $25,000, both of which are directly related to the decision to dispose of the segment. Also included is the segment's estimated operating loss of $100,000 for the period from May 1, 1998 through the disposal date. A $120,000 operating loss from January 1, 1998 through April 30, 1998 is *not* included in the estimated disposal loss of $480,000. Before income taxes, what amount should be reported in Carty's income statement for the year ended December 31, 1998 as the loss from the discontinued operations?
    A. $600,000
    B. $480,000
    C. $455,000
    D. $425,000 (AICPA adapted)

22. The effect of a material transaction that is infrequent in occurrence but NOT unusual in nature should be presented separately as a component of income from continuing operations when the transaction results in a:

	GAIN	LOSS
A.	Yes	Yes
B.	Yes	No
C.	No	No
D.	No	Yes

    (AICPA adapted)

Chapter 4

Exercises and Problems

1. Matching
    Required: Using the following key, classify the following transactions on the income statement of Polo Ranch:
    - A. Income from continuing operations
    - B. Income (loss) from discontinued operations
    - C. Extraordinary items
    - D. Cumulative effect of changes in accounting principle
    - E. Not included on the income statement

    _____ 1. Sale of aging racehorse at less than book value.
    _____ 2. Loss of crops due to heavy summer flooding.
    _____ 3. Winnings of racehorses.
    _____ 4. Salaries paid to horse trainers.
    _____ 5. Construction of new foaling barn.
    _____ 6. Filed a lawsuit against a veterinarian who allegedly crippled a valuable racehorse.
    _____ 7. Retirement of long-term debt at a gain.
    _____ 8. Adoption of FASB Statement No. 109, Accounting for Income Taxes.
    _____ 9. Correction of error in accounting for cost of feed.
    _____ 10. Loss resulting from disposition of a guest ranch, which had been owned and operated as a sideline business by Polo Ranch.
    _____ 11. Gain on the sale of investment in common stock of another company.
    _____ 12. Dividends paid to shareholders of Polo Ranch stock.
    _____ 13. Purchase of stallion to be used in breeding program.
    _____ 14. Accrual of wages owed to employees as of the end of the fiscal year.
    _____ 15. Interest earned on certificates of deposit.

2. Prepare an income statement
    Required: Based upon the information provided prepare, in good form, the 1997 multiple-step income statement for Dream Weavers, Inc., a basketry store and school.

Retained earnings, January 1	$ 226,500
Inventory, December 31	130,620
Selling expenses	144,700
Sales revenue	1,080,200
Interest expense	3,600
General and administrative expenses	46,900
Cost of goods sold	874,900
Gain on early retirement of debt (gross)	12,630
Tax rate	30%
Dividends declared this year	10,000
Average shares of common stock outstanding during the year	3,900

3. Prepare a corrected income statement
   You have received the following income statement for Gett's Record Store:

Gett's Record Store
Income Statement
For the Year Ending December 31, 1997

Sales revenue	$60,200
Cost of goods sold	30,600
Gross profit	$29,600
Selling expenses	14,000
General expenses	12,000
Income before tax	$ 3,600
Income tax (20%)	720
Net income	$ 2,880
Earnings per share (1,200 shares outstanding)	$2.40

Required: Upon review of the financial records for the company, you find that ending inventory was overstated by $820. No other errors were noted. Based upon this information, prepare a corrected income statement for 1997.

Critical Thinking Question: What would happen if you didn't discover the error in ending inventory?

SOLUTIONS TO TEST YOUR UNDERSTANDING

Fill-in-the-Blanks

1. financial capital maintenance
2. Losses
3. earnings process; substantially complete; earned
4. point-of-sale
5. unusual in nature; infrequent in occurrence
6. transactions
7. physical capital maintenance
8. single-step
9. comparative financial statements
10. parent; subsidiaries
11. Income; continuing operations
12. intraperiod tax allocation
13. Discontinued Operations
14. earnings per share
15. market value; multiple; earnings

Multiple Choice

1. B
2. B
3. A
4. D
5. C
6. B
7. A
8. A
9. C
10. C
11. A
12. B
13. A
14. D
15. A
16. A
17. B
18. A
19. D
20. D
21. A
22. A

Chapter 4

Exercises and Problems

1. Matching

    1. A
    2. A
    3. A
    4. A
    5. E (asset)
    6. E (contingent asset)
    7. C
    8. D
    9. A
    10. B
    11. A
    12. E (distribution to owners)
    13. E (asset)
    14. A
    15. A

2. Prepare an income statement

Dream Weavers, Inc.
Income Statement
For the Year Ending December 31, 1995

Sales revenue		$1,080,200
Cost of goods		874,900
Gross profit		$ 205,300
Operating expenses:		
Selling expenses	$144,700	
General and administrative expenses	46,900	
Interest expense	3,600	195,200
Income before taxes		$ 10,100
Income taxes (30%)		3,030
Income from continuing operations		$ 7,070
Extraordinary gain (net of tax expense of $3,789)		8,841
Net income		$ 15,911
Earnings per share:		
Operating income		$1.81
Extraordinary item		2.27
Net income		$4.08

3. Prepare a corrected income statement

Gett's Record Store
Corrected Income Statement
For the Year Ending December 31, 1997

Sales revenue	$60,200
Cost of goods sold*	31,420
Gross profit	$28,780
Selling expenses	14,000
General expenses	12,000
Income before tax	$ 2,780
Income tax expense (20%)	556
Net income	$ 2,224
Earnings per share (1,200 shares outstanding)	$1.85

*Cost of goods sold was understated when ending inventory was overstated. An overstatement of ending inventory means that inventory which was really gone (either through sales, shrinkage or disappearance) was erroneously counted as an asset, when it should have been expensed. Thus, correction of the error increases expense, i.e., cost of good sold, thus decreasing net income for the year.

Critical Thinking Question: What would have happened if the error in ending inventory had not been discovered? An overstatement of ending inventory leads to an overstatement of net income because cost of goods sold is understated. If last year's ending inventory was overstated, then this year's beginning inventory will be overstated. An overstatement of beginning inventory leads to an overstatement of goods available for sale, and thus, an overstatement of costs of goods sold, assuming no other errors are made. If cost of goods is overstated, then net income is understated. Keep in mind that if the error in last year's ending inventory was not discovered, then the amount of net income closed into retained earnings for last year would have been overstated. But, this year, since the beginning inventory was overstated, this year's net income will be understated, and thus, the amount of net income closed into retained earnings for this year will be understated. But, at the end of this year, the *balance* in retained earnings will be correct, because the errors in inventory counter-balance.

CHAPTER 5

THE STATEMENT OF CASH FLOWS

KEY POINTS

I. What Good is a Cash Flow Statement?
   A. Provides information not easily determined from either the balance sheet or the income statement.
      1. Recall the examples in the text, such as Circle K, a company that reported positive net income but incurred huge negative cash flows from operations. Eventually, Circle K was forced into financial distress.
   B. Provides information about the flows of cash: how was cash generated and how was cash used by the business?
      1. Cash flow information is clearly and succinctly presented in a one page statement.

II. Structure of the Cash Flow Statement
   A. Reconciliation of sources and uses of cash
   B. Define cash and cash equivalents
      1. Cash equivalents are those short-term, highly liquid investments that can readily be converted to cash.
   C. Classify sources and uses of cash according to business activity:
      1. Operating Activities
         a. Normal, ongoing, daily activities, related to the business purpose and mission.
         b. Examples: cash received from customers; cash paid to employees; interest received; dividends received.
      2. Investing Activities
         a. Transactions involving the purchase and sale of investment securities (not cash equivalents), property, plant, equipment, and other assets not generally held for resale. Also includes cash loaned and receipts of loan payments if lending is not the company's primary business activity.
         b. Examples: purchase a truck for $15,000; sell an idle building for $5,000; collections on nontrade long-term receivables.
      3. Financing Activities
         a. Transactions involving owners (equity financing) and creditors (debt financing), except interest payments which are operating activities.
         b. Examples: proceeds from the issuance of common stock; dividends paid to shareholders; issue long-term debt.
         c. Note: be sure to study carefully Exhibit 5-2 in your text.
   D. Presentation of noncash transactions
      1. Investing and financing transactions which do not immediately involve cash are presented in a separate schedule, not in the body of the cash flow statement.
         a. Example: purchase land with a mortgage; issue stock in exchange for land.

III. History of the Cash Flow Statement
   A. Promulgated by the FASB, FASB Statement No. 95 in 1987.
   B. Replaces statement of changes in financial position, APB Opinion No. 19.
   C. Impetus for cash flow statement came from a study by the Financial Executives Institute which suggested that financial executives, investors, and others really needed cash flow information and determined that the statement of changes in financial position was inadequate for their needs.

IV. Reporting Cash Flow From Operations
   A. FASB allows two formats for presentation of cash flows from operating activities:
      1. **Direct** method: presentation of gross cash receipts and disbursements from operating activities.
         a. Involves analysis of changes in balance sheet account balances and income statement items to restate accrual basis statements into cash basis.

Accrual	Adjustments	=	Cash Basis
Sales	+ Decrease/- Increase Accounts Receivable	=	Cash Collected From Customers
Cost of Goods Sold	+ Increase/- Decrease Inventory AND + Decrease/- Increase Accounts Payable	=	Cash Paid for Inventory
Wages Expense	+ Decrease/- Increase Accrued Wages Payable	=	Cash Paid For Wages
Other Operating Expenses (excluding depreciation)	+ Decrease/- Increase Related Accrued Liabilities AND + Increase/- Decrease Related Prepaid Expense Accounts	=	Cash Paid For Operating Expenses
Noncash operating expenses, such as depreciation	Eliminate		

2. **Indirect** method: begins with net income from the income statement and makes adjustments to reconcile to cash from operating activities.
   a. Adjustments required
      1) Adjustments for noncash items
         a) Depreciation is added as it is neither a source nor a use of cash.
         b) Likewise, amortization expense is also added.
      2) Adjustments for gains and losses on the sale of assets
         These items are investing activities, so they must be eliminated from the operating activities section of the cash flow statement, thusly:
         a) gains are subtracted.
         b) losses are added.
         c) proceeds will be accounted for in the investing section of the cash flow statement.
      3) Adjustments for changes in current operating accounts
         a) in general, increases in asset accounts represent a use of cash and thus, are subtracted from net income.
         b) in general, decreases in asset accounts represent a source of cash and are thus, added to net income.
         c) in general, increases in liability accounts represent sources of cash, and are thus, added to net income.
         d) in general, decreases in liability accounts are uses of cash and are deducted from net income.

Reconcile Accrual Net Income to Operating Cash Flow (Analysis Based Upon Changes in Account Balances During Period)

Current Asset and Current Liability Accounts	Adjustments Required to Convert Accrual to Cash Basis	
	ADD	DEDUCT
Accounts Receivable	Decrease	Increase
Inventory	Decrease	Increase
Prepaid Expenses	Decrease	Increase
Accounts Payable	Increase	Decrease
Accrued Wages Payable	Increase	Decrease
Accrued Liabilities Payable	Increase	Decrease

B. Both the direct and the indirect method result in exactly the same cash flow from operating activities number.
C. Although FASB stated a preference for the direct method, most companies use the indirect method.
D. The direct and indirect method are used only in the operating section; investing and financing presentations are not affected by the choice of presentation style in operating section.

V. Preparing a Complete Statement of Cash Flows
   A. Preparation involves five steps:
      1. Determine the change in cash and cash equivalents.
         a. The difference between the beginning and ending balances for the period in question.
         b. This is the "target" figure, to which the cash flow statement must reconcile.
      2. Determine cash provided by (used in) operating activities.
         a. Requires analysis of balance sheet and income statement accounts.
      3. Determine net cash provided by (used in) investing activities.
         a. Requires analysis of balance sheet and income statement accounts.
      4. Determine net cash provided by (used in) financing activities.
         a. Requires analysis of balance sheet and income statement accounts.
      5. Prepare the statement of cash flows, separating cash flows by activity (operating, investing and financing).
         c. Separate disclosure is required for all significant noncash transactions.
         d. Note: noncash items are NOT reported in the body of the cash flow statement.
   B. Statement of Cash Flows is headed "for the period ending on the fiscal year-end," indicating this is a flow statement.
      1. Compare to balance sheet heading, which is "as of."
      2. Compare to income statement heading, which is "for the period ending."

VI. Using Cash Flow Data to Assess Financial Strength
    A. Financial strength is a function of:
       1. liquidity
       2. profitability
       3. growth potential
       4. risk
    B. Cash flow statement contains data helpful to assess each factor of financial strength.
    C. Patterns of cash flow information can be helpful.
    D. Ratio analysis can also be helpful:
       1. (Cash flow from operations)/Net income
          a. Measure of earnings quality; how correlated accrual net income and cash flow from operations are.
          b. On average, this ratio tends to be greater than 1.
       2. (Capital expenditures + Acquisitions)/Cash from operations
          a. Measures relationships between investment spending and cash generated by operations.
          b. Indicates company's attitude towards reinvestment in long-lived productive assets.
       3. (Cash from operations + Interest paid + Taxes paid)/Interest expense
          a. Measures ability to service debt.
          b. Note the similarity between this ratio and the ratio, times interest earned.
          c. Generally, a higher ratio indicates more solvency.
       4. (Cash from operations + Interest paid + Taxes paid)/Total assets
          a. Measures efficiency of productivity of assets.

DEMONSTRATION PROBLEM

Before you test your understanding of the material in this chapter, you may want to work through the following problem. The problem presents comparative balance sheets for Big Horn Beverage for 1998 and 1997 and the income statement for 1998. The statement of cash flows will be created using the information from the balance sheets and the income statement. One additional piece of information is provided, namely, the amount of dividends paid during the year.

Chapter 5

Before working the demonstration problem, familiarize yourself with the information in the balance sheets and income statements:

Big Horn Beverage
Balance Sheet
December 31, 1998 and 1997

Assets	1998	1997
Cash	$ 43,000	$140,000
Accounts receivable	390,000	210,000
Inventory	360,000	450,000
Land	—	120,000
Total assets	$793,000	$920,000

Liabilities and Equities		
Accounts payable	$150,000	$140,000
Accrued liabilities payable	48,000	30,000
Mortgage payable	140,000	200,000
Common stock	250,000	250,000
Retained earnings	205,000	300,000
Total liabilities and equities	$793,000	$920,000

Big Horn Beverage
Income Statement
For the Year Ending December 31, 1998

Sales	$1,120,000
Cost of goods sold	750,000
Gross profit on sales	$ 370,000
Operating expenses	(360,000)
Loss on sale of land	(15,000)
Net loss	$ (5,000)

Additional information:
   Cash dividends declared and paid during the year: $90,000.

Next, plan the preparation of the statement of cash flows. What information do we need to compute first? First, we need to compute cash flows from operating activities. We have a choice in presentation style for this section of the statement of cash flows. Do you remember the two formats we could use? Yes, the direct and the indirect. Let's select the direct format for this demonstration problem.

Remember, the direct format affects only the operating section. Recall that the direct format looks like this:

Cash collected from customers	$XXXXXX
Less: Cash paid for merchandise	(XXXXXX)
Less: Cash paid for operating expenses	(XXXXXX)
Less: Cash paid for interest and taxes	(XXXXXX)
Net cash used in operating activities	$XXXXXX

Let's begin the computations:

First, cash received from customers:
Cash received from customers is a function of sales to customers and collections of amounts owed by customers (i.e., accounts receivables). So, by analyzing both sales and changes in the balance of accounts receivable, we can compute the amount of cash collected from customers.

In formula form, the computation is:

Sales	$1,120,000
+ Beginning accounts receivable	210,000
Maximum amount of cash we *could* collect	$1,330,000
– Ending accounts receivable	390,000
Cash collected from customers (the amount we *did* collect)	$ 940,000

Next, cash paid for merchandise:
Cash paid for merchandise is a function of inventory activity and how we financed the inventory. We assume we finance the inventory by trade payables, that is, credit from our customers. So, to determine the amount of cash paid for merchandise, we must analyze inventory activity and accounts payable activity. To do that, we need to first analyze inventory activity:

Cost of goods sold	$ 750,000
+ Ending inventory	360,000
Total goods available for sale	$1,110,000
– Beginning inventory	450,000
Purchases	$ 660,000

Notice that the analysis above looks like the cost of goods sold section of the income statement, backwards! Why did we do that? We needed to know the amount of purchases of inventory. Why? Because we will assume the purchases were financed with accounts payable so the total purchases for the period represents the maximum amount we could have charged to our suppliers.

We use that information to analyze accounts payable and determine cash paid to suppliers—for merchandise:

Beginning accounts payable	$140,000
+ Purchases	660,000
Maximum amount we *could* pay to suppliers	$800,000
– Ending accounts payable	150,000
Cash paid to suppliers for merchandise	$650,000

Next, cash paid for operating expenses:
Generally, depreciation is included in operating expenses on the income statement, and it will be eliminated from the analysis because depreciation does not represent a cash flow item for the current period.

In the case of Big Horn Beverage, however, there is no depreciation expense. How can we determine that there is no depreciation? There are no depreciable assets on the balance sheet, hence, there can be no depreciation expense. Therefore, no adjustment for depreciation is needed.

Accordingly, the analysis of cash paid for operating expenses becomes a straight-forward analysis of the changes in the accrued liabilities accounts and the amount of operating expenses reported on the income statement:

Operating expenses	$360,000
+ Beginning accrued liabilities	30,000
Maximum amount of cash we *could* pay for operating expenses	$390,000
– Ending accrued liabilities	48,000
Cash paid for operating expenses	$342,000

Now, we have analyzed all of the operating accounts, including sales, accounts receivable, cost of goods sold, inventory, accounts payable, operating expenses, and accrued liabilities, so we are ready to put together the operating section of the cash flow statement:

Cash collected from customers	$940,000
Less: Cash paid for merchandise	650,000
Less: Cash paid for operating expenses	342,000
Net cash used in operating activities	$(52,000)

Note: net cash from operating activities in this case is negative, indicating that operating activities did not generate cash. Rather, operating activities *used* cash. What does that mean in terms of the company's fiscal health? (It means the company is either having difficulty controlling expenses, it is not collecting receivables, its inventory is increasing, or its sales prices are too low. With any of the explanations comes the observation that negative cash flow from operations cannot continue indefinitely—recall the case of Circle K in your textbook).

On to the next two sections of the cash flow statement: cash flow from investing activities and cash flow from financing activities.

Let's begin with investing activities since that section is usually presented next in the cash flow statement:
Investing activities include those dealing with long-term investments in property, plant and equipment or other long-term investments. In the case of Big Horn Beverage, we observe from the comparative balance sheet a change in the balance in the land account, from a balance of $120,000 in 1997 to a balance of $-0- in 1998. Apparently, the land was sold or otherwise disposed of. The income statement will tell us what happened to the land: "Loss on the sale of land: $15,000."

We now know the land was sold at a loss, but for the cash flow statement we must determine the proceeds from the sale:

Sales price	$?????
Less: carrying value	(120,000)
Loss on sale of land	$(15,000)

Thus, the sales price must have been $105,000.

There were no other investing activities during 1998, so the entire investing section is:

Cash flows from investing activities:	
Proceeds from the sale of land	$105,000
Net cash provided by investing activities	$105,000

The financing section:
Financing activities include borrowing and repaying money, and activities with investors, such as issuing stock or paying dividends. Review the income statement and balance sheets for such activities.

The mortgage payable account decreased from $200,000 in 1997 to $140,000 in 1998, indicating a repayment of $60,000. Cash would have been used to repay the mortgage, so that cash flow must be included in the financing section.

Since the balance in the common stock account did not change from 1997 to 1998, there were no new issues of stock during 1998.

However, the supplemental information tells us that dividends of $90,000 were paid during the year, and this use of cash must be included in the financing section:

Cash flows from financing activities:
Payments of mortgage payable $ (60,000)
Payments of dividends (90,000)
Net cash used in financing activities $(150,000)

We're ready to put the entire statement together, complete with heading and reconciliation of cash:

Big Horn Beverage
Statement of Cash Flows
For the Period Ending December 31, 1998

Cash flows from operating activities:
    Cash collected from customers $940,000
    Less: Cash paid for merchandise   650,000
    Less: Cash paid for operating expenses   342,000
    Net cash used in operating activities $(52,000)

Cash flows from investing activities:
    Proceeds from the sale of land $105,000
    Net cash provided by investing activities   105,000

Cash flows from financial activities:
    Payments of mortgage payable $(60,000)
    Payments of dividends   (90,000)
    Net cash used in financing activities   (150,000)

Net decrease in cash $(97,000)
Cash at the beginning of the year   140,000
Cash at the end of the year $ 43,000

TEST YOUR UNDERSTANDING

Fill-in-the-Blanks

Required: Fill in the blanks to complete the following sentences.

1. The _____ _____ _____ _____ provides information about the cash receipts (inflows) and cash payments (outflows) of a company during a period of time.

2. The statement of cash flows is separated into cash flows from _____, _____, and _____ activities.

3. A _____ _____ is a short-term, highly liquid investment that can be converted easily into cash.

4. _____ _____ include transactions and events that normally enter into the determination of net income, including interest and taxes.

5. _____ _____ include purchases and sales of noncurrent assets such as land, buildings, equipment, machinery, and nontrading financial investments.

66 Chapter 5

6. _____ _____ include transactions and events whereby cash is obtained from or paid to owners or creditors.

7. Transactions relating to investing and financing activities that affect a company's financial position, but not the cash flows during the period are disclosed on a supplemental schedule to the cash flow statement as significant _____ _____ and _____ transactions.

8. The method of presenting cash flows from operating activities that is preferred by the FASB and which presents cash inflows and outflows by major operating activity is the _____ _____.

9. The method of presenting cash flows from operating activities that is most used by U.S. businesses and which presents only a reconciliation between accrual net income and cash flow from operating activities is the _____ _____.

10. The FASB has defined all transactions involving _____ - _____ - _____ and _____ - _____ - _____ securities as investing activities.

11. An increase in accounts receivable during the period represents a(n) _____ of cash collected from customers during the period.

12. Cash payments for income taxes paid is reported in the _____ activities section of the cash flow statement.

13. A decrease in prepaid insurance represents a(n) _____ in cash paid for operating expenses.

14. A decrease in accounts payable would be _____ to accrual net income to reconcile to cash provided by operating activities.

15. Depreciation expense would be _____ to accrual net income to reconcile to cash provided by operating activities.

Multiple Choice

Required: Circle the best answer.

1. Which of the following should be reported on the cash flow statement?
   A. Cash flow per share associated with investing activities
   B. Cash flow per share associated with operating activities
   C. Cash flow per share associated with financing activities
   D. All of the above
   E. Cash flow per share is not reported

2. In its 1998 income statement, the Pizza Company reported net sales of $2,000,000. Net income was $120,000. Accounts Receivable @12/31/97 = $60,000; and @ 12/31/98 = $70,000. Cash collected from customers during 1998 is:
   A. $2,000,000.
   B. $120,000.
   C. $1,990,000.
   D. $2,010,000.

3. In its 1998 income statement, the Pie Company reported cost of goods sold of $300,000. Other information:

	12/31/97	12/31/98
Accounts payable	27,000	18,000
Inventory	62,000	64,000
Accounts receivable	10,000	12,000

Cash paid to suppliers during 1998 is:
A. $311,000.
B. $300,000.
C. $327,000.
D. $302,000.

4. The following information is available from the financial statements of Generation X Clothing for the year ended December 31, 1997:

Net income	$286,000
Depreciation expense	82,000
Payment of dividends	50,000
Purchase of plant assets	68,000

An analysis of current operating accounts reveals the following changes in balance from the beginning of the year to the end:

	Increase	Decrease
Accounts receivable	$106,000	
Inventory		$90,000
Accounts payable	14,000	
Income taxes payable	15,000	

What amount of cash flow from operating activities should Generation X Clothing report for 1997?
A. $286,000
B. $348,000
C. $454,000
D. $351,000

5. During 1998, Columbia Printing sold a building for $200,000. The building cost $150,000 and had a book value of $110,000. How would the transaction be reported in Columbia Printing's 1998 financial statements?
A. Income Statement: Gain on the sale of $90,000
   Cash Flow: No impact
B. Income Statement: Gain on the sale of $90,000
   Cash Flow: Cash provided by investing activities of $90,000
C. Income Statement: Gain on the sale of $90,000
   Cash Flow: Cash provided by investing activities of $200,000; if the indirect method is used, adjustment to net income of $90,000
D. Income Statement: Gain on the sale of $90,000
   Cash Flow: Cash provided by investing activities of $200,000

6. During 1997, Rascal Fairs acquired equipment for $400,000, paying $50,000 in cash and signing a 5-year note for the remainder. How should the transaction be reported on Rascal Fairs' 1997 statement of cash flows?
A. Investing activities: Cash used $50,000; Noncash schedule: Note of $350,000; Operating activities: Cash paid for interest on the note
B. Investing activities: Cash used $400,000
C. Investing activities: Cash used $50,000; Financing activities: Cash provided $350,000; Financing activities: Cash used $350,000; Operating activities: Cash paid for interest
D. None of the above

Chapter 5

Questions 7 and 8 are based on the following information:

Doig, Inc. reported net income of $300,000 for 1997. Changes occurred in several balance sheet accounts as follows:

Equipment	$25,000 increase
Accumulated depreciation	$40,000 increase
Note payable	$30,000 increase

Additional information:
- During 1997, Doig sold equipment costing $25,000, with accumulated depreciation of $12,000 for a gain of $5,000.
- In December, 1997, Doig purchased equipment costing $50,000 with $20,000 cash and a 12% note payable of $30,000.
- Depreciation expense during the year was $52,000.

7. In Doig's 1997 statement of cash flows, net cash provided by operating activities should be:
   A. $340,000.
   B. $347,000.
   C. $352,000.
   D. $357,000. (AICPA adapted)

8. In Doig's 1997 statement of cash flows, net cash used in investing activities should be:
   A. $ 2,000.
   B. $12,000.
   C. $22,000.
   D. $35,000. (AICPA adapted)

9. A statement of cash flows includes certain supplemental disclosures. These are:
   A. cash paid for interest and taxes.
   B. reconciliation schedule (direct method only, reconciling net income to cash from operating activities).
   C. noncash investing and financing activities.
   D. all of the above.

10. Cash receipts and cash disbursements should be classified in the statement of cash flow as:
    A. operating, investing, and capital activities.
    B. operating, investing, and planning activities.
    C. operating, financing, and capital activities.
    D. operating, investing, and financing activities.

11. What are the two methods which may be used to calculate and present cash flows from operating activities?
    A. Current and noncurrent
    B. Single-step and multiple-step
    C. Direct and indirect
    D. Cash basis and accrual basis

12. Which of the following cash flows per share should be reported in the statement of cash flows?
    A. Primary cash flows per share only
    B. Fully diluted cash flows per share only
    C. Both primary and fully diluted cash flows per share
    D. Cash flows per share should not be reported (AICPA adapted)

13. Harold, Inc. had the following activities during 1997:
    - Acquired 2,000 shares of stock in Chester, Inc. for $26,000.
    - Sold an investment in Max Motors for $35,000; carrying value of the investment was $33,000.
    - Acquired a $50,000, 4-year certificate of deposit from a bank (during the year, interest of $3,750 was paid to Arf).
    - Collected dividends of $1,200 on stock investments.

In Harold's 1997 statement of cash flows, net cash used in investing activities should be:
A. $37,250.
B. $38,050.
C. $39,800.
D. $41,000. (AICPA adapted)

14. In a statement of cash flows, if used equipment is sold at a gain, the amount shown as a cash inflow from investing activities should be:
A. the carrying value of the equipment plus the gain.
B. the carrying value of the equipment plus the gain less the amount of tax attributable to the gain.
C. the carrying value of the equipment plus the gain and plus the amount of the tax attributable to the gain.
D. the carrying value of the equipment. (AICPA adapted)

15. How should a gain from the sale of used equipment for cash be reported on the statement of cash flows using the indirect method?
A. In investing activities as a reduction of the cash inflow from the sale
B. In investing activities as a cash outflow
C. In operating activities as a deduction from accrual net income
D. In operating activities as an addition to accrual net income (AICPA adapted)

16. A company acquired a building, paying a portion of the purchase price in cash and issuing a mortgage note payable to the seller for the balance. In a statement of cash flows, what amount is included in investing activities?
A. Cash payment
B. Acquisition price
C. Zero
D. Mortgage amount (AICPA adapted)

17. Which of the following represents a normal pattern of cash flows for a financially healthy corporation?

	Operating	Investing	Financing
A.	+	–	–
B.	–	–	–
C.	–	+	+
D.	–	+	–

18. In a statement of cash flows using the indirect method, depreciation expense is shown as an adjustment to net income because:
A. it affects the calculation of accrual-based net income but does not affect cash flow.
B. it involves cash but does not affect the calculation of accrual-based net income.
C. it is a source of cash.
D. it is an investing activity and must be eliminated from the operating section.

19. Perry Company had the following balances on December 31, 1997:
- Cash in checking account $350,000
- Cash in money-market account 250,000
- U.S. Treasury bill, purchased 1/1/97, maturing 2/28/97 800,000
- U.S. Treasury bond, purchased 3/1/97, maturing 2/28/98 500,000

Perry's policy is to treat as cash all highly-liquid investments with a maturity of three-months or less when purchased. What amount should Cook report as cash and cash equivalents in its December 31, 1997 balance sheet and statement of cash flows?
A. $600,000
B. $1,150,000
C. $1,400,000
D. $1,900,000 (AICPA adapted)

20. A company purchased a building, paying a portion of the purchase price with cash and issuing a mortgage note to the seller for the balance. In a statement of cash flows, what amount is included in financing activities for the transaction?
   A. Cash payment
   B. Acquisition price
   C. Zero
   D. Mortgage amount (AICPA adapted)

21. Mend Co. purchased a three-month U.S. Treasury bill. In preparing Mend's cash flow statement, this purchase would:
   A. have **no** effect.
   B. be treated as an outflow from financing activities.
   C. be treated as an outflow from investing activities.
   D. be treated as an outflow from operating activities. (AICPA adapted)

22. In 1997, a tornado completely destroyed a building belonging to Doyle Corp. The building cost $100,000 and had an accumulated depreciation of $48,000 at the time of the tornado. Doyle received a cash settlement from the insurance company and reported an extraordinary loss of $21,000. In Doyle's 1997 statement of cash flows, the net change reported in the cash flows from investing activities section should be a:
   A. $10,000 increase.
   B. $21,000 decrease.
   C. $31,000 increase.
   D. $52,000 decrease. (AICPA adapted)

23. The primary purpose of the statement of cash flows is to provide relevant information about:
   A. differences between net income and associated cash receipts and disbursements.
   B. an enterprise's ability to generate future positive net cash flows.
   C. the cash receipts and cash payments of an enterprise during the period.
   D. an enterprise's ability to meet cash obligations. (AICPA adapted)

24. During 1997, Monfredo Company entered into the following transactions:
   - Paid dividends of $10,000.
   - Received interest on savings account, $1,500.
   - Received dividends on investments, $2,000.
   - Paid interest on loans, $500.
   - Issued common stock, $100,000.

   In its 1997 statement of cash flows, how much should Monfredo report as financing cash flows?
   A. $103,500 cash inflow and $10,500 cash outflow
   B. $93,000 cash inflow
   C. $100,000 cash inflow and $10,000 cash outflow
   D. $90,000 net cash inflow

25. Which of the following is NOT disclosed on the statement of cash flows when prepared under the direct method, either on the face of the statement or in a supplemental schedule?
   A. The major classes of gross cash receipts and gross cash payments
   B. The amount of income taxes paid
   C. A reconciliation of net income to net cash flow from operating activities
   D. A reconciliation of ending retained earnings to net cash flow from operations (AICPA adapted)

Name: **Chapter 5**

Exercises and Problems

1. **Classification**

    Required: Indicate whether each of the following would be classified as a/an (O) operating activity, (I) investing activity, or (F) financing activity on the cash flow statement. If the item would not be reported on the cash flow statement so state.

    a) Cash collected from customers
    b) Cash paid for property taxes
    c) Cash paid to retire bonds
    d) Cash paid to acquire treasury stock
    e) Cash paid to acquire an interest in a producing oil well
    f) Cash paid for dividends
    g) Dividends received
    h) Paid a key employee the following bonus: cash of $18,000 and of company vehicle with a book value of $7,000
    i) Bad debt expense of $12,000
    j) Purchase of three-month Treasury bills
    k) Long-term debt retired by issuing stock
    l) Purchased a building for $200,000, with $50,000 down and a mortgage of $150,000
    m) Changed accounting methods; cumulative effect of the change, $14,000
    n) Cash paid to acquire inventory

2. **Analysis of cash flow patterns**

    Required: For each of the following cash flow patterns, write a brief explanation of the company's general activities and comment on the company's general fiscal health trends.

	Cash Flow from Operating Activities	Cash Flow from Investing Activities	Cash Flow from Financing Activities
1	+	–	+
2	+	+	+
3	–	–	–
4	–	+	–
5	+	–	–
6	+	+	–
7	–	+	+
8	–	–	+

Chapter 5

3. Statement of cash flows
   Sayers Corporation uses the direct method to prepare its statement of cash flows. Sayers' trial balances at December 31, 1997 and 1998 are as follows:

	1998	1997
Debits:		
Cash	$ 35,000	$ 32,000
Accounts Receivable	33,000	30,000
Inventory	31,000	47,000
Property, Plant, and Equipment	100,000	95,000
Unamortized Bond Discount	4,500	5,000
Cost of Goods Sold	250,000	380,000
Selling Expenses	141,500	172,000
General & Administrative Expenses	137,000	151,300
Interest Expense	4,300	2,600
Income Tax Expense	20,400	61,200
	$756,700	$976,100
Credits:		
Allowance for Uncollectible Accounts	$ 1,300	$ 1,100
Accumulated Depreciation	16,500	15,000
Trade Accounts Payable	25,000	17,500
Income Taxes Payable	21,000	27,100
Deferred Income Taxes	5,300	4,600
Bonds Payable (8% callable)	45,000	20,000
Common Stock	50,000	40,000
Additional Paid-In Capital	9,100	7,500
Retained Earnings	44,700	64,600
Sales	538,800	778,700
	$756,700	$976,100

Additional information:
- Sayers' purchased $5,000 in equipment during 1998.
- Depreciation expense is included in both selling and general and administrative expenses.
- Uncollectible accounts expense is included in general and administrative expenses.
- No uncollectible accounts were written off during 1998.
- The amortization of "unamortized bond discount" is included in interest expense, but involves no cash payments. (Hint: interest expense less amortized bond discount = cash paid for interest)
- The increase in deferred income taxes (a liability) is deducted from income tax expense because it represents the portion of income tax expense *not* paid in cash this year. The journal entry Sayers wrote for the transaction was:

          Income Tax Expense   20,400
          Income Tax Payable   6,100
             Cash   25,800
             Deferred Tax Liability   700

Required: Using the direct method, prepare a schedule indicating net cash provided by (used in) operating activities for Sayers Corporation for the year ending December 31, 1998.   (AICPA adapted)

4. Net cash flows computations

   The differences in Holmes Inc.'s balance sheet accounts at December 31, 1997 and 1998 are presented below:

	Increase (Decrease)
Assets	
Cash	$ 120,000
Short-term investments (classified as available-for-sale)	300,000
Accounts receivable, net	—
Inventory	80,000
Long-term investments	(100,000)
Plant assets	700,000
Accumulated depreciation	—
	$1,100,000
Liabilities and Equities	
Accounts payable and accrued liabilities	$ (5,000)
Dividends payable	160,000
Short-term bank debt	325,000
Long-term debt	110,000
Common stock, $10 par	100,000
Additional paid-in capital	120,000
Retained earnings	290,000
	$1,100,000

   Additional information:
   - Net income for 1998 was $790,000.
   - Cash dividends of $500,000 were declared in 1988.
   - A building costing $600,000 and having a carrying amount of $350,000 was sold for $350,000.
   - Equipment costing $110,000 was acquired through the issuance of long-term debt.
   - A long-term investment was sold for $135,000. There were no other transactions involving long-term investments.
   - 10,000 shares of common stock were issued for $22 per share.

   Required: Compute (1) net cash flows from operating activities; (2) net cash flows from investing activities; and (3) net cash flows from financing activities.

SOLUTIONS TO TEST YOUR UNDERSTANDING

Fill-in-the-Blanks

1. Statement of cash flows
2. operating, investing, financing
3. cash equivalent
4. Operating activities
5. Investing activities
6. Financing activities
7. noncash investing; financing
8. direct method
9. indirect method
10. available-for-sale; held-to-maturity

11. decrease
12. operating
13. decrease
14. added
15. added

Multiple Choice

1. E
2. C   Explanation:

Sales	$2,000,000
+ Beginning balance	60,000
– Ending balance	70,000
Cash received from customers	$1,990,000

3. A   Explanation:

Beginning inventory	$ 62,000
– Cost of goods sold	300,000
– Ending inventory	64,000
Purchases	$302,000
Beginning accounts payable	$ 27,000
+ Purchases	302,000
– Ending accounts payable	18,000
Cash paid for inventory	$311,000

4. D   Explanation:

Net income	$286,000
Depreciation expense	82,000
Increase in receivables	(106,000)
Decrease in inventory	90,000
Increase in payables	14,000
Decrease in income tax payable	(15,000)
Cash flow from operations	$351,000

5. C
6. A
7. B   Explanation:

Net income	$300,000
Depreciation	52,000
Gain on sale of equipment	(5,000)
Net cash flow from operations	$347,000

8. A   Explanation:

Proceeds from the sale of equipment	$18,000
Cash used to purchase equipment	(20,000)
Net cash used in investing activities	$(2,000)

9. D
10. D
11. C
12. D
13. D   Explanation:

Cash paid for Chester Inc. stock	$(26,000)
Cash proceeds from sale of Max Motors	35,000
Cash invested in certificate of deposit	(50,000)
Net cash used in investing activities	$(41,000)

14. A
15. C
16. A

Name: Chapter 5

17. A
18. A
19. C   Explanation:

Cash in checking account	$350,000
Cash in money-market account	250,000
U.S. Treasury bill (maturity is 3 months or less at purchase)	800,000
Total cash and cash equivalents	$1,400,000

20. C
21. A
22. C   Explanation:

Acquisition cost of building	$100,000
Accumulated depreciation	(48,000)
Net book value of building	$ 52,000
Extraordinary loss on income statement	(21,000)
Cash received from insurance company	$ 31,000

23. C
24. D
25. D

Exercises and Problems

1. Classification

    a) O   h) cash = O; noncash for the transfer
    b) O   i) noncash; reconciling item with indirect method
    c) F   j) cash equivalent
    d) F   k) Noncash
    e) I   l) I = $50,000; noncash $150,000
    f) F   m) Noncash; reconciling item with indirect method
    g) O   n) O

2. Analysis of cash flow patterns
   1. Company is using cash from operations and is borrowing (or issuing equity) to expand.
   2. Company is using cash generated from operations, sale of assets, and financing to stock-pile cash; this company is probably very liquid and may be looking for other companies to acquire.
   3. Company is using cash reserves to finance operational shortfall and to pay long-term creditors or investors.
   4. Company is financing operating cash flow shortages and payments to creditors or stockholders by selling fixed assets.
   5. Company is using cash flow generated by operating activities to buy fixed assets and to pay down debt or pay dividends to owners.
   6. Company is using cash from operating activities and from sale of fixed assets to pay down debt or to repay owners.
   7. Company's operating cash flow problems are covered by the sale of fixed assets and by borrowing from creditors or issuing equity to owners.
   8. Company is growing rapidly but has shortfalls in cash from operating activities and from the purchase of long-term assets; the shortfalls are financed either by debt or equity investment.

3. Statement of cash flows

Sayers Corporation
Statement of Cash Flows
For the Year Ending December 31, 1998

Cash flows from operating activities:
Cash receipts from customers $535,800
Cash payments for:
Inventory	$226,500	
Operating expenses	276,800	
Interest	3,800	
Income taxes	25,800	532,900
Net cash provided by operations		$ 2,900

Explanations:
Cash receipts from customers:
 Sales + Beginning accounts receivable – Ending accounts receivable
 $538,800 + $30,000 – $33,000 = $535,800

Cash paid for inventory:
Cost of goods sold	$250,000
+ Ending inventory	31,000
– Beginning inventory	(47,000)
– Ending trade payables	(25,000)
+ Beginning trade payables	17,500
Cash paid for inventory	$226,500

Cash paid for operating expenses:
Selling expenses	$141,500
+ General and administrative expenses	137,000
– Depreciation expense	(1,500)
– Uncollectible accounts expense	(200)
Cash paid for operating expenses	$276,800

Cash paid for income taxes was explained in the body of the problem

4. Net cash flows computations
   (1) $920,000
   Explanation:
   Net cash flows from operating activities can generally be computed using either the direct or the indirect methods. To use the direct method, we need information regarding sales, which we are not given in this problem, so we cannot use the direct method for this problem. Using the indirect method, then:

Net income	$790,000
Add: depreciation expense	250,000
Less: gain on sale of long-term investment	(35,000)
Less: increase in inventory	(80,000)
Less: decrease in accounts payable and accrued liabilities	(5,000)
Net cash provided by operating activities	$920,000

Computations:
Depreciation expense:
The balance in the accumulated depreciation account did not change from the beginning to the end of the year. However, we know that a building costing $600,000 with a carrying value of $350,000 was sold. The journal entry to facilitate that sale must have been:

Cash	350,000	
Accumulated Depr.	250,000	
Building		600,000

From this journal entry we can see that accumulated depreciation was debited during the year for the sale. Since the overall balance did not change during the year, the account must have also been credited for $250,000 at some point during the year. What transaction could bring about a credit to accumulated depreciation?

Depreciation Expense	250,000	
Accumulated Depr.		250,000

Therefore, depreciation expense must have been $250,000.

Gain on sale of long-term investment:
The only transaction affecting long-term investments was the sale for $135,000. However, the balance in the account decreased by $100,000, so the journal entry to record the sale must have been:

Cash	135,000	
Long-Term Investment		100,000
Gain on Sale		35,000

(2) $(1,005,000)
Explanation:

Purchase of short-term investments	$ (300,000)
Sale of long-term investments	135,000
Sale of building	350,000
Purchase of plant assets	(1,190,000)
Net cash used in investing activities	$(1,005,000)

Explanation of plant assets:

Building account:	
Cost of equipment acquired	$110,000
Cost of building sold	(600,000)
Cost of plant assets acquired	???
Net increase in plant assets account	$700,000

Therefore, cost of plant assets acquired must be $1,190,000.

The other amounts are given in the problem or are computed in net cash flows from operating activities.

(3) $205,000
Explanation:

Issuance of short-term debt	$325,000
Issuance of common stock	
(10,000 x $22)	220,000
Cash paid for dividends	(340,000)
Net cash provided by financing activities	$205,000

Computation of dividends paid:
Retained earnings increased by $290,000 during the period, but net income was much greater than that, namely, $790,000. Therefore, dividends of $500,000 must have been declared ($790,000 – $500,000 = $290,000).

However, dividends payable increased by $160,000, indicating that not all of the dividends declared this period were actually paid:

Dividends declared	$500,000
Increase in dividends payable	(160,000)
Dividends paid	$340,000

CHAPTER 6

THE REVENUE/RECEIVABLES/CASH CYCLE

KEY POINTS

I. The Operating Cycle of a Business
   A. Involves (in order):
      1. Purchase inventory (cash or on account)
      2. Sell inventory (often on account; receivable created) (revenue is usually recognized at this point also)
      3. Collect receivable
      4. Repeat 1, 2, 3
   B. Revenue:
      1. Recognize when earnings process is complete **and** cash is realized or realizable.
      2. Generally, revenue is earned at the point of sale, when title passes to buyer and receivable is created.
   C. Record revenue and cash collection
      1. Example:
         Lynley Company sells $10,000 of merchandise on account to a customer. Customer pays account 10 days later. Journal entries to record this sequence are:

Accounts Receivable	10,000	
Sales		10,000
Sale of merchandise on account.		
Cash	10,000	
Accounts Receivable		10,000
Customer pays on account		

      2. What if customer uses a credit card?
         a. Two likely scenarios:
            1) customer uses credit card from another company, such as American Express:

Accounts Receivable— American Express	10,000	
Sales		10,000

               When American Express settles it will deduct its fee from cash remitted. The fee is usually between 3% and 5%. Assuming the fee is 5% for Lynley:

Cash	9,500	
Credit Card Service Charge	500	
Accounts Receivable—American Express		10,000

            2) customer could use a bank credit card, such as VISA or MasterCard. In this case, Lynley will deposit credit card receipts directly into its bank account and service charge will be deducted immediately (assume a 5% service charge):

Cash	9,500	
Credit Card Service Charge	500	
Sales		10,000

   D. Classification of receivables
      1. **Receivables** are rights to receive money, goods, or services from others, generally expected to be settled by cash.
      2. **Trade receivables** result from normal operating activities and represents rights to receive cash from customers.
         a. Can be informal, such as *accounts receivable* or formal, such as *notes receivable*
         b. Both represent extensions of credit to customers.
      3. **Nontrade receivables** result from all other types of activities and represent all other types of receivables, such as advances to employees, claims for tax refunds, insurance claims for losses and damages, deposits with utility companies, dividends receivable, interest receivable, and purchase prepayments.
      4. Receivables are often classified by **maturity**, with **current receivables** including those items for which cash settlement is expected within a year or the company's normal operating cycle. **Noncurrent** or **long-term receivable** are those which will extend past a year of the company's normal operating cycle.

Chapter 6

II. Accounting for Sales Revenue
   A. Sales Discounts
      1. *Trade discounts*: gross selling price less designated amount; effect is to reduce "list" price to "net" price, which is the amount actually charged to the customer.
      2. *Cash (or sales) discount*: discount offered to customer for prompt payment; customer can take cash discount only if payment is remitted within time indicated on the invoice.
         a. Generally expressed as "2/10,n/30" which means 2% discount if paid within 10 days; total amount due within 30 days.
         b. Gross method to record sales discount:
            Example: Sales of $6,000, terms 1/15,n/30:

Accounts Receivable	6,000	
Sales		6,000

            To record sales on account.
            If payment is made within 15 days:

Cash	5,940	
Sales Discounts	60	
Accounts Receivable		6,000

            If payment is not made within 15 days but is made within 30 days:

Cash	6,000	
Accounts Receivable		6,000

   B. Sales Returns and Allowances
      1. Goods returned to seller in the normal course of business, due to damage, spoilage, error or contract agreement.
      2. Example: Assume merchandise costing $500 is sold and later returned, the journal entry to record the return is:

Sales Returns & Allowances	500	
Accounts Receivable		500

   C. The Valuation of Accounts Receivable—Accounting for Bad Debts
      1. In general, receivables are valued on the balance sheet at their **net realizable value**, which is also their expected cash value.
         a. Net realizable value is equal to the gross amount of the receivables less the allowance for uncollectible accounts, as this amount represents the expected cash flow. Sometimes, companies present both gross receivables and the allowance account on the balance sheet; other companies report only the net number. Look in your text: how does Microsoft report receivables?
      2. Generally, trade receivables are NOT valued as net present value because the timeliness of their collectibility diminishes the significance of the time value of money factor.
      3. Uncollectible accounts receivable are also called "bad debts." Uncollectible accounts arise when customers don't pay.
      4. There are two methods to account for uncollectible accounts receivable: (1) **direct write-off** and (2) **allowance method**.
         a. Direct method: when the receivable becomes uncollectible, write it off directly to expense as follows:

Doubtful Accounts Expense	XXX	
Accounts Receivable		XXX

            This method is required for tax purposes, but is not consistent with generally accepted accounting principles (GAAP). It is, however, simple, but it does not match revenue and expense and it does not value receivables at net realizable value.
         b. Allowance method: a valuation account, which is a contra-asset account is established by *estimating* the amount of uncollectible receivables. The account is established thusly:

Doubtful Accounts Expense	XXX	
Allowance for Doubtful Accounts		XXX

            When a receivable becomes uncollectible, the allowance account is debited because the expense has already been recognized, thusly:

Allowance for Doubtful Accounts	XXX	
Accounts Receivable		XXX

5. Estimating uncollectible accounts
   There are two methods commonly used to estimate uncollectible accounts: (1) **Sales method [income statement approach]** and (2) **Receivables balance method [balance sheet approach]**
   a. *Sales method [income statement approach]:* doubtful accounts are assumed to be a function of sales and thus, are estimated as a percentage of sales. In this method, the focus for accounting is the income statement, and thus, the amount to calculate is the *expense* amount. For example, assume credit sales of $4,000 and an estimated uncollectible percentage of 1% of credit sales, the journal entry would be:
   Doubtful Accounts Expense   40
       Allowance for Doubtful Accounts   40
   Note: This journal entry would be the same regardless of the balance in the Allowance account.
   b. *Receivables approach [balance sheet approach]:* doubtful accounts are assumed to be a function of granting credit and thus, are estimated by analyzing the receivables accounts. The analysis makes use of the accounts receivable aging, which is a listing of specific receivables by the length of time they have been outstanding. Generally, the longer a receivable has been outstanding the more likely it is to become uncollectible.
   The focus of the receivables approach (balance sheet approach) is the net realizable value of the receivables, so the balance in the Allowance account is considered when writing the journal entry. For example, consider the following:

   Accounts Receivable $10,000
   Allowance for Doubtful Accounts   1,000
   Net Realizable Value $ 9,000

   In this case, what is the percentage of expected uncollectible accounts, based upon receivables? (The answer is 10%, and that's a HUGE percentage of uncollectibles!) Ok, so what if the company agrees that the percentage is too high and decides the correct percentage should be 7%? This journal entry would be made:
   Doubtful Accounts Expense   300
       Allowance for Doubtful Accounts   300
   Thinking Question: Does it seem weird to you that we just a wrote a journal entry which REDUCED expense???? Yes, it is strange and probably unusual, but this problem illustrates the point of the balance sheet method: what counts in this case is the NET REALIZABLE VALUE of the receivables, and thus, the journal entry focuses on the balance sheet account and NOT on the income statement account.
D. Warranties for Service and Replacement
   1. Warranties are agreements provided by the seller to the buyer that obligates the seller to perform, at the customer's request, free service or repair or to replace defective units.
   2. Warranties generally extend for a specific period of time or over a specific amount of usage.
   3. Seller must estimate costs associated with warranty claims and must accrue those costs in the period the revenue was earned.
   4. Example:
      Havers Electronics sells and services personal computers. All computers sold carry a one-year warranty. Past experience indicates cost of warranty claims to be about 12% of total sales. If Havers' sales are $100,000, it would record estimated warranty liabilities:
      Warranty Expense   12,000
          Estimated Liability Under Warranties   12,000
      Assume actual warranty claims are $11,600 this year:
      Estimated Liability Under Warranties   11,600
          Cash   11,600
      Periodically, the warranty claims accrued should be analyzed to insure that it closely matches actual expense.

III. Monitoring Accounts Receivable
   A. To realize the maximum amount of cash from receivables requires careful monitoring by management.
   B. Ratio can be very helpful, and two ratios are commonly used: (1) accounts receivable turnover and (2) days' sales in receivables.
      1. Accounts receivable turnover measures the amount of time it takes to collect receivables.

a. Calculation:

$$\frac{\text{Net credit sales}}{\text{Average accounts receivable balance}}$$

b. Note: the result is the number of times receivables "turn" into cash during the year.
2. Days' sales in receivables is also a measure of collection period and is calculated:

$$\frac{365}{\text{Accounts receivable turnover}}$$

C. Once you have calculated receivables ratios, how do you know if the ratios are "strong" or "weak?"
1. Like most ratios, the answer is industry dependent.
2. Some industries, such as freight transportation have very quick collection periods, so "days' sales in receivables" will be very low.
3. Other industries, such as pawn shops, have very long collection periods (and high interest rates on receivables, too!), so "days' sales in receivables" will be very high.
4. See Exhibit 6-1 in your text for more examples.
D. Receivables are costly, and the longer they are outstanding, the more costly they are.
1. Costs associated with receivables include bookkeeping, bad debts, and indirect interest costs.

IV. Cash Management and Control
A. Cash is the single most important item on the balance sheet.
1. Involved directly or indirectly in every transaction a business undertakes.
2. Liquidity (the measure of cash on hand to meet current obligations) is key to business's survival.
3. Cash, left alone, is unproductive, however.
a. If left alone (not invested prudently) cash fails to earn interest and is thus, unproductive to the business.
B. Composition of cash
1. Cash on hand, also called demand deposits:
a. coin, paper money, and unrestricted funds on deposit at the bank.
b. reported on balance sheet as cash.
2. Time deposits
a. restricted cash in that funds are not available for immediate use.
b. examples include CD's (certificates of deposit) and money market certificates.
c. reported on the balance sheet as cash.
3. Money deposited in international banks
a. if available for immediate and unrestricted withdrawal from the international bank, consider as cash (and report on balance sheet as such).
4. Restricted cash balances
a. Sometimes management sets aside certain amounts of cash for certain purposes, such as travel or income tax payments.
b. Although this is technically cash, it is not unrestricted so it should be reported on the balance sheet separately from other cash balances.
5. Cash overdrafts
a. If the company writes checks in excess of the amount on deposit in the bank, the overdraft should be reported as a current liability, not as negative cash (although in practice you will see companies that report negative cash balances on the balance sheet).
6. Postage, Post-dated checks, IOU's, Not-sufficient funds (NSF) checks
a. Do not report these items as cash because they do not meet the test of available for immediate use as a medium of exchange.
7. Compensating balances
a. Often a company will agree, as part of an overall lending agreement, to maintain a certain balance in its bank account; this agreed-upon amount is called a "compensating balance."
b. Since the money on deposit as a compensating balance is not available for use by the company, it is not "cash on hand."
c. The SEC suggests separate disclosure of compensating balances in the "cash" section of the balance sheet.
d. Often the company will include a footnote disclosure as well.
C. Management and Control of Cash
1. Since cash is fungible and readily available for use, it is a temptation and frequent target for misuse.

2. Control implies safeguarding and managing to ensure that cash is used in the best interests of the company and for company purposes only.
3. Basic characteristics of a system of cash control:
   a. Specifically assigned responsibility for handling cash receipts.
   b. Separation of handling and recording cash receipts.
   c. Daily deposit of all cash received.
   d. Voucher system to control cash payments.
   e. Internal audits at irregular intervals.
   f. Double record of cash--bank and books, with reconciliations performed by someone outside the accounting function.

D. Petty Cash Fund
   1. Petty cash refers to the fund of currency on hand used to make periodic payments that are too small to justify the cost of writing a check (for large companies, the cost of writing a check can be quite large).
   2. The amount in the petty cash fund is insignificant to the business as a whole, but nonetheless, because it is cash, it is accounted for carefully.
   3. To open a petty cash fund, make the following entry:

Petty Cash	200	
Cash		200

      Entry to establish petty cash fund.

      (Note: this entry implies that $200 in currency has been transferred to a petty cash fund, and the currency is generally kept in a cash box, under the control and responsibility of one person.)
   4. As petty cash is spent, receipts for the expenditures are placed in the cash box, but no journal entries are written at this time.
   5. When the petty cash fund runs low, or at specified points in time, the petty cash fund is reconciled and replenished.
      a. Reconciling means that the remaining currency when added to the total amount on all the receipts in the cash box should equal the original petty cash amount, in this case, $200.
      b. Upon reconciliation, the expenses paid by petty cash are recorded, and the out-of-balance amount is recorded to an expense account, "Cash Short and Over."
      c. A journal entry might look like this:

Office Supplies Expense	35	
Postage Expense	35	
Cash Over and Short	10	
Cash		80

      What does this journal entry tell you? (It should tell you that when the petty cash box was counted, $80 had been spent but there were receipts in the box for $70, so the difference is charged to "over and short.")
      d. To replenish the fund:

Petty Cash	80	
Cash		80

E. Bank Reconciliations
   1. When a business writes a check, it is authorizing the bank to pay to the holder of the check funds from the business's bank account. Likewise, when a business deposits other business's checks into its accounts it is asking the bank to add those funds to its account.
   2. At the end of each month, the bank sends to each customer a summary of checks it has cleared, deposits it has made, and fees it has charged for services.
   3. The bank's summary, called a bank statement, must be reconciled to the records the company has kept of such transactions in the form of a **bank reconciliation**.
   4. Generally, bank reconciliations are made monthly, because banks will only accept responsibility for their errors for a few months after the error's occurrence.
   5. Bank reconciliations for businesses are just like your personal bank reconciliations--just with more transactions and maybe more money involved!
   6. **Reconciling items** are those differences between activities recorded on the bank's books and the business's. Four common reconciling items include:
      a. a deposit made by the business (and thus recorded in its books) has not been received and/or recorded by the bank (and thus, is not on the bank statement).

1) *Deposits in transit*, as these are called, must be added to the bank's reported balance to reconcile with the business's books.
    b. Checks written and mailed by the business (and thus, recorded as reductions in cash) have not cleared the bank yet (and thus, the bank has not deducted the amount from the business's account).
        1) *Outstanding checks*, as these items are called, must be deducted from the balance on the bank statement to reconcile with the business's books.
    c. Banks generally charge fees for servicing accounts, and they usually automatically deduct fees from the customer's account. The amount of the fees is generally not known by the business until the bank statement arrives, so the business generally has not recorded the fees.
        1) Fees must be deducted from the business's cash balance to reconcile with the bank's statement. A journal entry is written to accomplish this:
            Bank Fees Expense   15
                Cash   15
        2) When business's deposit checks to their accounts, sometimes some of the checks are not depositable because the person or business writing them didn't have enough money in his/its account to cover the check. Such checks are called "NSF" for "not-sufficient funds" or "bad checks." When NSF checks are returned, the bank will deduct the amount on them from the business's bank account, so the business must acknowledge this reduction in money in a manner similar to the recording of bank fees. Banks often charge a fee for NSF funds, too, and the business must journalize those fees as well.
    d. Sometimes a third party will make a deposit directly to the business's account, and occasionally, the business may not have recorded this amount. So, when the bank statement is received the business must journalize the receipt of cash.
        1) What kinds of transactions do you think might be handled in this manner? (Hint: think about your own checking account--does the bank pay you interest on your account? If so, when do you record the interest? Right! When you get your bank statement.)
7. What happens if you analyze all the common reconciling items, and the bank statement still does not reconcile to the books?
    a. Now, you have to look for errors.
        1) Bank errors usually involve recording someone else's transactions in your account (Note: this happens *very* rarely, so don't count on it.)
        2) Book errors usually involve misrecording of deposits (adding the deposit incorrectly or recording the amount on a deposited check incorrectly) or misrecording checks (writing the check itself for one amount and journalizing it for another).
    b. Sometimes, errors are really hard to find and the search can be very frustrating!
8. Preparing the reconciliation
    a. The formal reconciliation can take on several different formats, but the basic idea is the same in each of them: to adjust both the bank and the books to arrive at the "true" account balance.
    b. After preparing the reconciliation, the depositor should record items appearing on the bank statement and requiring recognition on depositor's books. Corrections for errors must be made.
    c. At this point, the account is "reconciled."

V. Presentation of Sales and Receivables in the Financial Statements
   A. Present current receivables in the current asset section.
   B. Any long-term trade and nontrade receivables are reported as "other noncurrent assets."
   C. Allowances are also generally presented in the balance sheet.
   D. Footnotes are often used to supplement information in the balance sheet.

EXPANDED MATERIAL KEY POINTS

VI. Accounts Receivable as a Source of Cash
    Three major strategies:
    A. Assignment of Accounts Receivable
        1. Borrow money by pledging accounts receivable as security on the loan.
        2. General assignment: all receivables are assigned; presents no accounting problems; loan and repayment are recorded normally. Footnote disclosure of assigned receivables is necessary, however.

3. Assign specific receivables: borrower should transfer the balance of those accounts to a special account and clearly identify the account as assigned receivables.
   B. Factoring accounts receivable
      1. Sale of accounts receivable without recourse is factoring.
      2. The buyer of the receivable is the "factor."
      3. Factor assumes the burden of billing and collecting accounts receivables.
      4. Factor generally charges fees in excess of the interest charges on a loan with assignment of receivables. Often factor fees are as much as 30% of the net receivables.
   C. Transfer of Accounts Receivable with Recourse
      1. Transferee (usually a bank or finance company) advances cash for accounts receivable but retains the right to collect from transferor if the transferor's customers fail to pay.
      2. Accounting question: is the transaction a *borrowing* transaction (like assignment) or *sale* transaction (like factoring)?
         a. Borrowing: record liability and difference between proceeds received and net receivables transferred as finance cost (i.e., interest).
         b. Sale: difference between transfer price (amount received) and net amount of receivables transferred represents at gain or loss on sale (authoritative literature in this case is FASB Statement No. 77).

VII. Notes Receivable
   A. Like accounts receivable, issues regarding accounting for notes receivable center around three themes: (1) recognition, (2) valuation, and (3) as a source of cash. The accounting treatments for notes receivable differ from those relating to accounts receivable.
   B. **Thinking Question:** Why? To answer this question think about the differences and similarities between accounts and notes receivable. Both represent rights to receive money sometime in the future, but notes receivable are accompanied by formal agreements (promissory notes) which legally bind the borrower to pay.
   C. Recognition
      Similar to accounts receivable:

Notes Receivable	XXX	
Sales		XXX

      -or-

Notes Receivable	XXX	
Accounts Receivable		XXX

   D. Valuation
      Different than accounts receivable:
      Notes receivable are recorded at **present value**, (remember, accounts receivable are recorded at net realizable value).
      Also, notes receivable contain **interest**, either explicit (the interest rate is stated on the note) or implicit (the interest element is buried in the note).
      Thinking Question: Have you seen commercials on TV that advertise "no interest for one full year?" How can companies lend you money for one full year and not charge interest? ..... RIGHT!! They don't--the interest is implicit and is buried in the price of the item you purchase.
      Thinking Question: Recording a note with explicit interest should be straightforward:

Notes Receivable	XXX	
Sales		XXX
Interest Receivable	XX	
Interest Revenue		XX

      But, what about notes with implicit interest? The challenge in this case is to determine the amount of implicit interest--usually the implicit interest rate to use is the same rate the company would normally charge or receive if interest was explicit. To record, we back out the interest portion and book it as a "discount on notes receivable" or as "unearned interest:"

Notes Receivable	XXX	
Sales		XXX
Discount on Notes Receivable		XX

      Then, as time passes, the discount is recognized as interest revenue:

Discount on Notes Receivable	XX	
Interest Revenue		XX

      When the note is settled the discount will have been entirely recognized as interest revenue.

Chapter 6

VIII. Notes Receivable as a Source of Cash
  A. Notes can be turned to cash by selling them to a financial institution--somewhat in the same manner as factoring or selling accounts receivable.
  B. The difference, however, is that the amount of the note which is sold is the **maturity value**, which is the principal amount of the note plus the amount of interest which will be earned on the note during its tenure.
  C. The process of selling the note prior to maturity is often called "discounting."
  D. Like factoring and selling accounts receivable, discounting notes receivable is costly as the financier will charge interest and will generally not assume credit risk--in other words, the sale is with recourse.
  E. Steps in the discounting an interest-bearing note:
    1. Determine the maturity value of the note:
       Maturity value = face amount + interest
       Interest = face amount x interest rate x interest period
       Interest period = date of note to date of maturity
    2. Determine the amount of the discount:
       Discount = maturity value x discount rate x discount period
       Discount period = date of discount to maturity date
    3. Determine proceeds:
       Proceeds = maturity value – discount

IX. Impact of Uncollectible Accounts on the Statement of Cash Flows
  A. Uncollectible accounts affect cash flow from operations.
  B. If indirect method is used, consider changes in net receivables (i.e., receivables less allowance and taking into account write-offs).
  C. If direct method is used and accounts receivables are analyzed "net," write-offs have been impounded.
    1. However, sales must be reduced by amount of bad debts expense for the period because bad debt expense reduces net receivables balance but does not generate cash.

X. Using a Four-Column Bank Reconciliation
  A. Four-column bank reconciliation is also called a *proof of cash*.
  B. Method of reconciling checking account that is designed to check itself for accuracy.
    1. Both receipts and disbursements are used to determine correct cash balance.
    2. Reconciles both beginning of month and end of month balances.

TEST YOUR UNDERSTANDING

Fill-in-the-Blanks

Required: Fill in the blanks to complete the following sentences.

1. Inflows or other enhancements of assets of an entity or settlements of its liabilities, or a combination of both from delivering or producing goods, rendering services, or other activities that constitute the entity's ongoing major or central operations are called _____.

2. An extension of short-term credit to customers is recorded in _____ _____.

3. The _____ _____ is a reduction in the "list" sales price of an item to the "net" sales price actually charged the customer.

4. A reduction in the selling price, allowed if payment is received within a specified short period of time is called a _____ _____.

5. _____ _____ _____ is the amount of cash expected to be received from the conversion of assets in the normal course of business.

6. The _____ _____, which is required by GAAP, is the method of recognizing the estimated losses from uncollectible accounts as expenses during the period in which the sales occur.

Name: _____ Chapter 6   87

7. Obligations of a company to provide free service on units failing to perform satisfactorily or to replace defective goods are called _____.

8. Net credit sales divided by average accounts receivable for a period is the formula for _____ _____ _____.

9. The average number of days from the sale to the eventual collection of cash is called _____ _____ _____ _____ _____ _____.

10. _____ _____ are funds deposited in a bank that can be withdrawn upon demand.

11. _____ _____ are funds deposited in a bank that legally require prior notification before they can be withdrawn.

12. A credit balance in the cash account is called a _____ _____.

13. A portion of a demand deposit that must be maintained as support for existing borrowing arrangements is called a _____ _____.

Expanded Material Items:

14. Borrowing money with receivables pledged as security on the loan is called _____ of accounts receivable.

15. The sale of receivables without recourse is called _____.

16. The transfer of receivables _____ _____ is a hybrid form of receivables financing, which may, depending upon the specific nature of the arrangement, result in either a factoring arrangement or an assignment arrangement.

17. A four-column bank reconciliation is called a _____ _____ _____, and is useful because it checks itself for accuracy by reconciling both the beginning cash balance and the ending cash balance.

Multiple Choice

Required: Circle the best answer.

1. The method of estimating doubtful accounts based upon a percentage of credit sales emphasizes:
   A. the balance sheet.
   B. the income statement.
   C. the statement of cash flows.
   D. specific accounts which are uncollectible.

2. Information taken from the books of ToyCo reveals:
   Accounts Receivable $20,000
   Allowance for Doubtful Accounts   1,500 (credit)
   Credit Sales   99,000

   If Doubtful Accounts are estimated to be 2% of credit sales, what journal entry should ToyCo write this year:
   A. Doubtful Accounts Expense   480
         Allowance for Doubtful Accounts   480
   B. Doubtful Accounts Expense   1,980
         Allowance for Doubtful Accounts   1,980
   C. Doubtful Accounts Expense   1,980
         Accounts Receivable   1,980
   D. Doubtful Accounts Expense   480
         Accounts Receivable   480

3. When the allowance method is used to account for uncollectible accounts, the write-off of an uncollectible account will:
   A. increase net income.
   B. decrease net income.
   C. have no impact on net income.
   D. decrease net realizable value of receivables.

4. An analysis of Accounts Receivable at Doo Company reveals the following:

Accounts Receivable	$500,000
Allowance for Doubtful Accounts (before adjustment)	40,000 (credit)
Estimated uncollectible accounts	60,000

   The net realizable value of Doo Company's receivables is:
   A. $440,000.
   B. $460,000.
   C. $400,000.
   D. $480,000.

5. Use the following information to determine the balance which should appear in the Cash account for JJ's Sports Company:
   (1) Year-end bank statement balance: $36,500
   (2) Deposits in transit: $2,400
   (3) Coins and currency in cash drawer: $800
   (4) Postage stamps on hand: $40
   (5) Customer checks in cash drawer, held on deposit for bicycle rentals: $400
   (6) IOU's from two employees: $20
   (7) Outstanding checks: $600

   The amount JJ's Sports Company should show as the Cash balance is:
   A. $39,100.
   B. $39,500.
   C. $40,100.
   D. $39,520.

6. During May, 1997, Lynley Company entered into the following transactions:
   (1) Sold goods to customers, on account, $120,000.
   (2) Shipped goods on approval to customer, $30,000.
   (3) Shipped goods on consignment to customer, $16,000.
   (4) Received goods returned from customers, $10,000.
   (5) Offered a 10% cash discount to a customer for prompt payment; customer did not pay within the time frame of the discount.

   No other transaction occurred during May. Net revenue for the month is:
   A. $120,000.
   B. $166,000.
   C. $110,000.
   D. $153,000.

7. Mason Company had the following account balances at December 31, 1997:

Cash in banks	$2,250,000
Cash on hand	125,000
Cash legally restricted for additions to plant (expected to be distributed in 1998)	1,600,000

   Cash in banks includes $600,000 in compensating balances against short-term borrowing arrangements. The compensating balances are not legally restricted as to withdrawal by Mason. In the current assets section of Mason's December 31, 1997 balance sheet, total cash should be reported at:

A. $1,775,000.
B. $2,250,000.
C. $2,375,000.
D. $3,975,000. (AICPA adapted)

8. Havers Corporation's checkbook balance on December 31, 1997 was $5,000. In addition, Havers held the following items in its safe:
   - Check payable to Havers Corporation, dated January 2, 1998, in payment for a sale made on December 15, 1997, and not included in the December 31, 1997 checkbook balance, in the amount of $2,000.
   - Check payable to Havers Corporation, deposited December 15 and included in the checkbook balance, but returned from the bank on December 30, stamped "NSF." The check was redeposited on January 5, 1998 and cleared the bank on January 9, 1998. The check amount is $500.
   - Check drawn on Havers' account, payable to a vendor, dated and recorded in the books on December 31, but not mailed until January 10, 1998. The check amount is $300.

   The proper amount to be shown as Cash on Havers' December 31, 1997 balance sheet is:
   A. $4,800.
   B. $5,300.
   C. $6,500.
   D. $6,800. (AICPA adapted)

9. At October 31, 1997, Accent, Inc. had cash accounts at four different banks. One account is segregated solely for a November 15, 1997 payment to a special bond retirement fund. A second account, used for branch operations, is overdrawn. The third account, used for regular corporate operations, has a positive balance. The fourth account, maintained in a foreign country, is restricted for use in the foreign country only, and it has a positive balance. How should these accounts be classified on Accent's October 31, 1997 balance sheet?
   A. The segregated account should be reported as a noncurrent asset, the regular account and the foreign account should be reported as current assets, and the overdraft should be reported as a current liability.
   B. The segregated account, the regular account and the foreign account should be reported as current assets, and the overdraft should be reported as a current liability.
   C. The segregated account and the foreign account should be reported as noncurrent assets, and the regular account should be reported as a current asset, net of the overdraft.
   D. The segregated and regular accounts should be reported as current assets, the foreign account should be reported as a current asset with appropriate allowances for possible noncollectibility, and the overdraft should be reported as a current liability. (AICPA adapted)

10. The following accounts were taken from ABC Co.'s unadjusted trial balance at December 31, 1997:

	Debit	Credit
Accounts Receivable	$1,000,000	
Allowance for Uncollectible Accounts	3,000	
Net Credit Sales		$3,000,000

    ABC estimates that 3% of the gross accounts receivable will become uncollectible. After adjustment at December 31, 1997, the allowance for uncollectible accounts should have a credit balance of:
    A. $90,000.
    B. $82,000.
    C. $38,000.
    D. $30,000. (AICPA adapted)

11. The following accounts were taken from ABC Co.'s unadjusted trial balance at December 31, 1997:

	Debit	Credit
Accounts Receivable	$1,000,000	
Allowance for Uncollectible Accounts		$ 3,000
Net Credit Sales		3,000,000

    ABC estimates that 1% of all credit sales will be uncollectible. After adjustment at December 31, 1997, the allowance for uncollectible accounts will have a credit balance of:

A. $10,000.
B. $13,000.
C. $33,000.
D. $30,000. (AICPA adapted)

12. XYZ Co. prepared an aging of its accounts receivable at December 31, 1997 and determined that the net realizable value of the receivables was $250,000. Additional information is available as follows:

Allowance for uncollectible accounts at 1/1/97, credit balance	$ 28,000
Accounts written off as uncollectible during 1997	23,000
Accounts receivable at 12/31/97	270,000
Uncollectible accounts recovery during 1997	5,000

For the year ended December 31, 1997, XYZ's uncollectible account's expense would be:
A. $23,000.
B. $20,000.
C. $15,000.
D. $10,000. (AICPA adapted)

13. Edgar Inc. had the following bank reconciliation at March 31, 1997:

Balance per bank statement, 3/31/97	$46,500
Add: deposit in transit	10,300
	$56,800
Less: outstanding checks	12,600
Balance per books, 3/31/97	$44,200

Data per bank for the month of April, 1997:
Deposits	$58,400
Disbursements	49,700

All reconciling items at March 31, 1997 cleared the bank in April. Outstanding checks at April 30, 1997 totaled $7,000. There were no deposits in transit at April 30, 1997. What is the cash balance per books at April 30, 1997?
A. $48,200
B. $52,900
C. $55,200
D. $58,500 (AICPA adapted)

14. On the December 31, 1997 the balance sheet of Dexter Company, the current receivables consisted of the following:

Trade accounts receivable	$ 93,000
Allowance for uncollectible accounts	(2,000)
Claim against shipper for goods lost in transit (November 1997)	3,000
Selling price of unsold goods sent by Dexter on consignment at 130% of cost (goods NOT included in Dexter's ending inventory)	26,000
Security deposit on lease of warehouse used for storing inventory	30,000
Total	$150,000

At December 31, 1997, the correct total of Dexter's net receivables is:
A. $94,000.
B. $120,000.
C. $124,000.
D. $150,000. (AICPA adapted)

15. Fargo Shoe Store had sales of $1,000,000 during December 1997. Experience has indicated that merchandise totaling 7% of sales will be returned within 30 days of purchase, and an additional 3% will be returned within 90 days. Returned merchandise is readily resalable. In addition, merchandise totaling 15% of sales will be exchanged for merchandise of equal or greater value. What amount should Fargo report for net sales in its income statement for the month of December, 1997?
    A. $900,000
    B. $850,000
    C. $780,000
    D. $750,000 (AICPA adapted)

16. Plains Co. estimates its uncollectible accounts expense to be 2% of credit sales. Plains' credit sales for 1997 were $1,000,000. During 1997, Plains wrote off $18,000 of uncollectible accounts. Plains' allowance for uncollectible accounts had a $15,000 credit balance on January 1, 1997. In its income statement for the year ending December 31, 1997, what amount should Plains report as uncollectible accounts expense?
    A. $23,000
    B. $20,000
    C. $18,000
    D. $17,000 (AICPA adapted)

17. The following information relates to Walton's accounts receivable at December 31, 1997:

Days Outstanding	Amount	Estimated % Uncollectible
0 – 60	$120,000	1%
61 – 120	90,000	2%
Over 120	100,000	6%
	$310,000	

    During 1997, Walton wrote off $7,000 in receivables and recovered $4,000 that had been written off in previous years. The December 31, 1996 allowance for uncollectible accounts had a credit balance of $22,000. Under the aging (balance sheet) method, what amount of allowance for uncollectible accounts will Walton report at December 31, 1997? (Hint: the account will have a credit balance)
    A. $9,000
    B. $10,000
    C. $13,000
    D. $19,000 (AICPA adapted)

18. A company uses the allowance method to recognize uncollectible accounts expense. What is the effect at the time of collection of an account previously written off on each of the following?

	Allowance for Uncollectible Accounts	Uncollectible Accounts Expense
A.	No effect	Decrease
B.	Increase	Decrease
C.	Increase	No effect
D.	No effect	No effect

    (AICPA adapted)

19. During 1997, Gumshoe Company introduced a new product carrying a two-year warranty against defects. The estimated warranty costs related to dollar sales are 2% within 12 months following the sale and 4% in the second 12 months following the sale. Sales and actual warranty expenditures for 1997 and 1998 are:

	Sales	Actual Warranty Expenditures
1997	$150,000	$2,250
1998	250,000	7,500
	$400,000	$9,750

    What amount should Gumshoe report as estimated liability in its December 31, 1998 balance sheet?
    A. $2,500
    B. $4,250
    C. $11,250
    D. $14,250 (AICPA adapted)

Chapter 6

20. Archer Company sells to wholesalers on terms of 2/15, n/30. Archer has no cash sales, but 50% of Archer's customers take advantage of the cash discount. Archer uses the gross method of recording sales and trade receivables. An analysis of Archer's trade receivables at December 31, 1997 reveals the following:

Age	Amount	Collectible
0 – 15 days	$100,000	100%
16 – 30 days	60,000	95%
31 – 60 days	5,000	90%
over 60 days	2,500	$500
	$167,500	

    In its December 31, 1997 balance sheet, what amount should Archer report as an allowance for discounts?
    A. $1,000
    B. $2,000
    C. $1,675
    D. $0 (AICPA adapted)

21. (Expanded material) The sale of receivables without recourse to a third party is also called:
    A. assignment of receivables.
    B. discounting receivables.
    C. pledging receivables.
    D. factoring receivables.

22. (Expanded material) Chapin Company has an 8% note receivable dated June 30, 1997, in the original amount of $150,000. Payments of $50,000 in principal plus accrued interest are due on July 1, 1998, 1999, and 2000. In its June 30, 1999 balance sheet, what amount should Chapin report as a current asset for interest on the note receivable?
    A. $0
    B. $4,000
    C. $8,000
    D. $12,000 (AICPA adapted)

23. (Expanded material) On Harold's April 30, 1997 balance sheet a note receivable was reported as a noncurrent asset and its accrued interest for eight months was reported as a current asset. Which of the following terms fits Harold's note receivable?
    A. Both principal and interest amounts are payable on August 31, 1997 and August 31, 1998.
    B. Principal and interest are due on December 31, 1997.
    C. Both principal and interest amounts are payable on December 31, 1997 and December 31, 1998.
    D. Principal is due August 31, 1998, and interest is due August 31, 1997 and August 31, 1998.
    (AICPA adapted)

24. (Expanded material) Rossman received from a customer a one-year, $500,000 note bearing annual interest of 8%. After holding the note for six months, Rossman discounted the note at Waverly Bank at an effective interest rate of 10%. What amount of cash did Rossman receive from the bank?
    A. $540,000
    B. $523,810
    C. $513,000
    D. $495,238 (AICPA adapted)

25. (Expanded material) Which of the following is a method to generate cash from accounts receivable?

	Assignment	Factoring
A.	Yes	No
B.	Yes	Yes
C.	No	Yes
D.	No	No

    (AICPA adapted)

Name: Chapter 6   93

26. (Expanded material) On July 1, 1997, ABC Corp. sold equipment to Partners Company for $100,000. ABC accepted a 10% note receivable for the entire sales price. The note is payable in two equal installments of $50,000 plus accrued interest on December 31, 1997 and December 31, 1998. On July 1, 1998, ABC discounted the note at a bank at an interest rate of 12%. ABC's proceeds from the discounting are:
   A. $48,400.
   B. $49,350.
   C. $50,350.
   D. $51,700.   (AICPA adapted)

27. (Expanded material) After being held for 40 days, a 120-day, 12% interest-bearing note receivable was discounted at a bank at 15%. The proceeds from the bank equal:
   A. maturity value less discount at 12%.
   B. maturity value less discount at 15%.
   C. face value less discount at 12%.
   D. face value less discount at 15%.   (AICPA adapted)

Exercises and Problems

1. Accounts Receivable balance
   Required: Use the following information to compute the year-end balance in Accounts Receivable for BA and Company:

(a)	Beginning balance	$16,000
(b)	Accounts written off	1,200
(c)	Beginning inventory	22,000
(d)	Purchases of inventory	96,000
(e)	Ending inventory	48,000
(f)	Gross profit margin	60%
(g)	Customer collections	$179,000
(h)	All sales are credit	

2. Adjusting entries
   The following information is available for Sophie's Sophisticates:

Beginning Accounts Receivable	$ 38,000
Ending Accounts Receivable	36,000
Sales (net and all credit)	100,000
Allowance for Uncollectible Accounts	1,400 (cr)

   Required: Write the necessary adjusting entry assuming each of the following independent scenarios:

   a) Uncollectible accounts are estimated to be 2.2% of sales.
   b) A detailed analysis of accounts receivables reveals:
Accounts determined to be uncollectible	$800
Accounts determined to be doubtful	$900
   c) Sophie wants to write off the entire account of Charlotte's Niceties because she heard Charlotte has declared bankruptcy. Charlotte's Niceties' account balance is $1,500.
   d) Uncollectible accounts are estimated to be 1.2% of sales.
   e) A detailed analysis of accounts receivable reveals no uncollectible accounts and doubtful accounts in the amount of $600.

3. Wagon Box Stables
   Wagon Box Stables breeds, raises, trains, and sells cattle working horses. The owner, Joe Sutton is well known as a champion horse breeder and trainer. Joe guarantees all of his horses for medical soundness and performance capability at the level advertised. Thus, if a customer buys a horse from Wagon Box Stables and becomes

dissatisfied with it, the horse can be returned to the Stables for a full refund. Because the horses Joe trains and sells are champion stock, the selling prices tend to be quite high, often in the $15,000 and $20,000 range. Accordingly, Joe began granting credit to certain customers a few years ago. Generally, the credit arrangement is quite informal, a handshake, but occasionally Joe makes a deal with the customer to share in the horse's winnings. Two of the horses Joe sold this year are in the "Incentive Fund," which means the Association in which the horses are registered pays an incentive for every point the horse earns during the year. In the case of both Incentive Fund horses Joe sold, the customer agreed to split the Incentive Fund winnings with Wagon Box Stables.

Wagon Box Stables is in the process of preparing its year-end financial statements, and the bookkeeper is having difficulty valuing the accounts receivable. He asked your study group to help. He supplied the following information about accounts receivable activities during the current year for your review:

Beginning Balance		$32,000
Smokey's Timber	$10,000	
Candy Barr	10,000	
Talbot's Dream	10,000	
Festus	2,000	
Sales on credit:		
Smokey's Fire	$15,000	
Sugar Candy	20,000	
Marshall Dillon*	17,000	
Miss Kitty*	16,000	
Payments received:		
Smokey's Timber	$10,000	
Candy Barr	8,000	
Talbot's Dream	4,000	
Festus	2,000	
Smokey's Fire	10,000	
Sugar Candy	--0--	
Marshall Dillon	17,000	
Miss Kitty	--0--	

* Incentive Fund horses

Additional information:
- Current year winnings, as reported by owners; neither of the owners remitted payment with the notification of winnings:
  - Marshall Dillon $1,200
  - Miss Kitty $1,000
- Miss Kitty was returned to the stable because the owner didn't like her; Joe agreed to refund the customer's money, but since no money had been paid, the bookkeeper didn't do anything about it.
- The buyer of Sugar Candy pledged all of the horse's earnings to Joe as collateral for the purchase. The buyer agreed to pay Joe not only all the winnings Sugar Candy earned, but also to pay the rest of the purchase price, should the earnings not be enough. Joe and the bookkeeper have confirmed that Sugar Candy has won several major events and has earnings in excess of $60,000 for the prior year. Both Joe and the bookkeeper have called the owner about payment on Sugar Candy, and while the owner has promised to pay, no money has arrived. Last month, Joe called the Association in which Sugar Candy is registered and began proceedings to have her registration rescinded (if the Association rescinds the horse's registration to the customer, that person would be unable to enter the horse in any further Association sponsored events). Joe informed the buyer of the action (in writing), but Joe has heard nothing from the buyer at this point.
- The $4,000 payment on Talbot's Dream was received at the beginning of the year, and no communication has come from the customer. A check of Association sponsored events reveals that Talbot's Dream has entered (and done well) in several events during the year, so the bookkeeper assumes the horse is alive and well.
- Four quarterly payments of $2,000 each were received during the year on Candy Barr.

Required: Value the accounts receivable for Wagon Box Stables. Be certain you consider possible doubtful accounts, sales returns, and the Incentive Fund activities.

Name: *Chapter 6*

4. **Scrip program**

   Your study group has been asked to help a neighborhood school PTA with its Scrip Program. The Scrip Program works like this: the PTA buys "scrip" from several local businesses, including grocery stores, restaurants, and department stores. The scrip is purchased in various denominations, such as $5, $10, and $25. For each dollar of scrip purchased the retailer rebates 5% (or $.05) to the PTA. The PTA then sells the scrip for face value, and the purchasers of the scrip can redeem it for goods and services equal to the face value. The scrip does not expire, so purchasers can redeem it at the store the scrip was purchased from any time after purchase. To set up the program, the PTA purchased $10,000 worth of scrip from 5 different businesses ($2,000 from each business). Scrip is sold every Friday morning before school on the school campus. Volunteers advertised the program extensively, and the initial $10,000 of scrip was sold within two weeks, thus netting the PTA a "profit" of $500. The Scrip Program was undertaken by the PTA as a fund-raising activity, and as the President of the PTA pointed out to you, the initial reaction to the program has been quite positive. However, the program has become a bookkeeping and control nightmare for the volunteers involved, and they have asked your study group for assistance.

   Required: Design a system to help the PTA manage and control the Scrip Program. Be sure to consider the type of organization the PTA is and its goals with the Scrip Program when you design the system. Also keep in mind the potential control problems the PTA faces with several volunteers handling the scrip (keep in mind the scrip is just like money, except it can only be redeemed at certain places). Be sure your system contains a mechanism to reconcile and audit scrip purchases, sales, and inventory.

   Hint: Consider how scrip is similar to cash and how it differs from cash. How would these similarities and differences affect your system if it was designed for cash instead of scrip?

5. **Scrip, "On the Road"**

   Assume the PTA's Scrip Program has been in existence for a year or so and has been quite successful. Lately, however, the PTA noticed a decrease in sales of scrip. The issue was discussed at a recent PTA meeting, and one member suggested a means to increase scrip sales. "Why don't you let some of us take scrip to our offices and sell it there?" suggested Ted Everson, a local businessman. "I'm sure the people in my office would gladly buy scrip," he added. After considerable discussion, the members of the PTA agree that "taking the Scrip Program on the road" might indeed increase sales. One member, however, expressed doubts, "Even if sales do increase," she said, "we will lose a lot of control over the scrip, what with having so many people carrying scrip around with them. I'm afraid some scrip might get lost in the process, and if that happens, we could actually lose money." The president of the PTA agreed and decided to return to your study group for help.

   Required: Design a system to control and manage the Scrip Program if it goes "on the road."

6. **Petty cash fund**

   The accountant for Streamline Company established a petty cash fund of $1,400. During August, 1997, the fund was depleted by the following activities:

Shipping expense	$740
Travel expense	240
Postage expense	230
Miscellaneous supplies	170

   In addition to the receipts for the items above, the petty cash box contained $8 in coins and an IOU for $8 from the secretary holding the fund. The company has decided to decrease the fund to $1,000.

   Required: Prepare, in good form, the journal entries necessary to:
   a) Establish the petty cash fund;
   b) Replenish the petty cash fund;
   c) Record the decrease in the petty cash fund.

7. **Bank reconciliation**

   The books of Master Service, Inc. disclosed a cash balance of $68,757 on June 30, 1997. The bank statement as of June 30, 1997 showed a balance of $54,780. Additional information:
   a. Check number 1233 for $3,000 was originally recorded in the books as $4,500.

Chapter 6

b. A customer's note dated March 5 was discounted on April 12. The note was dishonored on June 29, the maturity date. The bank charged Master Service's account $14,265, which included the bank's fees.
c. The deposit of June 24 was recorded in the books as $2,895, but it was actually a deposit of $2,700.
d. Outstanding checks totaled $9,885 as of June 30.
e. Bank service charges for June were $210.
f. The bank charged the account $1,296 for a customer's NSF check.
g. Master Service made a deposit of $600 on June 3, but the deposit was not recorded by the bank.
h. Receipts of June 30 were $13,425 and were recorded by the bank on July 2.
i. A bank memo stated that a customer's note for $4,500 and interest of $165 had been collected on June 27; the bank charged a collection fee of $36 on the transaction.

Required: Prepare a bank reconciliation statement.

8. Credit card sales
Dream Weavers, Inc., a weaving shop, accepts cash and VISA credit cards from its customers. In addition, the store occasionally extends short-term credit to certain customers. During September, the shop had total sales of $130,000, composed of $37,000 cash; $83,000 credit cards; and $10,000 on account. The bank charges a 3% fee on credit card sales.

Required: Prepare, in good form, the journal entry to reflect the sales transactions for September.

9. (Expanded material) Assignment of accounts receivable
Specific customer accounts receivable totaling $1,850,000 were assigned to Otoe Finance Company by ABC Inc. as collateral for a loan of $1,470,000. The finance company charged a 3% service fee on the total accounts receivable assigned. The note bears interest at 12% per year.

During the first month, ABC collected $680,000 on the assigned receivables. This amount plus one month's interest was remitted to the finance company.

Required:
a) Prepare, in good form, all necessary journal entries concerning the assignment, the loan, and the remittance on ABC's books.
b) Prepare the section of ABC's balance sheet to reflect the assignment at the end of the first month.

10. (Expanded material) Factoring accounts receivable
On June 1, 1997, Capstone Corporation needed cash to meet current operating obligations. Capstone decided to factor some of its receivables. Capstone factored $600,000 of receivables to Valley Bank for $511,400. An allowance for doubtful accounts of 2% of the receivables balance is maintained by Capstone. The bank withheld 5% of the purchase price as protection against sales returns and allowances. Sales returns against factored receivables totaled $1,600.

Required:
a) Prepare, in good form, the journal entry to reflect the factoring (sale) of the accounts receivable.
b) Prepare, in good form, the journal entry to record the final settlement of the accounts receivable factoring.

SOLUTIONS TO TEST YOUR UNDERSTANDING

Fill-in-the-Blanks

1. revenue
2. Accounts Receivable
3. trade discount

4. cash discount
5. Net realizable value
6. allowance method
7. warranties
8. accounts receivable turnover
9. number of days' sales in receivables
10. Demand deposits
11. Time deposits
12. cash overdraft
13. compensating balance
14. assignment
15. factoring
16. with recourse
17. proof of cash

Multiple Choice

1.	C	8.	A	15.	A	22.	C
2.	B	9.	D	16.	B	23.	D
3.	C	10.	D	17.	A	24.	C
4.	A	11.	C	18.	C	25.	B
5.	A	12.	D	19.	D	26.	D
6.	C	13.	A	20.	A	27.	B
7.	C	14.	A	21.	D		

Exercises and Problems

1. Accounts Receivable balance
   Ending balance = $10,800
   Calculations:
   Step 1: Think about what you are trying to calculate and how the balance sheet and income statement relate to each other.
   Step 2: Look at the information you do have, including the data to calculate sales.
   Step 3: Calculate sales (Why??? Because sales increase receivables)

Beginning inventory	$ 22,000
Add: purchases	96,000
Goods available for sale	$118,000
Less: ending inventory	48,000
Cost of goods sold	$ 70,000

   Gross profit margin is 60%, so cost of goods sold must be 40% of sales (.4Sales = Cost of goods sold or .4Sales = $70,000), so sales must be $175,000.
   Step 4: Add sales to accounts receivable:
   $ 16,000
   175,000
   $191,000--this represents the total amount of receivables that could be collected or written off during the year.
   Step 5: Consider uncollectible accounts:
   Subtract from the total amount of possible receivables ($191,000) the amount written off ($1,200).
   Step 6: Then consider customer payments:
   the payments of $179,000 reduce the balance in accounts receivable

98   Chapter 6

Step 7: Put it all together:
Beginning balance	$ 16,000
Add: sales	175,000
Subtract: uncollectibles	(1,200)
Subtract: customer payments	(179,000)
Ending balance	$ 10,800

2. Adjusting entries
   a) Uncollectible Accounts Expense   2,200
       Allowance for Uncollectible Accounts   2,200

   Calculations:
   Uncollectibles are assumed to be a function of sales in this case, so the focus in this case is the income statement. Thus, the entry focuses upon the expense side of the journal entry, which is calculated by multiplying the estimated uncollectible percentage by the total amount of credit sales: .022 X $100,000.

   b) Allowance for Uncollectible Accounts   800
       Accounts Receivable   800
       To write off uncollectible accounts.

       Uncollectible Accounts Expense   300
       Allowance for Uncollectible Accounts   300
       To increase provision for uncollectible accounts.

   Calculations:
   Note there are two journal entries in this case. In the first entry, the uncollectible account is written off. In the second entry, the provision for uncollectible accounts is updated to reflect the current analysis of the status of the receivables. The allowance account begins with a balance of $1,400, but the analysis of the receivables indicates $1,700 ($800 + $900) is needed, so the account is adjusted to the required amount. The approach in this case is a balance sheet approach with the emphasis being valuation and the balance in the allowance account.

   c) Uncollectible Accounts Expense   1,500
       Allowance for Uncollectible Accounts   1,500
       To increase provision for uncollectible accounts.

       Allowance for Uncollectible Accounts   1,500
       Accounts Receivable   1,500
       To write off account of Charlotte's Niceties.

   Calculation:
   In this case, two journal entries were written, one to increase the provision and the other to write off the uncollectible account. Normally, we'd think we would just write off the uncollectible, but notice that the provision is not large enough to sustain a $1500 write-off. This indicates that the demise of Charlotte's Niceties was a surprise to Sophie's Sophisticates and thus, the account was not considered in the provision.

   Another alternative in this case might be the direct write-off method:
   Uncollectible Accounts Expense   1,500
       Accounts Receivable   1,500
   Thinking Question: Why might the direct write-off method be allowable in this case???? [Answer: because the provision was not large enough to handle all of the uncollectible accounts.]

   d) Uncollectible Accounts Expense   1,200
       Allowance for Uncollectible Accounts   1,200

   Calculation:
   In this case, the focus is the expense side of the journal entry and bad debts are assumed to be a function of sales; thus, the expense is calculated by multiplying the estimated percent (1.2%) times the annual credit sales ($100,000). Notice that the balance in the allowance account is now $2,600.

Name: Chapter 6   99

   e) Allowance for Uncollectible Accounts   800
       Uncollectible Accounts Expense   800

Calculation:
An analysis of accounts receivable indicates that the allowance account is overstated: the balance in the allowance account is $1400, and the amount needed in the account is only $600. Therefore, the allowance account must be adjusted downward to the required amount of $600. Thus, the journal entry contains a debit to the allowance account. Another way of looking at this particular example is to think about the amount of expense which has been incurred over the years. Since the allowance account is overstated, no charge to expense is necessary this period; in fact, expense has been apparently overstated in prior periods, so during this period a credit to expense is warranted.

3. Wagon Box Stables
The goal in this problem is to determine net realizable value of Wagon Box Stables accounts receivable.

First, we need to recap the activity in Accounts Receivable:

Accounts Receivable

Smokey's Timber	10,000	10,000	Smokey's Timber
Candy Barr	10,000	8,000	Candy Barr
Talbot's Dream	10,000	4,000	Talbot's Dream
Festus	2,000	2,000	Festus
Smokey's Fire	15,000	10,000	Smokey's Fire
Sugar Candy	20,000	—	Sugar Candy
Marshall Dillon	17,000	17,000	Marshall Dillon
Miss Kitty	16,000	—	Miss Kitty
Marshall Dillon	600	16,000	Miss Kitty returned
Miss Kitty	500		
Balance	34,100		

Next, we need to analyze each customer's account to determine if there are any doubtful accounts. Generally, we estimate doubtful accounts using either a percentage of sales or accounts receivable balance, but those methods are not realistic in this case. Wagon Box Stables has few accounts, and each account is a significant amount. In this case, it is more realistic to analyze each individual account rather than estimate uncollectible accounts based on aggregate data.

Smokey's Timber has been paid in full, so that account is closed.
Candy Barr has a balance outstanding of $2,000, but the owner has been making regular payments, so that account is not likely doubtful.
Talbot's Dream has a balance outstanding of $6,000; no payment has been received since the beginning of the year, and Joe has heard nothing from the buyer; this account is doubtful.
Festus is paid in full.
Smokey's Fire has an outstanding balance of $5,000. We need further information about this account to make a determination about its collectibility. Let's assume Joe tells us the owner is making regular payments; in that case, the account is probably not doubtful.
Sugar Candy has an outstanding balance of $20,000, and no payments have been made on the horse. Further, attempts to collect from the buyer have been unsuccessful, and Joe has begun proceedings to have Sugar Candy's registration suspended. This account is doubtful.
Miss Kitty was returned, and the account credited. However, notice that the account also included $500 for Incentive Fund winnings that Joe is to receive from the buyer who had Miss Kitty for part of the year. Since the horse has been returned to Joe, it is doubtful the buyer will pay the $500. Therefore, the $500 is doubtful.

Recapping our analysis of the individual accounts, we find doubtful accounts total $26,500. An allowance for doubtful accounts should be established in this amount, making the net realizable value of the receivables $7,600.

Chapter 6

4. **Scrip program**

    Scrip behaves very much like cash, and therefore, is subject to many of the same risks and temptations that plague cash. The PTA must establish a strong system of scrip control that would mirror a strong cash control system.

    Basic to the system is the notion of separation of duties; this means the person who orders the scrip should be someone other than the person who counts the scrip, who should be someone other than the person who deposits the money received from the scrip, and so on. Scrip should be kept well monitored and stored in a locked secure place. Another feature the system may need is a tracking system for individual scrip certificates. Perhaps the certificates themselves are numbered or have an identifying feature which could be recorded and reconciled. Finally, scrip "inventory" must be reconciled with scrip monetary receipts and disbursements to ensure safeguarding of the scrip. Refer to the Study Guide Key Points and to your text for more commentary in this area.

5. **Scrip,"On the Road"**

    Stewardship of the scrip is seriously compromised when physical control is relinquished. The scrip could be prenumbered and the person who "signs out" scrip "on the road" could maintain a list of who has which scrip. You might suggest to the PTA that if it takes scrip on the road, the person(s) who take physical control of the scrip also agree to be financially responsible for any lost or stolen scrip. All in all, however, the idea of taking large amounts of scrip into various unsecured locations is not wise.

6. **Petty cash fund**

    a) Petty Cash   1,400
          Cash   1,400

    b) Shipping Expense   740
       Travel Expense   240
       Postage Expense   230
       Miscellaneous Supplies   170
       Employee Receivable   8
       Cash Over and Short   4
          Cash   1,392

    c) Cash   400
          Petty Cash   400

7. **Bank reconciliation**

    Master Service, Inc.
    Bank Reconciliation
    For the Period Ending June 30, 1997

Balance per bank statement, June 30		$54,780
Add: Deposits in transit	$13,425	
Bank error, deposit not recorded	600	14,025
		$68,805
Less: Outstanding checks		9,885
Corrected bank balance		$58,920
Balance per books, June 30		$68,757
Add: Book error on check 1233	$1,500	
Customer note collected by bank	4,665	6,165
		$74,922
Deduct: Dishonored note:	$14,265	
Book error on deposit	195	
NSF check	1,296	
Bank service charges	246	16,002
Corrected book balance		$58,920

8. Credit card sales
   Cash ($37,000 + [$83,000 - 2,490])   117,510
   Accounts Receivable   10,000
   Credit Card Service Fee ($83,000 x 3%)   2,490
       Sales   130,000

9. Assignment of accounts receivable
   a) Journal entries:
      Accounts Receivable Assigned   1,850,000
          Accounts Receivable   1,850,000

      Cash   1,414,500
      Assignment Finance Charge (.03 x $1,850,000) 55,500
          Notes Payable   1,470,000

      Cash   680,000
          Accounts Receivable Assigned   680,000

      Notes Payable   680,000
      Interest Expense ($1,470,000 x .12 x 1/12)   14,700
          Cash (680,000 + 14,700)   694,700

   b) Current assets section of balance sheet:
      Accounts Receivable Assigned $1,170,000
      Less: Note Payable   790,000
      Net $ 380,000

10. Factoring accounts receivable
    a) Journal entry to record factoring:
       Cash ($511,400 – $25,570)   485,830
       Receivable From Factor (.05 x $511,400)   25,570
       Allowance for Doubtful Accounts*   12,000
       Loss on Factoring*   76,600
           Accounts Receivable   600,000

       *Calculations:
          Allowance: .03 x $600,000 = $12,000
          Loss: ($600,000 – $12,000) – $511,400 = $76,600

    b) Journal entry to record the final settlement of sales returns and allowances:
       Sales Returns and Allowances   1,600
       Cash ($25,570 - 1,600)   23,970
           Receivable From Factor   25,570

CHAPTER 7

COMPLEXITIES OF REVENUE RECOGNITION

KEY POINTS

I. Revenue Recognition
   A. Revenue is *earned* when two conditions are met:
      1. Revenue is realizable (amount and timing of the cash flows is reasonably well known) AND
      2. The earnings process is substantially complete (the seller has fulfilled the bulk of his obligations to the buyer).
      3. NOTE THAT BOTH CONDITIONS MUST BE MET.
      [Keep this in mind whenever you deal with revenue recognition issues!]
   B. The term, *recognition*, refers to the time when transactions are recorded on the company's books.
   C. Normally, revenue is earned at the point of sale, so normally revenue is recognized at the point of sale.
   D. Under special circumstances, revenue can be earned *prior* to the point of sale or *after* the point of sale.

II. Revenue Recognition Prior to Delivery of Goods or Performance of Services
   A. What circumstances suggest revenue recognition prior to delivery of goods?
      1. Usually, the construction or performance period is lengthy (longer than one year), but progress towards completion is being made throughout the period.
   B. How can revenue be recognized in these cases?
      1. First, amount and timing of cash flows must be reasonably known.
         a. In a long-term construction contract, the total revenue is specified by the contract (so the total revenue is known), and cash payment dates are generally specified in the contract as well (so the timing of the cash flow can be estimated).
      2. Second, seller has to *earn* revenue
         a. In a long-term contract, generally, the seller is making progress throughout the contract, and while the product or service is acceptable to the buyer only when it's completed, the seller is working towards that, so we can account for recognition of *part* of the revenue as the progress is being made.
   C. Two accounting methods
      1. Percentage-of-completion (proportional performance)
         a. Recognize revenue as measurable milestones of the total product or service are achieved.
         b. Preferred method, also acceptable for tax purposes
      2. Completed-contract
         a. Used only when conditions for percentage-of-completion cannot be met.
         b. Contractors prefer this method for tax purposes, but tax rules have severely limited its use.
   D. Percentage-of-Completion
      1. Necessary conditions for use:
         a. Dependable estimates can be made of contract revenues, contract costs, and extent of progress towards completion of the project.
         b. Contract clearly specifies rights and responsibilities of all parties to the contract.
         c. Buyer can be expected to perform.
         d. Contractor (seller) can be expected to perform.
      2. Measuring percentage of completion
         a. Input measures
            1) Cost-to-cost method
               a) Percentage complete = $\dfrac{\text{Actual Costs Incurred to Date}}{\text{Total Estimated Costs of Project}}$
               b) Used when costs and progress are correlated, but not useful in projects in which "up front" or early construction costs are very high relative to total actual progress on the project.
               c) Cost-to-cost is the most commonly used method.

104 *Chapter 7*

        2) Efforts-expended method
           a) Percentage completed is a function of work performed, based upon labor hours, machine hours or material quantities.
           b) Often produces results similar to cost-to-cost method.
      b. Output measures
        1) Percentage complete is a function of output, such as units produced, value added, or contract milestones achieved.

III. Accounting for Long-Term Construction-Type Contracts
    A. All costs associated with the project (direct and indirect) are charged to an inventory account, Construction in Progress.
    B. Contract generally specifies a billing schedule. It is recorded by:
        Accounts Receivable   XXX
            Progress Billings on Construction Contracts   XXX
    C. Accounts Receivable is the current asset account, indicating the contractual obligation on the part of the buyer to pay.
    D. Progress Billings is a deferred account, which is offset against the inventory account, Construction in Progress **Thinking question:** When the Progress Billings account is offset against the Construction in Progress account, what is the result? [answer: the value of the inventory (or project to date) for which the customer has not yet been billed]
    E. Cash payments by customer are recorded:
        Cash   CCC
            Accounts Receivable   CCC
    F. Using percentage-of-completion: cost-to-cost method
       1. Total revenue on the project will be spread over the life of the contract based upon percentage complete.
          a. Cumulative revenue to date: total estimated revenue multiplied by percentage complete to date.
          b. Cumulative cost to date: total estimated construction cost multiplied by percentage complete to date.
          c. Cumulative gross profit: cumulative revenue less cumulative cost.
       2. Current year revenue:
          a. (Percentage complete x Total revenue) less prior years' revenues.
       3. Current year costs:
          a. If cost-to-cost method is used, generally current year costs will be equal to actual period costs.
       4. Gross Profit (revenue less expense) is added to the Construction in Progress account, thereby valuing inventory at net realizable value.
       5. Note: amounts recognized as revenue and expense do not affect the progress billings or accounts receivable accounts as these accounts are established by contract.
    G. Revision of estimates
       1. Generally, cost estimates are the ones which change because the contract price (i.e., revenue) is set by the contract.
       2. Generally, cost estimates are revised upward, so total gross profit over the life of the project is less than originally planned.
       3. The new cost estimate must be used and the "catch-up" impact of the new estimates will be reflected in current year cost and gross profit.
    H. Reporting anticipated contract losses
       1. In some cases, an increase in total estimated costs can result in an expected loss on the total contract.
       2. The loss will be recognized in the year in which the cost estimates have changed.
       3. Recording the anticipated loss
          a. Completed-contract method
            1) The amount of expected net loss is recorded in its entirety in the year it is anticipated, and the inventory asset will be reduced to new net realizable value:
                Anticipated Loss on Long-Term
                    Construction Contracts   LLL
                    Construction in Progress   LLL

b. Percentage-of-completion
   1) The entire amount of the expected loss is recorded in the year it is first anticipated.
   2) However, since revenues, costs, and gross profit may have already been recognized in prior periods, the accounting treatment required is:
      a) cumulative loss = cumulative recognized revenue plus anticipated loss.
      b) loss this period = cumulative recognized revenue less cumulative recognized cost.
      c) year-end journal entry:
         Cost of Long-Term Construction Contracts   XX
            Revenue from Long-Term Construction Contracts   XX
            Construction in Progress   XX
      d) Note: the credit to the construction in progress account reduces inventory to net realizable value, and represents the loss recognized this year.

IV. Accounting for Long-Term Service Contracts: The Proportional Performance Method
   A. No FASB Statement dealing specifically with accounting for long-term service contracts.
      1. Authoritative literature cited in text follows recommendations of AICPA's Accounting Standards Division.
   B. Proportional performance method is preferable.
      1. Progress can be measured using either input or output measures.
         a. Measure used should tie to activity performed.
      2. Revenue derives from service contract fee and will be allocated to each accounting period in which activity occurs, using measure in 1.a.
      3. Service contracts have three types of costs:
         a. Initial costs (obtain and perform initial services)
         b. Direct costs (related to performing the service under the contract)
         c. Indirect costs (overhead costs to maintain the organization)
      4. If cost-to-cost method used:
         a. Indirect cost should be excluded from the costs incurred to date; i.e., only direct costs are relevant, and they must be charged to expense when incurred.
         b. Indirect costs should be charged to expense as period costs.
         c. Anticipated loss recognized in the year it becomes apparent.
      5. Note: proportional performance is very conservative because no revenue is recognized until service is performed, even though cash may be received well prior to that date.
         a. Generally, the signing of the contract is an event which triggers revenue recognition, because at that point initial service activities have been performed.

V. Revenue Recognition After Delivery of Goods or Performance of Services
   A. Why wait to recognize revenue after the point of sale (delivery of goods)?
      1. Collection of cash is uncertain.
      2. Timing of cash flows is uncertain.
      3. Seller has significant work left to perform for the buyer.
   B. Methods to account for revenue recognition after the point of sale or as cash is received:
      1. Installment sales
      2. Cost recovery
      3. Cash
   C. Installment sales method
      1. Most commonly applied method for dealing with uncertainty of cash flows, though still used much less than full accrual.
      2. Be sure to distinguish the accounting method from "installment sales," (sales in which the product is paid for in a series of payments or installments; normally, these sales are accounted for using the accrual method)
      3. Installment sales method for merchandise
         a. Information needed:
            1) Sales amount
            2) Gross profit on sales
            3) Cash collections of sales

b. Method
1) Record sales and cost of sales similar to full accrual:

Installment Accounts Receivable	SSS	
Installment Sales		SSS
Cost of Installment Sales	CSC	
Inventory		CSC

2) Record cash collections normally:

Cash	CCC	
Installment Accounts Receivable		CCC

3) At year-end, close installment sales and cost of sales AND defer gross profit:

Installment Sales	SSS	
Cost of Installment Sales		CSC
Deferred Gross Profit		DGP

4) Recognize gross profit proportional to cash collections:

Deferred Gross Profit	PPP	
Realized Gross Profit on Installment Sales		PPP

c. Important points
1) A separate gross profit account must be established for each year.
2) Accounts receivable collections must also be accounted for by year.
d. Interest on installment sales
1) Interest portion of the contract payments is always recognized when the cash is received and the remainder of the cash payment is treated as a collection of the installment sale.

4. Cost recovery method
a. No income is recognized on sales until the total cost of the sales has been recovered through cash collections.
b. No interest income is recognized until total cost of sales has been recovered through cash collections.
c. Method
1) Record sales and cost of sales similar to full accrual:

Cost Recovery Accounts Receivable	SSS	
Cost Recovery Sales		SSS
Cost of Cost Recovery Sales	CSC	
Inventory		CSC

2) Record cash collections normally:

Cash	CCC	
Cost Recovery Accts. Receivable		CCC

3) At year-end, close installment sales and cost of sales AND defer gross profit:

Cost Recovery Sales	SSS	
Cost of Cost Recovery Sales		CSC
Deferred Gross Profit		DGP

4) Recognize gross profit ONLY after all costs of sales have been recovered through cash collections; after full cost recovery, cash collections would be recorded normally, and that portion of deferred gross profit would be recognized:

Deferred Gross Profit	PPP	
Realized Gross Profit on Cost Recovery Sales		PPP

c. Important points
1) A separate gross profit account must be established for each year.
2) Accounts receivable collections must also be accounted for by year.

5. Full accrual, installment sales, and cost recovery compared
a. Gross profit ultimately recognized is the same regardless of method.
b. Timing of the recognition varies, with full accrual generally recognizing gross profit earliest; next is installment sales, and finally cost recovery.

6. Cash method
a. Rarely used in merchandising or real estate.
b. Used in service contracts when collectibility is very uncertain.

c. Defers recognition of revenue until cash is collected.
d. Recognizes expense as incurred.

VI. Accounting for the Transfer of Assets Prior to the Recognition of Revenue
   A. Deposit method—general
      1. Cash is collected before a sales contract is sufficiently defined to recognize revenue.
         a. Examples: certain real estate transactions, certain prepaid services (see the text for an example of SCI, a funeral provider)
   B. Deposit method—franchising industry
      1. What is a franchise?
         a. Franchisors sell the rights to use the company name, sell certain company products, and/or offer certain company services to franchisees.
         b. Franchisees purchase the rights and conduct business.
         c. Franchisors often are obligated to perform certain tasks or services for the franchisee after the agreement is made.
         d. Franchisees often continue to pay franchisors, either fees or percentages of the business they generate after the agreement is made.
         e. Examples: McDonalds, Subway, Motel 6, 7-11.
      2. Accounting challenges
         a. When the franchisor can recognize revenue, especially with respect to the initial franchise fee.
            1) Franchisors used to recognize the fee as soon as the cash was received.
            2) If the fee was large, and the franchisor had significant obligations after the agreement was made, recognition of the entire fee currently was inappropriate.
            3) For an example of how misleading this treatment can be, see the text (story about Western Savings in Texas).
         b. Preferred accounting treatment of initial franchise fee
            1) Book fee as a deposit (liability).
            2) Recognize revenue when franchisor has performed substantially all required services.
   C. Consignment sales
      1. What is a consignment sale?
         a. Consignor (owner/seller) delivers goods to consignee who agrees to market and sell the goods (consigned inventory).
         b. Until the goods are sold, title rests with consignor, though goods in the possession of consignee.
         c. Examples: art is often displayed at galleries on consignment; crafts, needlework, and basketry are also often sold on consignment.
      2. Accounting treatments
         a. Consignor keeps the inventory on its books, though in a special account.

TEST YOUR UNDERSTANDING

Fill-in-the-Blanks

Required: Fill in the blanks to complete the following sentences.

1. _____ refers to the time when transactions are recorded on the books.

2. Revenues and gains are generally recognized when: (1) they are _____ (or _____) and (2) the earnings process is _____ _____.

3. Normally revenue is recognized at the _____ _____ _____.

4. The _____-_____ _____ is an accounting method that recognizes revenues and expenses on long-term construction contracts only when completed.

5. The _____-_____-_____ _____ is an accounting method for long-term construction contracts that recognizes revenue and related expenses prior to delivery of the goods, based on either an input or an output measure of the earnings process.

6. The _____ _____ _____ is an accounting method for recording service revenue and related expenses prior to the completion of a service contract.

7. The method for determining the percentage of completion for long-term construction contracts using a ratio of the actual cost incurred to date to the estimated total costs is the _____-_____-_____ method.

8. The _____ _____ _____ is a revenue recognition method that recognizes revenue and related expenses as cash is received.

9. When using the installment sales method, a separate _____ _____ _____ account is kept for each year and _____ _____ collections must be accounted for by year.

10. The _____ _____ method requires recovery of the total investment prior to recognition of revenue.

11. In the _____ method, all costs are charged to expense as incurred, and revenue is recognized as collections are made.

12. In the _____ method, the receipt of cash and the unearned revenue are recognized prior to the completion of the contract.

13. Under the provisions of FASB Statement No. 45, revenue and related expense from franchising operations cannot be recognized prior to _____ _____ of the services covered by the initial fee.

14. Under the provisions of FASB Statement No. 45, monetary assets received prior to substantial performance under the terms of the franchising agreement should be offset by a _____ or a _____ _____ account; costs related to the services rendered should be _____ until revenue is recognized.

15. A _____ is a transfer of property without the transfer of title or the risk of ownership; the recipient of the property is the _____, who acts as a selling agent for the owner of the property, the _____.

Multiple Choice

Required: Circle the best answer.

1. Revenue can be recorded in the books when:
   A. it is realized or realizable or when the seller delivers the product or completes the service for the buyer.
   B. the seller delivers the product or completes the service for the buyer.
   C. the cash is received.
   D. the seller delivers the product or completes the service for the buyer and the amount and timing of cash flows can be reasonably known.

2. Revenue is often recognized at the point of sale. Why?
   A. Title has transferred, indicating the buyer's acceptance of the product or service.
   B. The amount and timing of the cash flows are generally known because the invoice specifies them.
   C. A and B together.
   D. Either A or B.

Name: *Chapter 7*

3. Construction in Progress will include both indirect and direct costs and income (or loss) associated with a contract in progress under which accounting method(s)?

	Percentage-of-Completion	Completed-Contract
A.	Yes	Yes
B.	Yes	No
C.	No	Yes
D.	No	No

4. Which of the following would be used in the calculation of the income recognized in the final year of a construction contract that has been in progress for several years and has been accounted for using the percentage-of-completion method?

	Contract Price	Actual Total Costs	Income Previously Recognized
A.	Yes	Yes	Yes
B.	Yes	Yes	No
C.	Yes	No	No
D.	No	Yes	Yes

5. Consider a three-year construction project for which a profit is forecast. At the end of the first year, the balance in the Construction in Progress account using the percentage-of-completion method would be:
   A. zero.
   B. the same as the completed-contract method.
   C. higher than the completed-contract method.
   D. lower than the completed-contact method.   (AICPA adapted)

6. Which of the following classification schemes is correct?

	Construction In Progress	Progress Billings
A.	Current Asset (inventory)	Deferred account (offset to inventory)
B.	Current Asset (inventory)	Revenue Account
C.	Deferred Asset	Current Asset (receivable)
D.	Current Asset (inventory)	Current Asset (receivable)

7. A two-year contract with a contract price of $3,000,000 will be accounted for using the percentage-of-completion method. Other information relating to the contract:

	1997	1998
At year-end:		
Percent complete	20%	60%
Estimated total costs	$2,250,000	$2,400,000
Total income recognized	$150,000	$360,000

What is the amount of contract costs incurred during 1997?
A. $600,000
B. $150,000
C. $450,000
D. $360,000

8. Farley Construction entered into a long-term construction contract during 1998 with a contract price of $2,000,000. The company uses the *completed-contract method* of accounting for long-term contracts. The following data relates to the contract during 1998:

Costs incurred	$ 385,000
Estimated costs to complete	1,640,000
Progress billings	960,000
Cash collections	580,000

Chapter 7

How much loss should Farley recognize during 1998?
A. $380,000
B. $25,000
C. $5,000
D. $0

9. Farley Construction entered into a long-term construction contract during 1998 with a contract price of $2,000,000. The company uses the *percentage-of-completion method* of accounting for long-term contracts. The following data relates to the contract during 1998:

Costs incurred	$ 385,000
Estimated costs to complete	1,640,000
Progress billings	960,000
Cash collections	580,000

How much loss should Farley recognize during 1998?
A. $380,000
B. $25,000
C. $5,000
D. $0

10. Redwall Construction uses the percentage-of-completion method of accounting for its long-term construction contracts. During 1997, Redwall began work on a $4,500,000 project, which was completed during 1998. The accounting records disclose the following data relating for 1997:

Progress billings	$1,650,000
Costs incurred	1,350,000
Cash collections	1,300,000
Estimated costs to complete	2,700,000

How much income should Redwall have recognized during 1997 on this contract?
A. $105,000
B. $150,000
C. $300,000
D. $350,000

11. The following data relate to a construction job begun during 1997:

Total contract price	$300,000
Actual costs incurred during 1997	60,000
Estimated remaining costs	120,000
Progress billings	90,000
Cash collections	30,000

If the completed-contract method is used, how much gross profit will be recognized during 1997?
A. $0
B. $30,000
C. $40,000
D. $90,000

12. The following data relate to a construction job begun during 1997:

Total contract price	$300,000
Actual costs incurred during 1997	60,000
Estimated remaining costs	120,000
Progress billings	90,000
Cash collections	30,000

If the percentage-of-completion method is used, how much gross profit will be recognized during 1997?
A. $0
B. $40,000
C. $80,000
D. $90,000

13. The Broken Bow Corporation had the following data relating to sales accounted for under the installment sales method:

	1997	1998
Installment Sales	$50,000	$60,000
Cost of installment sales	35,000	36,000
Collections of 1997 sales	10,000	15,000
Collections of 1998 sales	0	25,000

How much gross profit should Broken Bow recognize during 1998?
A. $3,000
B. $25,500
C. $14,500
D. $10,000

14. Enterprise Corporation uses the installment sales method to account for certain sales. As of January 1, 1998, Customer Rider's accounts receivable balance was $40,000, and the gross profit was 15% on sales. Customer Rider defaulted on January 2, 1998, and merchandise with a fair market value of $25,000 was repossessed. At the time of the default, what is the balance in the Deferred Gross Profit account relating to Customer Rider's account?
A. $25,000
B. $40,000
C. $6,000
D. Cannot be determined with the information provided.

15. Enterprise Corporation uses the installment sales method to account for certain sales. As of January 1, 1998, Customer Rider's accounts receivable balance was $40,000, and the gross profit was 15% on sales. Customer Rider defaulted on January 2, 1998, and merchandise with a fair market value of $25,000 was repossessed. What is Enterprise's gain or loss on the repossession?
A. $15,000 loss
B. $40,000 loss
C. $25,000 gain
D. $9,000 loss

16. Grand Island Company uses the cost recovery method to account for certain sales. Information regarding the sales is as follows:

	1997	1998
Cost recovery sales	$50,000	$60,000
Cost of sales	35,000	36,000
Collections of 1997 sales	17,000	19,000
Collections of 1998 sales	0	30,000

What amount of realized gross profit should Grand Island recognize during 1998?
A. $17,700
B. $1,000
C. $300
D. $19,000

17. Franchise fees are recognized as revenue when:
    A. the cash is received.
    B. the franchise agreement is signed.
    C. the franchisor has substantially performed all required services.
    D. the franchise has begun operations.

18. Goods on consignment should be included in the inventory of:
    A. both the consignor and the consignee.
    B. the consignor but not the consignee.
    C. the consignee but not the consignee.
    D. neither the consignor nor the consignee.

19. Verb Company uses the installment method of revenue recognition. The following data pertain to Verb's installment sales for the years ended December 31, 1997 and 1998:

	1997	1998
Installment receivables at year-end on 1997 sales	$60,000	$30,000
Installment receivables at year-end on 1998 sales	—	69,000
Installment sales	80,000	90,000
Cost of sales	40,000	60,000

    What amount should Verb report as deferred gross profit in its December 31, 1998 balance sheet?
    A. $23,000
    B. $33,000
    C. $38,000
    D. $43,000   (AICPA adapted)

20. It is proper to recognize revenue prior to the sale of merchandise when:
    I. The revenue will be reported as an installment sale.
    II. The revenue will be reported under the cost recovery method.

    A. I only
    B. II only
    C. Both I and II
    D. Neither I nor II   (AICPA adpated)

21. On October 1, 1997, Rahn's Fuel Company sold 100,000 gallons of heating oil to Schroeder's Farms at $3 per gallon. Fifty thousand gallons were delivered on December 15, 1997, and the remaining 50,000 were delivered on January 15, 1998. Payment terms were: 50% due on October 1, 1997; 25% due on first delivery, and the remaining 25% due on second delivery. What amount of revenue should Rahn's Fuel Company recognize from this sale during 1997?
    A. $ 75,000
    B. $150,000
    C. $225,000
    D. $300,000   (AICPA adapted)

22. How would the proceeds received from the advance sale of non-refundable tickets for a theatrical performance be reported in the seller's financial statement before the performance?
    A. Revenue for the entire proceeds
    B. Revenue to the extent of related costs expended
    C. Unearned revenue to the extent of related costs expended
    D. Unearned revenue for the entire proceeds   (AICPA adapted)

23. Friedman's is a retailer of home appliances and offers a service contract on each appliance sold. Friedman's sells appliances on installment contracts, but all service contracts must be paid in full at the time of the sale. Collections received for service contracts should be reported as an increase in a:
    A. deferred revenue account.
    B. sales contracts receivable valuation account.
    C. stockholders' valuation account.
    D. service revenue account.   (AICPA adapted)

24. Noun Company began operations on January 1, 1997. Noun appropriately uses the installment method of accounting to record revenue. The following information is available for the years ended December 31, 1997 and 1998:

	1997	1998
Sales	$1,000,000	$2,000,000
Gross profit realized on sales made in:		
1997	$150,000	$ 90,000
1998	—	200,000
Gross profit percentages	30%	40%

    What amount of installment accounts receivable should Noun report in its December 31, 1998 balance sheet?
    A. $1,225,000
    B. $1,300,000
    C. $1,700,000
    D. $1,775,000   (AICPA adapted)

25. Cash collection is a critical event for income recognition in the:

	Cost recovery method	Installment method
A.	No	No
B.	Yes	Yes
C.	No	Yes
D.	Yes	No

    (AICPA adapted)

26. Tug Company began operations on January 1, 1997. Tug appropriately uses the installment sales method of accounting. The following information is available for 1997:

Installment sales receivable, December 31, 1997	$800,000
Deferred gross profit, December 31, 1997 (Before recognition of realized gross profit for 1997)	560,000
Gross profit on sales	40%

    For the year ended December 31, 1997, cash collections and realized gross profit on sales should be:

	Cash Collections	Realized Gross Profit
A.	$400,000	$320,000
B.	$400,000	$240,000
C.	$600,000	$320,000
D.	$600,000	$240,000

    (AICPA adapted)

27. Chee Company sells equipment on installment contracts. Which of the following statements best justifies Chee's use of the cost recovery method of revenue recognition to account for these installment sales?
    A. The sales contract provides that title to the equipment only passes to the purchaser when all payments have been made.
    B. No cash payments are due until one year from the date of sale.
    C. Sales are subject to a high rate of return.
    D. There is **no** reasonable basis for estimating collectibility.   (AICPA adapted)

114   Chapter 7

28. According to the cost recovery method of accounting, gross profit on the installment sale is recognized in income:
    A. after cash collections equal to the cost of sales have been received.
    B. in proportion to the cash collections.
    C. on the date the final cash collection is received.
    D. on the date of sale.   (AICPA adpated)

29. On December 31,1997, Utah, Inc. authorized Ted to operate as a franchisee for an initial fee of $150,000. Of this amount, $60,000 was received upon signing the agreement and the balance, represented by a note, was due in three annual payments of $30,000 each, beginning December 31, 1998. The present value on December 31, 1997 of the three annual payments is approximately $72,000. According to the agreement, the non-refundable down payment represents a fair measure of the services already performed by Utah, Inc. However, substantial future services are required of Utah, Inc. Collectibility of the note is reasonably certain. In Utah, Inc.'s December 31, 1997 balance sheet, unearned franchise fees from Ted's franchise should be reported as:
    A. $132,000.
    B. $100,000.
    C. $ 90,000.
    D. $ 72,000.   (AICPA adapted)

30. Each of Ben's Bagel Company's 21 new franchises contracted to pay an initial franchise fee of $30,000. By December 31, 1997, each franchisee had paid a non-refundable $10,000 fee and signed a note to pay $10,000 principal plus market rate of interest on December 31, 1998 and December 31, 1999. Experience indicates that one franchisee will default on the additional payments. Services for the initial fee will be performed in 1998. What amount of unearned franchise fees would Ben's Bagel Company report at December 31, 1997?
    A. $400,000
    B. $600,000
    C. $610,000
    D. $630,000   (AICPA adapted)

Exercises and Problems

1. Complete the table
    Required: Complete the following table. Which method is most conservative? Why? Develop scenarios under which each method would be appropriate (keep in mind that there are no clear cut GAAP guidelines in this area, but rather, accountants rely upon professional judgement).

Method	Timing of Revenue and/or Income Recognition	Treatment of Product Costs or Direct Costs Under Service Contracts
Full Accrual		
Installment Sales		
Cost Recovery		
Cash		

Name: Chapter 7 115

2. Complete the table
   Required: Complete the following table.

   LONG-TERM CONTRACTS
   ACCOUNTING TERMS

Account	Type of Account	Definition & Meaning
Construction in Progress		
Progress Billings on Construction Contracts		
Net of Construction in Progress and Progress Billings		

3. Percentage-of-completion and completed-contract method
   AAA entered into a contract in 1997 to construct a parking structure at a contract price of $5,000,000. Construction data:

	1997	1998	1999
Construction costs incurred	$750,000	$2,700,000	$650,000
Estimated costs to complete	$3,000,000	$550,000	-0-
Progress billings	$550,000	$3,600,000	$850,000
Collections from customer	$450,000	$3,300,000	$1,250,000

   Required: Prepare the necessary journal entries to record the contract using:
   a) Percentage-of-completion method
   b) Completed contract method
   Note: Carry percentage calculations to two decimal places.

4. Long-term contract with anticipated loss
   BBB entered into a contract in 1997 to construct a building at a contract price of $5,000,000. Construction data:

	1997	1998	1999
Construction costs incurred	$750,000	$2,700,000	$1,655,000
Estimated costs to complete	$3,000,000	$1,680,000	-0-
Progress Billings	$550,000	$3,600,000	$850,000
Collections from customer	$450,000	$3,300,000	$1,250,000

116   **Chapter 7**

Required: Write the journal entries to record the contract using:
    a) Percentage of completion method
    b) Completed contract method.
Note: Carry percentage calculations to two decimal places.

5. Installment sales and cost recovery methods
    The following information relates to sales for Carl's Company during 1997 and 1998:

	1997	1998
Installment sales	$50,000	$80,000
Cost of sales	35,000	60,000
Collections of 1994 sales	25,000	25,000
Collections of 1995 sales		62,000

    Required: Journalize these transactions assuming:
        1) Carl's Company uses the installment sales method.
        2) Carl's Company uses the cost recovery method.

6. Franchises
    Rainbow Toys charges a franchise fee of $150,000. The franchise agreement requires the franchisee to make an initial payment of $25,000 and sign a non-interest bearing note for $125,000. The note is to be paid in 5 installments of $25,000, beginning one year from the agreement date. The initial fee is refundable until the day the franchisee opens the toy store. The franchisee's normal borrowing rate is 10%. The franchisor agrees to find a store location, train employees and set up the initial store display. Initial direct costs of the franchise agreement are $66,000.

    Required: Prepare the journal entries on the franchisor's books to record the initial franchise fee under each of the following scenarios:
        1) Franchisor has not performed the services agreed upon in the contract and collection of the note is reasonably certain.
        2) Franchisor has performed substantially all of the contracted services and collection of the note is reasonably certain.
        3) Franchisor has performed substantially all of the contracted services, but collection of the note is doubtful.

SOLUTIONS TO TEST YOUR UNDERSTANDING

Fill-in-the-Blanks

1. Recognition
2. realized (realizable); substantially complete
3. point of sale
4. completed-contract method
5. percentage-of-completion method
6. proportional performance method
7. cost-to-cost
8. installment sales method
9. deferred gross profit; accounts receivable
10. cost recovery
11. cash

12. deposit
13. substantial performance
14. deposit; deferred credit; deferred
15. consignment; consignee; consignor

Multiple Choice

1.	D	9.	B	17.	C	24.	C
2.	C	10.	B	18.	B	25.	B
3.	B	11.	A	19.	C	26.	D
4.	A	12.	B	20.	D	27.	D
5.	C	13.	C	21.	B	28.	A
6.	A	14.	C	22.	D	29.	D
7.	C	15.	D	23.	A	30.	C
8.	B	16.	B				

Exercises and Problems

1. Complete the table

Method	Timing of Revenue and/or Income Recognition	Treatment of Product Costs or Direct Costs Under Service Contracts
Full Accrual	Recognize revenue when it is earned, generally at the point of sale	Recognize when incurred
Installment Sales	Recognize revenue as cash is collected, based upon gross margin on sales	Recognize as cash is collected, based upon gross margin on sales
Cost Recovery	Recognize revenue only after all costs have been recovered through cash collections	Recognize as cash is collected
Cash	Recognize revenue as cash is collected	Recognize costs as incurred

2. Complete the table

LONG-TERM CONTRACTS
ACCOUNTING TERMS

Account	Type of Account	Definition & Meaning
Construction in Progress	Current asset, inventory	total costs expended to date on the contract.
Progress Billings on Construction Contracts	Deferred account, offsetting Construction in Progress	total amount billed to the customer on the long-term contract to date
Net of Construction in Progress and Progress Billings	Asset	value of the project not yet billed to the customer; rarely will the balance be a credit (rarely will progress billings exceed costs expended)

3. Percentage-of-completion and completed-contract method
   Percentage-of-completion method
   1997:

   Percentage complete = $\dfrac{\text{actual costs to date}}{\text{total expected costs}}$ = $\dfrac{\$750,000}{\$3,750,000}$ = .20

Construction in Progress	750,000	
Materials, Cash, etc.		750,000
Accounts Receivable	550,000	
Progress Billings on Long-Term Contract		550,000
Cash	450,000	
Accounts Receivable		450,000
Cost of Long-Term Contract	750,000	
Construction in Progress	250,000	
Revenue from Long-Term Contract		1,000,000
[.20 x $5,000,000]		

   1998:

   Percentage complete = $\dfrac{\$750{,}000 + \$2{,}700{,}000}{\$750{,}000 + \$2{,}700{,}000 + \$550{,}000}$ = $\dfrac{\$3{,}450{,}000}{\$4{,}000{,}000}$ = .86

Construction in Progress	2,700,000	
Materials, Cash, etc		2,700,000
Accounts Receivable	3,600,000	
Progress Billings on Long-Term Contract		3,600,000
Cash	3,300,000	
Accounts Receivable		3,300,000

Cost of Long-Term Contract	2,700,000	
Construction in Progress	600,000	
Revenue from Long-Term Contract		3,300,000
[(.86 x $5,000,000) - $1,000,000]		

1999:
Project is complete.

Construction in Progress	650,000	
Materials, Cash, etc.		650,000
Accounts Receivable	850,000	
Progress Billings on Long-Term Contract		850,000
Cash	1,250,000	
Accounts Receivable		1,250,000
Cost of Long-Term Contracts	650,000	
Construction in Progress	50,000	
Revenue from Long-Term Contract		700,000
[$5,000,000 - $1,000,000 - $3,300,000]		
Progress Billings on Long-Term Contract	5,000,000	
Construction in Progress		5,000,000

<u>Completed-contract method</u>
1997:

Construction in Progress	750,000	
Materials, Cash, etc.		750,000
Accounts Receivable	550,000	
Progress Billings on Long-Term Contract		550,000
Cash	450,000	
Accounts Receivable		450,000

1998:

Construction in Progress	2,700,000	
Materials, Cash, etc.		2,700,000
Accounts Receivable	3,600,000	
Progress Billings on Long-Term Contract		3,600,000
Cash	3,300,000	
Accounts Receivable		3,300,000

1999:

Construction in Progress	650,000	
Materials, Cash, etc.		650,000
Accounts Receivable	850,000	
Progress Billings on Long-Term Contract		850,000
Cash	1,250,000	
Accounts Receivable		1,250,000
Cost of Long-Term Contracts	4,100,000	
Construction in Progress	900,000	
Revenue from Long-Term Contract		5,000,000

Progress Billings on Long-Term Contract	5,000,000	
Construction in Progress		5,000,000

4. Long-term contract with anticipated loss
   Percentage-of-completion method
   1997:

$$\text{Percentage complete} = \frac{\text{actual costs to date}}{\text{total expected costs}} = \frac{\$750,000}{\$3,750,000} = .20$$

Construction in Progress	750,000	
Materials, Cash, etc.		750,000
Accounts Receivable	550,000	
Progress Billings on Long-Term Contract		550,000
Cash	450,000	
Accounts Receivable		450,000
Cost of Long-Term Contract	750,000	
Construction in Progress	250,000	
Revenue from Long-Term Contract		1,000,000
[.20 x $5,000,000]		

1998:
Note: a loss is anticipated at this time. The total amount of the anticipated loss is $130,000.
[calculation: contract revenue - total estimated cost =$5,000,000 - ($750,000 + $2,700,000 + $1,680,000)]
So, we know we will be recognizing the entire amount of the loss this year, which means we will have to "unrecognize" the profit we recognized on the contract last year.
And, the percentage of completion must also be computed, thusly:

$$\% \text{ complete} = \frac{\text{actual total costs to date}}{\text{estimated total costs}} = \frac{\$750,000 + \$2,700,000}{\$750,000 + \$2,700,000 + \$1,680,000} = .67$$

The journal entries to record actual costs, progress billings, and cash receipts are not affected by the projected loss:

Construction in Progress	2,700,000	
Materials, Cash, etc.		2,700,000
Accounts Receivable	3,600,000	
Progress Billings on Long-Term Contract		3,600,000
Cash	3,300,000	
Accounts Receivable		3,300,000

The journal entry to record the current period revenues and expenses are affected by the projected loss. As in the case of a projected profit on a project, revenue is equal to the percent complete multiplied by the total contract revenue. Notice, however, that the expense amount exceeds the actual costs spent, and that the inventory account, Construction in Progress, is credited by an amount such that the total loss is impounded into the account during this period:

Cost of Long-Term Contract	2,730,000 *	
Construction in Progress		380,000
Revenue from Long-Term Contract		2,350,000 **

*[cost to recognize this period = (revenue recognized to date + amount of projected loss) – prior periods' costs = ($2,350,000 + $1,000,000 + $130,000) – $750,000 = $2,730,000]
**[revenue this period = (% complete x total contract revenue) – prior periods' revenue = (.67 x $5,000,000) – ($1,000,000) = $2,350,000]

1999:
The project is completed during 1999, and while it loses money overall, it does not lose as much as projected in 1998. Therefore, a profit will be reported during 1999, but overall, a loss of $105,000 will be recognized on this project.

Construction in Progress	1,655,000	
Materials, Cash, etc.		1,655,000
Accounts Receivable	850,000	
Progress Billings on Long-Term Contract		850,000
Cash	1,250,000	
Accounts Receivable		1,250,000
Cost of Long-Term Contracts	1,625,000 *	
Construction in Progress	25,000	
Revenue from Long-Term Contract		1,650,000 **

*[expense this period = total project cost – prior periods' costs = (750,000 + 2,700,000 + 1,655,000) -(750,000 + 2,730,000)]

**[revenue this period = total contract revenue – prior periods' revenue = $5,000,000 – 1,000,000 – 2,350,000]

Progress Billings on Long-Term Contract	5,000,000	
Construction in Progress		5,000,000

<u>Completed contract method</u>
1997:

Construction in Progress	750,000	
Materials, Cash, etc.		750,000
Accounts Receivable	550,000	
Progress Billings on Long-Term Contract		550,000
Cash	450,000	
Accounts Receivable		450,000

1998:
A loss on the project is projected this period, and the entire amount of the loss ($130,000) will be recognized during 1998.

Construction in Progress	2,700,000	
Materials, Cash, etc.		2,700,000
Accounts Receivable	3,600,000	
Progress Billings on Long-Term Contract		3,600,000
Cash	3,300,000	
Accounts Receivable		3,300,000
Anticipated Loss on Long-Term Contract	130,000	
Construction in Progress		130,000

1999:
The project is completed and the loss is actually $105,000.

Construction in Progress	1,655,000	
Materials, Cash, etc.		1,655,000
Accounts Receivable	850,000	
Progress Billings on Long-Term Contract		850,000

Cash	1,250,000	
Accounts Receivable		1,250,000
Cost of Long-Term Contracts	4,975,000	
Construction in Progress	25,000	
Revenue from Long-Term Contract		5,000,000
Progress Billings on Long-Term Contract	5,000,000	
Construction in Progress		5,000,000

5. Installment sales and cost recovery methods
   <u>Installment sales method</u>
   1997:

Installment Accounts Receivable (97)	50,000	
Installment Sales		50,000
Cost of Installment Sales	35,000	
Inventory		35,000
Cash	25,000	
Installment Accounts Receivable (97)		25,000
Installment Sales	50,000	
Cost of Installment Sales		35,000
Deferred Gross Profit (97)		15,000
Deferred Gross Profit (97)	7,500 *	
Realized Gross Profit		7,500

*[.30 x $25,000]

1998:

Installment Accounts Receivable (98)	80,000	
Installment Sales		80,000
Cost of Installment Sales	60,000	
Inventory		60,000
Cash	25,000	
Cash	62,000	
Installment Accounts Receivable (97)		25,000
Installment Accounts Receivable (98)		62,000
Installment Sales	80,000	
Cost of Installment Sales		60,000
Deferred Gross Profit (98)		20,000
Deferred Gross Profit (97)	7,500	
Deferred Gross Profit (98)	15,500	
Realized Gross Profit		23,000

<u>Cost recovery method:</u>
1997:

Installment Accounts Receivable (97)	50,000	
Installment Sales		50,000
Cost of Installment Sales	35,000	
Inventory		35,000

Cash	25,000	
Installment Accounts Receivable (97)		25,000
Installment Sales	50,000	
Cost of Installment Sales		35,000
Deferred Gross Profit (97)		15,000

No gross profit recognized during 1997 since cost has not been fully recovered through cash collections

1998:

Installment Accounts Receivable (98)	80,000	
Installment Sales		80,000
Cost of Installment Sales	60,000	
Inventory		60,000
Cash	25,000	
Cash	62,000	
Installment Accounts Receivable (97)		25,000
Installment Accounts Receivable (98)		62,000
Installment Sales	80,000	
Cost of Installment Sales		60,000
Deferred Gross Profit (98)		20,000
Deferred Gross Profit (97)***	15,000	
Deferred Gross Profit (98)**	2,000	
Realized Gross Profit		17,000

**[cost of sales was $60,000 and cash collections totaled $62,000 so $2,000 of gross profit can be realized this year]
*** [cost was fully recovered during 1998; in fact, receivables were fully collected so the total gross profit on the 1997 sales can be recognized during 1998]

6. Franchises

   1)
Cash	25,000	
Note Receivable	94,770 *	
Deposit on Franchise		119,770

      *Calculation: Present value of annuity of $25,000, for 5 periods at 10% interest.

Deferred Cost of Franchise Revenue	66,000	
Cash		66,000

   2)
Deposit on Franchise	119,770	
Franchise Fee Revenue		119,770
Cost of Franchise Fee Revenue	66,000	
Deferred Cost of Franchise Fee Revenue		66,000

   3) Use the installment method in this case because collectibility of the note is in doubt.

Deposit on Franchise	119,770	
Franchise Fee Revenue		119,770
Cost of Franchise Fee Revenue	66,000	
Deferred Cost of Franchise Fee Revenue		66,000
Franchise Fee Revenue	119,770	
Cost of Franchise Fee Revenue		66,000
Deferred Gross Profit on Franchise		53,770

Deferred Gross Profit on Franchise	11,250	
Realized Gross Profit on Franchise		11,250 *

*Calculation:

$$\frac{\$53,770}{\$119,770} \quad 45\% \text{ gross profit}$$

45% gross profit x $25,000 = $11,250.

CHAPTER 8

COST OF GOODS SOLD AND INVENTORY—IDENTIFICATION AND VALUATION

KEY POINTS

Note: Three key questions are associated with accounting for inventory:
1. What items should be included in inventory?
2. What costs should be included in the cost of inventory?
3. At the end of the accounting period, what assumptions should be made about which inventory units remain and which were sold?

Note: This chapter focuses on these three questions, specifically with respect to inventory valuation. Almost all companies in the U.S. use one or more of three basic inventory valuation methods:
     LIFO   FIFO   Average Cost

Note: The objective of valuation:
Divide total cost of inventory available for sale between goods sold during the period and goods remaining (in inventory) at the end of the period.

Keep these three notes in mind as you study this chapter.

I. What is inventory?
   A. *Inventory*: goods held for manufacture and eventual sale in the normal course of business.
      1. *Merchandise inventory*: goods held for sale by merchandising or retailing companies.
      2. Inventories of manufacturing companies:
         a. *Raw materials*: goods acquired for use in the production process.
         b. *Work in process (also called "goods in process")*: materials partially processed and requiring further work before they can be sold. Work in process inventory includes three cost elements: *direct materials, direct labor,* and *manufacturing overhead* (overhead consists of all the costs necessary to make production happen but which cannot be specifically identified with a particular product. Examples include electricity, insurance, wages of supervisory personnel).
         c. *Finished Goods*: manufactured products awaiting sale.
         d. Classifications between raw materials, work in progress, and finished goods are company specific, so what's raw material for one company may be finished goods for another. For example, thread and cloth are raw materials for a garment manufacturer, but the same thread and cloth would be finished goods for thread manufacturers or cloth manufacturers.
      3. **Important point:** Flow of product through the organization has great financial impact: while goods are on hand (either as raw materials, work in progress, or finished goods, they are listed on the balance sheet; once sold or otherwise disposed of, goods' costs are charged to expense and appear on the income statement).

II. Inventory Systems
   A. Means of keeping track of both costs and units of inventory.
   B. Two major inventory systems are:
      1. *Periodic inventory system*: after periodic physical verification of inventory on hand (via counting, measuring, or weighing), values are assigned to the items to calculate the amount to be shown on the balance sheet.
         a. Accounting:
            1) Purchases are charged to the purchases account (an expense account) not to Inventory.
            2) End-of-period adjusting entry is made to charge Purchases either to Cost of Goods Sold or to Inventory, based upon the physical measurement of the inventory on hand at that time.
            3) Inventory account is not used during the period to record transactions such as purchases and sales of inventory.

2. *Perpetual inventory system*: all inventory-type transactions are recorded during the period through the inventory account, with balance in account at the end of the period confirmed by a physical inventory.
   a. Accounting:
      1) Purchases charged to inventory account (an asset account on the balance sheet).
      2) Cost of sold inventory is credited (removed) from the inventory account at the time the sale is made (a debit to the expense account, cost of goods sold, and a credit to the inventory account for the amount of the cost of inventory sold).
      3) End of period adjustments to Inventory are made based upon physical count of inventory on hand. The adjustments generally represent *shrinkage* of inventory.
      4) **Important point:** note, with the perpetual system, the company always knows how much inventory it has on hand, while with the periodic system, the company knows only at the end of the period.

III. Whose Inventory Is It?
   A. Goods should be included in the inventory of the party holding title to the goods.
   B. Goods in transit:
     1. *FOB (free on board) shipping point*: title passes to the buyer when goods are loaded at the point of shipment, and usually buyer pays freight.
       a. Even if this inventory has not physically arrived at the buyer's location by year-end, it must be included in the buyer's books because title has passed.
       b. On the other side of the transaction, the seller records the sale and the reduction in inventory at the time the inventory is shipped.
     2. *FOB (free on board) destination*: title transfers when the goods arrive at the buyer's location, and usually seller pays freight.
       a. Technically, inventory shipped FOB destination is not included in the buyer's books until it arrives at its destination.
       b. Difficulties encountered by the sellers in determining exactly when the goods arrive at the buyer's location often prompt seller's to recognize the sale and the decrease in inventory at the time the goods are shipped.
   C. Consigned Goods
     1. Inventory physically housed in one party's location, (such as the dealer's gallery), but for which title rests with another party (namely, the owner).
       a. For example, art is often displayed in galleries on consignment. The artist is the owner. The gallery is the dealer. The artist retains title to the art until it is sold by the gallery. Until the art is sold, it remains on the artist's books.
       b. Consigned inventory should be listed on the book's of the party that has title to it.

IV. What Is Inventory Cost?
   A. Items to include in cost
     1. Generally, include all expenditures necessary to acquire, prepare, and place inventory for sale.
     2. Examples: purchase price, freight, storage costs, allocated overhead. These are called *product costs* or *inventoriable costs*.
     3. Some expenditures are difficult to specifically assign to inventory, such as insurance, so those are usually charged to the income statement as *period costs*.
     4. Allocating overhead costs to inventory
       a. Traditionally, overhead has been allocated to inventory based on the amount of direct labor used in production.
       b. A new system, *Activity Based Costing (ABC)*, allocates overhead based upon clearly defined *cost drivers*, which are characteristics of the production process.
   B. Discounts as reductions in cost
     1. Purchase discounts should be treated as a reduction of cost assigned to inventory.
       a. *Trade discount*: difference between catalog price and price charged to customer; purchase should be recorded at the price charged to the customer, which is the invoice price.

b. *Cash discount:* reduction from invoice price granted for payment of invoice within a limited time.
   1) generally listed on invoice as terms, such as "2/10, n/30," which means 2 percent discount if invoice is paid within 10 days, total invoice is due within 30 days.
2. Purchases can be recorded *gross* or *net*.
3. *Gross* means the purchase price is recorded without consideration of any possible cash discounts for early payment.
   a. If cash discounts are taken, the discount is credited to inventory at the time payment is made.
   b. Example: Buy $900 worth of inventory. Cash discount of 2% is available if the invoice is paid in 10 days. To record the purchase, at gross:

Inventory	900	
Accounts Payable		900

   If invoice is paid within the discount period, the journal entry would be:

Accounts Payable	900	
Inventory		18
Cash		882

   If invoice is paid after the discount period, the journal entry would be:

Accounts Payable	900	
Cash		900

4. *Net* means the purchase is recorded net of the discount, so the example above would be:

Inventory	882	
Accounts Payable		882

   If payment is made within discount period:

Accounts Payable	882	
Cash		882

   If payment is made after discount period:

Accounts Payable	882	
Discounts Lost (expense)	18	
Cash		900

V. Inventory Valuation Methods
   (*Caution*: this section is detailed and complicated. Be prepared to take your time and study this section carefully.)
   A. Companies can choose the cost allocation method
      1. Different types of inventory owned by the company can be valued with different cost allocation methods.
      2. Predominant method of cost allocation of inventory must be disclosed in the footnotes to the financial statements.
      3. Companies cannot change cost allocation methods without disclosing the impact of the change on the financial statements.
      4. Because cost allocation method affects both the balance sheet (the asset, inventory) and the income statement (the expense, cost of goods sold), the choice of method is very important to companies.
      5. Four common methods of inventory cost valuation:
         a. Specific identification
         b. FIFO
         c. LIFO
         d. Average cost
      6. FIFO and LIFO are both popular choices (see text, page 428 for more details regarding companies' choices).
   B. Specific Identification
      1. Costs are allocated to units of inventory according to the actual costs of specific units.
      2. Assumption is that costs attach, and thus, costs allocated to inventories should follow the physical flow of inventory through the company.
      3. Strong theoretical foundation for this method.
      4. Practically, the method is difficult to apply when inventory consists of many fungible units.
      5. Conceptually, accounting is simple, but requires constant dedication to detail.
      6. Used in practice generally only for large distinctive items, such as executive pleasure boats, purebred (registered) horses, and artwork.

C. Average Cost Method
1. Based upon the assumption that costs in inventory are fungible, and thus, variations in prices paid during the period should be averaged out among the total number of units purchased and sold.
2. If a periodic inventory system is used, the average cost method becomes a *weighted average cost*.
3. If a perpetual inventory system is used, the average cost method becomes a *moving average cost*.
4. Refer to the following data:
    Beginning balance: 160 units @ $2.00 per unit
    Sept. 1   Purchase 100 units @ $1.00 per unit
    Sept. 5   Sell 150 units
    Sept. 7   Purchase 250 units @ $3.00 per unit
    Sept. 10   Sell 180 units
    Sept. 10   Purchase 50 units @$4.00
    Let's use this data to analyze ending inventory and cost of goods sold using average cost.
    a. If the company uses a *periodic* inventory system:

Beginning balance	160 @ $2.00	$ 320.00
9/1	100 @ $1.00	100.00
9/7	250 @ $3.00	750.00
9/10	50 @ $4.00	200.00
Total	560 units	$1,370.00 total cost

    Average: $1.370/560 = $2.446
    So, cost of goods sold is 330 units x $2.446 or $807.00 (rounded)
    Ending inventory is 230 units x $2.446 or $563.00 (rounded)
    Important point: Notice that regardless of the cost allocation method we used we are still allocating total costs of $1,370 between cost of goods sold and ending inventory.
    b. If the company uses a *perpetual* inventory system:
    A recalculation of the average cost is required, as each purchase and sale occurs.
    As of 9/1, the average cost is: $420.00 / 260 units or $1.615.
    So, cost of goods sold for the 9/5 sale would be:
       150 units @ $1.615 or $242.25.
    When the purchase of 9/7 is recorded, the moving average changes again to reflect the average cost of the total number of units currently in inventory:
       360 units with a total cost of $927.75, for an average of $2.577.
    Cost of goods sold on 9/10 is:
       180 units x $2.577 or $463.86.
    At the end of the period, 230 units remain in inventory, with a total cost of $663.89 (average is 663.89/230 or $2.886).
    Total cost of goods sold is $463.86 + $242.25 or $706.11.
D. FIFO (first-in, first-out) Method
1. Based upon the assumption that costs should be charged to expense (cost of goods sold) in the order in which costs are incurred.
2. Thus, inventory on the balance sheet is stated in terms of the most recent costs.
3. Method is logical and often matches the physical flow of inventory, especially when the inventory is perishable or subject to style-related obsolescence.
4. Using the same data we used to compute average cost, let's compute inventory costs using FIFO:
    First, cost of goods sold will be calculated based upon the first costs incurred, so let's calculate the cost of goods sold for the September 5 sale:
       150 units @ $2.00, or $300.
    Note: after we've charged 150 units to cost of goods sold, there are still 10 units from the beginning balance of 160, so the next sale must take those into account, thus:
    September 10 sale of 180 units:

10 units @ $2.00 =	$ 20.00
100 units @ $1.00 =	100.00
70 units @ $3.00 =	210.00
total cost of goods sold for the September 10 sale:	$330.00

What is total cost of goods sold? $300 + $330 = $630.
What is the balance in ending inventory:

180 units @$3.00 =	$540.00
50 units @$4.00 =	200.00
Total	$740.00

Important point: notice that cost of goods sold in this method (FIFO) always reflects the costs associated with the earliest acquisitions of inventory and the inventory account on the balance sheet always reflects the costs of the latest purchases of inventory.

Thinking question: What will be the impact on the financial statements if, as in the example you just read, inventory costs are constantly rising?

Important point: Notice that we've still allocated total costs of $1,370 between income statement and balance sheet.

E. LIFO (last-in, first-out) Method
1. Based upon the assumption that the last costs incurred during the period should be charged to that period's income statement.
2. Method does not assume that costs attach, and thus, this method rarely matches physical flow of inventory with cost flow.
Thinking question: There are some exceptions. Can you think of any industries in which the last inventory produced or purchased is the first inventory sold? (Hint: think about steel production, coal mining or gravel excavation.)
3. LIFO was developed as a means of deferring illusionary inventory profits which can exist when prices are constantly rising. The method has been acceptable for tax purposes since 1938.
4. Generally, companies which adopt LIFO for tax purposes must also use LIFO for book reporting.
Thinking question: Why do you think there's a requirement to match book and tax reporting (this is the only major example of required conformity between book and tax reporting in the U.S.)? Why might companies be motivated to use LIFO for tax purposes and another method, such as FIFO for book purposes?
5. Example using LIFO with a periodic system:
Using the data from "C" above, calculate cost of goods sold and ending inventory. Before we begin, what is the total amount of cost to allocate between cost of goods sold and inventory? $1,370, correct!

Cost of goods sold:
330 total units sold:

50 @ $4.00	$200.00
250 @ $3.00	750.00
30 @ $1.00	30.00
Total	$980.00

Ending Inventory of 230 units:

70 @ $1.00	$ 70.00
160 @ $2.00	320.00
Total	$390.00

Important point: Note that during periods of rising prices (as in this example), LIFO produces the highest cost of goods sold; thus, LIFO produces the lowest net income. So, if companies could use this method for tax purposes, notice that taxable income would be lowest using LIFO (if prices are rising), and therefore, income tax paid would also be lowest.

Another important point: Purchases during the period are the same regardless of inventory valuation method used.

VI. More About LIFO
A. LIFO layers
1. When the quantity of units purchased or produced in the year exceeds the quantity sold, a new "layer" of inventory is created, representing the difference between the amount produced and the amount sold.
2. When a new layer is created, the old layers (i.e., excesses from prior years) remain untouched.

3. After a few years, then, the LIFO assumption results in ending inventory containing very old inventory prices.
    a. Since LIFO layers are created when prices are rising, the "value" on the year-end balance sheet of ending inventory does not reflect current value of existing inventory.
4. The difference between the LIFO ending inventory and the ending inventory that would be obtained using another valuation assumption is called the *LIFO reserve*.
    a. Most companies report the LIFO reserve on the balance sheet or in a footnote.
5. Example

Carter Company began operations in 1997. During the year Carter purchased 100 units at $5 per unit. Ending inventory was 20 units. During 1998, Carter purchased 200 units at $6 per unit and had 70 units in inventory at the end of the year. During 1999, Carter purchased 160 units at $7 per unit, and had 100 units in inventory at the end of the year. The following table demonstrates the accounting for Carter's inventory over the three-year period using LIFO.

	1997	1998	1999
Beginning inventory	-0-	(97)20 x $5 = $100	(97)20 x $5 = $100 (98)50 x $6 = $300
Purchases	100 x $5 = $500	200 x $6 = $1,200	160 x $7 = $1,120
Cost of goods sold	80 x $5 = $400	150 x $6 = $750	130 x $7 = $910
Ending inventory	(97)20 x $5 = $100	(97)20 x $5 = $100 (98)50 x $6 = $300	(97)20 x $5 = $100 (98)50 x $6 = $300 (99)30 x $7 = $210

B. LIFO liquidation
1. If the number of units sold during the period exceeds the number of units purchased during the period, inventory costs from old LIFO layers will be "sold."
    a. This is called *LIFO liquidation*.
    b. The effect of LIFO liquidation is disclosed in footnotes.
    Example
    Continuing the example above, let's assume that in the year 2000, the company purchases 100 units at $8 per unit, and let's further assume the company sells 140 units during the year. Because the company sold more units than it purchased during the year, LIFO liquidation occurs, and will be measured:
    Beginning inventory:
        (97) 20 x $5 = $100
        (98) 50 x $6 = $300
        (99) 30 x $7 = $210
    (Add) purchases during 2000:
        100 x $8 = $800
    (Total) goods available for sale:
        200 units
    (Total) goods sold during the period: 140 units:
        (00) 100 x $8 = $800
        (99) 30 x $7 = $210
        (98) 10 x $6 = $ 60
    (Remaining) Ending inventory:
        (97) 20 x $5 = $100
        (98) 40 x $6 = $240
3. Note: when a company experiences LIFO liquidation during times of rising prices, cost of goods sold decreases and net income increases, causing the so-called "LIFO liquidation effect."

C. LIFO and income taxes
1. LIFO was developed as a means of deferring illusionary inventory profits that can exist when prices are constantly rising.

2. LIFO has been acceptable for tax purposes since 1938.
    a. Generally, companies that adopt LIFO for tax purposes must also use LIFO for financial reporting purposes (this is the "LIFO conformity rule").
3. **Important point:** Note that during periods of rising prices (as in this example), LIFO produces the highest cost of goods sold; thus, LIFO produces the lowest net income. So, if companies could use this method for tax purposes, notice that taxable income would be lowest using LIFO (if prices are rising), and therefore, income tax expense would also be lowest.

VII. Overall Comparison of FIFO, LIFO, and Average Cost
   A. Companies choose inventory valuation methods weighing four factors:
      1. Income tax effects
      2. Bookkeeping costs
      3. Impact on financial statements
      4. Industry comparison
   B. As you study the common methods of inventory valuation keep in mind the differences in these four factors for each method.

VIII. Using Inventory Information for Financial Analysis
   A. Key Ratio: *inventory turnover*
      1. Measures efficiency in managing and using inventory.
      2. Calculation: $\dfrac{\text{Cost of Goods Sold}}{\text{Average Inventory}}$
      3. Result indicates the number of times the inventory is replaced during the year.
         a. For example, an inventory turnover of 6 means the inventory is replaced 6 times during the year, which also implies the company has on hand at any given time enough inventory to satisfy about 2 months worth of sales demand.
      4. Generally, the higher the inventory turnover the better, indicating the company is well anticipating the products its customers want and is supplying them very quickly.
         a. However, turnover can be too high; if a company does not maintain sufficient quantities of inventory on hand, it may experience shortages in inventory and may be unable to fully satisfy demand for its product.
         b. **Thinking question:** Can you think of a case in which inventory of a certain product is "undersupplied?" (Hint: remember Beanie Babies during the winter and spring of 1997 or Tickle Me Elmo at Christmas 1996?)
   B. Another key ratio: *Number of days' sales in inventory*
      1. Provides information regarding the average time taken to turn inventory.
      2. Calculation: $\dfrac{365}{\text{Inventory turnover}}$

EXPANDED MATERIAL KEY POINTS

IX. LIFO Pools
   A. Used to simplify the inventory valuation process, primarily useful for companies that have large amounts of various types of goods in inventory.
   B. LIFO inventory pool is a group of inventory items that are essentially the same.
   C. At the end of the period, the quantity of items in each pool is determined and costs are assigned by pool.
   D. Calculations are similar to LIFO calculations with only one type of item in inventory except that there are calculations for each inventory pool.

X. Dollar-Value LIFO
   A. Recall LIFO layers represent excess *quantities* of products (or purchases) of inventory over sales by year.
   B. Dollar-value LIFO determines layers based upon total *dollar* change in inventory rather than *unit* changes.
   C. Dollar-value LIFO is the most widely used adaptation of LIFO.
   D. All similar inventory items are grouped into pools, and the layers are based upon total dollar changes rather than unit level changes.

E. All goods in the inventory pool are treated as though they are identical.
F. Beginning and ending inventories in each pool are valued at "**base-year**" prices.
G. If ending inventory (valued at base-year prices) is greater than beginning inventory (valued at base-year prices), a new LIFO layer is created.
   1. **Thinking question**: if ending inventory is less than beginning inventory (both valued at base-year prices), what happens? (*Answer:* most recent LIFO layer is reduced).
   2. **Inventory pool** is a critical concept in dollar-value LIFO. Computationally, the fewer the pools, generally the greater the benefit associated with dollar-value LIFO. So, most companies define inventory pools as "natural business units," which means each pool contains goods which are similar. Ideally, then, the company which manufactures one basic type of product (for example, semiconductors) might make the point that it has one inventory pool. Companies also define pools along product lines.
H. **Base-year** prices are the prices in effect at the date the LIFO inventory method is adopted by the company. So, this varies by company.
I. A common method to determine ending inventory at base-year prices is double extension (using all of the inventory).
J. How to do the double extension method (with an index)
   1. Determine ending inventory in the pool at year-end prices.
   2. Convert ending inventory to base-year prices using the year-end price index.
   3. Determine the inventory layers in base-year dollars.
   4. Adjust the inventory to dollar-value LIFO by applying the appropriate indexes to each base-year layer.
K. **Thinking Question:** Where do companies get the indexes? (*Answer:* two sources are commonly used: [1] internally generated indexes can be computed by calculating the ratio of inventory costed at year-end prices to inventory extended at base-year prices or [2] externally generated indexes can be located from various governmental and trade sources.)
L. **Study Tip:** Dollar-value LIFO is computationally and philosophically difficult to understand. But dollar-value LIFO is also widely used. So, as a student, you need to find out how much emphasis your instructor places on this concept.

TEST YOUR UNDERSTANDING

Fill-in-the-Blanks

Required: Fill in the blanks to complete the following sentences.

1. Three key questions are associated with accounting for inventory. They are:
   a. What _____ should be included in inventory?
   b. What _____ should be included in the cost of inventory?
   c. At the end of the accounting period, what _____ should be made about which inventory items remain and which have been sold?

2. Almost all companies in the U.S. use one or more of three basic inventory valuation methods. The methods are _____, _____, and _____ _____.

3. Assets held for sale in the normal course of business or assets held to be used in the production process are called _____.

4. Inventory acquired by a manufacturer for use in the production process is called _____ _____.

5. _____ _____ are items used directly in the production of goods and represent the primary physical materials of the final product.

6. _____ _____ are items that are necessary to facilitate the production process but are not directly incorporated in the final product.

7. _____ _____ _____ is inventory of a manufacturer that is partly processed and requires further work before it can be sold.

8. All manufacturing costs other than direct materials and direct labor are referred to as _____ _____.

9. Manufactured products for which the manufacturing process is complete are referred to as _____ _____.

10. In a _____ inventory system, the cost of goods sold is not determined as each sale is made; rather, purchases are recorded to a purchases account and ending inventory is determined by physical count.

11. In a _____ inventory system, detailed records of each inventory purchase and sale are maintained, purchases are recorded to the inventory account, and cost of goods sold is determined at the time of sale.

12. The amount of inventory that is lost, stolen, or spoiled is _____.

13. When goods are shipped _____ _____ _____, title passes to the purchaser at the point of shipment.

14. When goods are shipped _____ _____, title passes to the purchaser at the point of destination.

15. _____ _____ are inventory items that are physically located at the dealer, but ownership is retained by the shipper until the dealer sells the inventory.

16. _____ _____ are also referred to as _____ _____ and represent costs included in the total cost of manufacturing inventory.

17. In an _____-_____ _____, (_____), system overhead is allocated on the basis of clearly identified characteristics of the production process that are known to create overhead costs; the characteristics of the production process that are known to create overhead costs are called _____ _____.

18. When a _____ _____ is given, a reduction in the selling price is granted because the customer pays the invoice within a specified (and usually quite short) period of time.

19. An inventory valuation method that assigns the actual cost of inventory items sold to cost of goods sold is the _____ _____ method.

20. The _____ _____ method of inventory valuation assigns the same average cost to each unit of inventory sold and to each item in inventory.

21. The inventory method which assumes that the first units sold are the first ones purchased or manufactured is the _____-_____, _____-_____ or _____ method.

22. The inventory method which assumes that the first units sold are the last units purchased or manufactured is the _____-_____, _____-_____ or _____ method.

23. An incremental group of LIFO inventory items created in any year in which the quantity of units purchased or produced exceeds the quantity of units sold is defined as a _____ _____.

24. The _____ _____ is the difference between LIFO ending inventory and the amount obtained using another method such as FIFO or average cost.

Chapter 8

25. _____ _____ refers to the reduction or elimination of old LIFO layers because total purchases or production in the current period is less than sales.

Multiple Choice

Required: Circle the best answer.

1. On December 15, 1997, the Kline Manufacturing Company purchased goods costing $40,000, FOB destination. Additional costs associated with the acquisition and delivery of the goods:

Special packaging costs	$1,000
Special insurance costs	2,000
Shipping fees	1,500

   The goods were received on December 21, 1997, and none were sold as of December 31, 1997. On Kline's December 31, 1997 balance sheet, what amount should be included in inventory for these goods?
   A. $40,000
   B. $41,000
   C. $43,000
   D. $41,500

2. On December 31, 1997 RobCo conducted a physical inventory and determined inventory to be $600,000 priced at cost. Included in the physical inventory were the following items:
   - $20,000 of goods held on consignment for Dart Company. ✗ not included
   - $30,000 of goods billed and shipped to a customer on December 30, with terms FOB shipping point. ✗ not inc
   - $10,000 of goods billed and shipped to a customer on December 30, with terms FOB destination.

   Not included in the physical inventory was an invoice for goods shipped from a supplier on December 30, with terms FOB shipping point in the amount of $15,000.

   As of December 31, 1997 RobCo's inventory balance on the balance sheet should be:
   A. $600,000.
   B. $565,000.
   C. $580,000.
   D. $540,000.

3. Ralson Company uses the net method to record purchases of inventory, and uses a perpetual inventory system. On April 6, Ralson purchased 200 units of inventory for $2.00 per unit. Freight costs on the shipment were $70. Terms of the invoice were 2/10, n/30. The amount recorded into the inventory account for this purchase should be:
   A. $70 for freight and $400 for units.
   B. $70 for freight and $408 for units.
   C. $68.60 for freight and $392 for units.
   D. $70 for freight and $392 for units.

4. Using the following information determine the inventoriable cost:

Merchandise purchased for resale	$500,000
Freight in	6,000
Freight out	7,000
Purchases returns	10,000

   A. $500,000
   B. $506,000
   C. $513,000
   D. $496,000

5. LLB Company sells a single product, the cost of which has been steadily decreasing for several years. LLB Company maintains a constant level of inventory of the product in terms of units. Sales of the product are constant and level throughout the year. All other factors being equal, the method which reports the highest cost of goods sold for LLB Company would be:
   A. LIFO.
   B. FIFO.
   C. average cost.
   D. specific identification.

6. During periods of rising prices, ending inventory would be the same using either a perpetual or a periodic inventory system if which inventory cost allocation method is used?
   A. FIFO
   B. LIFO
   C. Average cost
   D. Dollar-value LIFO

7. Which of the following would NOT be recorded as inventory?
   A. Cattle held and owned by a feedlot
   B. Partially completed automobiles at an auto manufacturing facility
   C. Land acquired for resale by a real estate development company
   D. Land owned by a farmer

8. Which of the following inventory cost allocation methods matches the most current costs with current revenues?
   A. FIFO
   B. LIFO
   C. Average cost
   D. Specific identification

9. Which inventory cost allocation method most closely matches recorded cost flows with physical product flows?
   A. FIFO
   B. LIFO
   C. Average cost
   D. Dollar-value LIFO

10. Relevant information for Blackstone Company:
Beginning inventory	$600,000
Ending inventory	500,000
Sales	900,000
Cost of Goods Sold	700,000

    Inventory turnover for Blackstone Company is:
    A. 1.17 times.
    B. 1.4 times.
    C. 1.27 times.
    D. 1.6 times.

11. S&S Distributors sells a variety of products and its product lines change regularly. Inventory costs are generally increasing. Which inventory cost allocation method will likely give S&S Distributors the highest cost of goods sold?
    A. FIFO
    B. Average cost
    C. Dollar-value LIFO
    D. LIFO

12. Which of the following is NOT an advantage of the periodic inventory system?
    A. Ease of use
    B. Physical inventory verification is required to complete calculation
    C. Intraperiod matching of revenues and inventory costs
    D. All of the above

13. In a period of rising prices, the inventory cost allocation method that tends to result in the lowest tax expense is:
    A. LIFO.
    B. FIFO.
    C. average cost.
    D. specific identification.

14. In which of the following types of inventories and businesses would you expect to encounter the use of specific identification as an inventory cost allocation method?
    A. Cattle on a cattle ranch
    B. Recreational vehicles at an RV dealership
    C. CD's at a music store
    D. Perishable foods in a grocery store

15. A company decided to change its inventory valuation method from FIFO to LIFO in a period of rising prices. What was the result of the change on ending inventory and net income in the year of the change?

	Ending inventory	Net income
A.	Increase	Increase
B.	Increase	Decrease
C.	Decrease	Decrease
D.	Decrease	Increase

    (AICPA adapted)

16. The following information applies to Alaskan Products, Inc. for 1997:

Merchandise purchased for resale	$400,000
Freight-in	10,000
Freight-out	5,000
Purchase returns	2,000

    Alaskan Products, Inc.'s 1997 inventoriable cost was:
    A. $400,000.
    B. $403,000.
    C. $408,000.
    D. $413,000.

    (AICPA adapted)

17. On June 1, 1997, Harrison Corporation sold merchandise with a list price of $5,000 to Pratt on account. Harrison allowed trade discounts of 30%. Credit terms were 2/15,n/40, and the sale was made FOB shipping point. Harrison prepaid $400 of delivery costs for Pratt as an accommodation. On June 1, 1997, Harrison received from Pratt a remittance in full payment amounting to:
    A. $3,500.
    B. $3,430.
    C. $3,900.
    D. $3,830.

    (AICPA adpated)

18. According to the net method, which of the following items should be included in the cost of inventory?

	Freight costs	Purchase discounts not taken
A.	Yes	No
B.	Yes	Yes
C.	No	Yes
D.	No	No

    (AICPA adapted)

19. The average cost method of inventory valuation is applicable to which of the following inventory systems?

	Periodic	Perpetual
A.	Yes	Yes
B.	Yes	No
C.	No	Yes
D.	No	No

    (AICPA adapted)

20. During periods of rising prices, a perpetual inventory system would result in the same dollar of ending inventory as a periodic inventory system under which of the following inventory valuation methods?

	FIFO	LIFO
A.	Yes	No
B.	Yes	Yes
C.	No	Yes
D.	No	No

    (AICPA adapted)

21. (Expanded material) On January 1, 1997, Shugat Company adopted the dollar-value LIFO inventory method. Shugat's entire inventory constitutes a single pool. Inventory data for 1997 and 1998 are as follows:

Date	Inventory at Current Year Cost	Inventory at Base Year Cost	Relevant Price Index
1/1/97	$150,000	$150,000	1.00
12/31/97	220,000	200,000	1.10
12/31/98	276,000	230,000	1.20

    Shugat's LIFO inventory value at December 31, 1998 is:
    A. $230,000.
    B. $236,000.
    C. $241,000.
    D. $246,000.

    (AICPA adapted)

22. (Expanded material) When the double extension approach to the dollar value LIFO inventory method is used, the inventory layer added in the current year is multiplied by an index number. Which of the following correctly states how components are used in the calculation of this index number?
    A. In the numerator, the average of the ending inventory at base year cost and at current year cost.
    B. In the numerator, the ending inventory at current year cost, and in the denominator, the ending inventory at base year cost.
    C. In the numerator, the ending inventory at base year cost, and the denominator at current year cost.
    D. In the denominator, the average of the ending inventory at base year cost and at current year cost.

    (AICPA adapted)

Exercises and Problems

1. Classify costs

   Treasured Stitches is a store specializing in custom quilt making. The records of Treasured Stitches indicate the following cost categories:
   1. Fabric, to be used in custom quilts.
   2. Quilt tops, (quilts that are pieced and stitched but which have not been backed or quilted to make a finished quilt).
   3. Thread, for use in custom quilting.
   4. Wages of employees who make quilts.
   5. Salary of the president of the company.
   6. Utilities: heat, electricity, air conditioning, telephone, fax, and insurance for the store.
   7. Wages for the bookkeeper.
   8. Depreciation on sewing machines used to make custom quilts.

9. Property tax on the store building.
10. Advertising.

Required: For each category, indicate whether the cost is an inventory cost (I), or if the cost represents a period cost, to be expensed (E) as incurred. For each inventory cost (I), indicate whether the cost is a direct material (DM), direct labor (DL) or manufacturing overhead (MOH).

2. Country Collectibles
Country Collectibles is a retail store specializing in handmade quilts and wall hangings. The company uses the FIFO method of inventory costing with a perpetual inventory system. During the first half of 1997, Country Collectibles purchased several quilts, paying cash for each purchase:

Date	Units	Cost per unit
1/15	6	$200
2/15	4	200
3/15	5	400
4/15	4	400
5/15	1	300
6/15	2	350

Prior to January 15, Country Collectibles had no quilts in inventory. Between January 15 and June 30, Country Collectibles sold 16 quilts for a total of $6,400. On June 30, a store clerk took inventory and determined that there were 7 quilts in the store. While it was true that there were 7 quilts in the store, two of the quilts had been sold (and paid for), but the customers had not yet taken delivery of the quilts.

Calculate the gross profit Country Collectibles made on quilt sales during the first half of 1997. Be sure to correct the store clerk's error in your calculations and take into account any inventory shrinkage.

If Country Collectibles used the average cost method for inventory allocation, what would its gross profit be for the first half of 1997? What would the gross profit be if Country Collectibles used LIFO? Which method makes the most sense for this company?

3. Inventory and cost of goods computations using different cost allocation methods
Required: Using the data provided below for B&B Distributing, calculate cost of goods sold and ending inventory for the month of January using (1) a periodic inventory system and (2) a perpetual inventory system. Calculate cost of goods sold and ending inventory with the following inventory cost flow assumptions: (a) FIFO, (b) LIFO and (c) Average cost.

Date	Activity	Units	Price per unit	Extension
1/1	Beginning inventory	300	$16.00	$4,800
1/4	Purchase inventory	100	16.10	1,610
1/5	Purchase inventory	100	17.00	1,700
1/15	Sell inventory	220	21.00	
1/19	Purchase inventory	400	17.50	7,000
1/20	Sell inventory	300	21.20	
1/22	Purchase inventory	100	18.00	1,800
1/25	Sell inventory	180	21.50	
1/31	Ending inventory	300		

4. Calculate beginning inventory
   The following information is available for Land's Sand and Gravel for 1997:

Freight-in	$ 6,000
Purchases (net)	60,000
Sales	96,000
Ending inventory	16,000
Gross profit percentage	40%

   Required: Calculate the beginning inventory for Land's Sand and Gravel for 1997.

5. (Expanded material) Dollar-value LIFO
   On January 1, 1997, Mel's Sand and Gravel adopted the dollar-value LIFO inventory method for income tax and external financial reporting purposes. However, Mel continued to use the FIFO inventory method for internal accounting and management purposes. In applying the LIFO method, Mel uses the double-extension method for determining price indexes and the multiple-pools approach under which substantially identical inventory items are grouped into LIFO inventory pools. The following data were available for Inventory Pool No. 1, which is comprised of two sizes of gravel, "fines" and "sand."

	FIFO Basis per Records		
	Units	Unit Cost	Total Cost
Inventory 1/1/97			
Fines	20,000	$30	$600,000
Sand	7,000	25	175,000
			$775,000
Inventory 12/31/97			
Fines	23,000	$35	$805,000
Sand	5,000	28	140,000
			$945,000
Inventory 12/31/98			
Fines	16,000	$40	$640,000
Sand	6,000	32	192,000
			$832,000

   Required:
   1) Prepare a schedule to compute the price indexes for 1997 and 1998, using the double-extension method.
   2) Prepare a schedule to compute the inventory amounts at December 31, 1997 and December 31, 1997, using the dollar-value LIFO inventory method. (AICPA adapted)

SOLUTIONS TO TEST YOUR UNDERSTANDING

Fill-in-the-Blanks

1. items; costs; assumptions
2. FIFO, LIFO, average cost
3. inventory
4. raw material
5. Direct materials
6. Indirect materials
7. Work in process
8. manufacturing overhead
9. finished goods
10. periodic
11. perpetual
12. shrinkage

Chapter 8

13. FOB shipping point
14. FOB destination
15. Consigned goods
16. Product costs; inventoriable costs
17. activity-based cost (ABC); cost drivers
18. cash discount
19. specific identification
20. average cost
21. first-in, first-out; (FIFO)
22. last-in, first-out; (LIFO)
23. LIFO layer
24. LIFO reserve
25. LIFO liquidation

Multiple Choice

1.	A	9.	A	16.	C
2.	B	10.	C	17.	D
3.	D	11.	C	18.	A
4.	D	12.	C	19.	B
5.	B	13.	A	20.	A
6.	A	14.	B	21.	C
7.	D	15.	C	22.	B
8.	B				

Exercises and Problems

1. Classify costs
   1. I; DM
   2. I; DM (This cost category could also be work in process inventory, but because the cost category was included in the problem, it appears that perhaps Treasured Stitches may purchase quilt tops and then pay its own employees to finish them.)
   3. I; DM
   4. I; DL
   5. E
   6. E
   7. E
   8. I; MOH
   9. E
   10. E

2. Country Collectibles
   Before analyzing cost of goods sold and determining gross profit, let's first reconcile units of inventory:

Beginning inventory	0
Purchases	<u>22</u>
Total available for sale	22
Sold	<u>(16)</u>
Ending inventory should be	6

   But, wait, ending inventory is only 5. (Yes, there are 7 quilts in the store at the end of the period, but recall that two of those have been sold so they should not be included in ending inventory.)

Notice, that Country Collectibles is short one quilt. This shortage represents shrinkage, which for a store like Country Collectibles, is a serious problem this year. Inasmuch as the store has only handled 22 quilts in the period, and one has disappeared, the company may have serious internal control problems. (Do you recall studying internal control in Chapter 6?)

How should we account for shrinkage? In this case, we will charge it to cost of goods sold.

FIFO
Cost of goods sold:

Units	Price	Total cost	
6	$200	$1,200	
4	200	800	
5	400	2,000	
1	400	400	
16		$4,400	
1	400	400	Shrinkage
17		$4,800	

Gross profit:
Sales	$6,400
Less: Cost of goods sold	4,800
Gross profit	$1,600

Average cost

22 quilts purchased during the period had a total cost of $6,600, so the average cost is $300 each. We will have to use this calculation because we have no data regarding the date of each sale so we cannot update average cost as we normally would in a perpetual system.

Cost of good sold:	16 units @ $300	$4,800
Shrinkage:	1 unit @ $300	300
Total cost of goods sold		$5,100

Gross profit:
Sales	$6,400
Cost of goods sold	5,100
Gross profit	$1,300

LIFO
Cost of good sold:

Units	Price	Total cost	
2	$350	$ 700	
1	300	300	
4	400	1,600	
5	400	2,000	
4	200	800	
16		$5,400	
1	200	200	shrinkage
17		$5,800	

Gross profit:
Sales	$6,400
Cost of goods sold	5,800
Gross profit	$ 600

Evaluation of methods
Gross profit is highest using FIFO, and it is lowest using LIFO. So, from a tax standpoint, LIFO is advantageous. However, the price of quilts does not seem to be rising steadily, so the advantage to LIFO may be temporary. Average cost is also acceptable as the price of quilts seems somewhat steady. So the use of average cost does not skew either cost of goods sold nor inventory.

Specific identification may, however, be a better alternative than either of the three more common methods. Recall that specific identification is useful for unique inventory items, such as works of art. Quilts may be considered works of art in this case. In addition, because there are few quilts handled during any given period, the bookkeeping costs associated with specific identification would not be onerous. Furthermore, specific identification may have helped determine exactly which quilt was missing at the end of the period.

3. Inventory and cost of goods computations using different cost allocation methods
   Important note: regardless of the inventory cost allocation method used, the total costs to account for during the period are the same. In this case, total costs are $16,910. These costs will be allocated this period between cost of goods sold and ending inventory.

   1) Periodic
      a) FIFO

Date	Activity	Units	Price per unit	Extension
January	Cost of Goods Sold	300	$16.00	$ 4,800
		100	16.10	1,610
		100	17.00	1,700
		200	17.50	3,500
Total	Cost of Goods Sold	700		11,610
	Ending inventory	200	17.50	3,500
		100	18.00	1,800
Total	Ending inventory	300		5,300
	Total costs			$16,910

   Note: cost of goods sold and ending inventory are the same when the FIFO cost allocation method is used, regardless of whether a periodic or a perpetual inventory system is maintained.

      b) LIFO

Date	Activity	Units	Price per unit	Extension
January	Cost of Goods Sold	100	$18.00	$ 1,800
		400	17.50	7,000
		100	17.00	1,700
		100	16.10	1,610
Total	Cost of Goods Sold	700		12,110
	Ending inventory	300	16.00	4,800
Total	Costs			$16,910

c) Average cost

Date	Activity	Units	Price per unit	Extension
January	Cost of Goods Sold	700	$16.91*	$11,837
1/31	Ending Inventory	300	16.91*	5,073
	Total costs			$16,910

* To determine the weighted average cost per unit with a periodic system, add the total cost associated with all the goods available for sale during the period (total cost of $16,910) and divide by the total number of units available for sale during the period (1,000 units).

2) Perpetual
   a) FIFO

Date	Activity	Units	Price per unit	Extension
1/15	Cost of Goods Sold	220	$16.00	$ 3,520
1/20	Cost of Goods Sold	80	16.00	1,280
		100	16.10	1,610
		100	17.00	1,700
		20	17.50	350
1/25	Cost of Goods Sold	180	17.50	3,150
	Total Cost of Goods	700		11,610
1/31	Ending inventory	200	17.50	3,500
		100	18.00	1,800
	Total ending inventory	300		5,300
	Total costs			$16,910

b) LIFO

Date	Activity	Units	Price per unit	Extension
1/15	Cost of Goods Sold	100	$17.00	$ 1,700
		100	16.10	1,610
		20	16.00	320
1/20	Cost of Goods Sold	300	17.50	5,250
1/25	Cost of Goods Sold	100	18.00	1,800
		80	17.50	1,400
	Total Cost of Goods	700		12,080
1/31	Ending inventory	280	16.00	4,480
		20	17.50	350
	Total ending inventory	300		4,830
	Total costs			$16,910

Chapter 8

c) Average cost

Date	Activity	Units	Price per unit (rounded)	Extension (rounded)
1/15	Cost of Goods Sold	220	$16.22*	$ 3,568
1/20	Cost of Goods Sold	300	16.97**	5,091
1/25	Cost of Goods Sold	180	17.19***	3,094
	Total Cost of Goods	700		11,753
1/31	Ending inventory	300	17.19***	5,157
	Total costs			$16,910

* To calculate weighted average cost per unit, first calculate the total costs associated with the goods available for sale at the time of the sale (in this case, there are 500 units available for sale, with a total cost of $8,110). Divide the total cost by the number of units, to get $16.22 per unit.

** At the time of the 1/20 sale, there were 280 units in inventory with a cost of $16.22 per unit allocated to them. The purchase of 400 units had a cost of $17.50 per unit. The weighted average cost, then of this 680 units would be $16.97.

*** At the time of the 1/25 sale, there were 380 units in inventory with a cost allocated per unit of $16.97 and the purchase of 100 units at $18.00 per unit. Thus, the weighted average cost of the total goods available for sale (480 units) would be $17.19 per unit.

At the end of the period, this is the cost allocated per unit to the ending inventory.

4. Calculate beginning inventory
   Land's Sand and Gravel Beginning Inventory is **$7,600**.
   This problem tests your knowledge of the relationships between items on the income statement. To solve this problem, begin with the information you do know and work into the information you do not know (i.e., what you need to calculate). First, keep in mind the fundamental relationships on the income statement:
   Sales - Cost of Goods Sold = Gross Profit

   Beginning inventory + Purchases + Freight = Goods Available for Sale

   Goods Available for Sale - Ending Inventory = Cost of Goods Sold

   In this problem, Sales are given ($96,000) as is Gross Margin (40%); therefore, we know Cost of Goods Sold must be $57,600.

   If Cost of Goods Sold is $57,600 and Ending Inventory is $16,000, then Goods Available for Sale must be $73,600.

   If Goods Available for Sale are $73,600 and Purchases are $60,000 and Freight is $6,000, then Beginning Inventory must be **$7,600**.

5. Dollar-value LIFO
   1) Computation of internal conversion price index using double-extension method:

	December 31, 1997	December 31, 1998
Current inventory at current year cost:		
Fines	23,000 x $35 = $805,000	16,000 x $40 = $640,000
Sand	5,000 x $28 = 140,000	6,000 x $32 = 192,000
	$945,000	$832,000

Current inventory at base cost:

Fines	23,000 x $30 = $690,000	16,000 x $30 = $480,000
Sand	5,000 x $25 = 125,000	6,000 x $25 = 150,000
	$815,000	$630,000

Price Index:
1997: $945,000/$815,000 = 1.16   1998: $832,000/$630,000 = 1.32

2) Computation of dollar-value LIFO:

	Current Inventory at Base Cost	Price Index	Inventory at LIFO Cost
December 31, 1997			
Base inventory	$775,000	1.00	$775,000
1997 layer	40,000	1.16	46,400
	$815,000		$821,400
December 31, 1998			
Base inventory	$630,000	1.00	$630,000
1997 layer	0	1.16	0
1998 layer	0	1.32	0
	$630,000		$630,000

(AICPA adapted)

CHAPTER 9

COST OF GOODS SOLD AND INVENTORY—
ESTIMATION AND NONCOST VALUATION

KEY POINTS

I. Inventory Valuation at Other Than Cost
   A. Lower of Cost or Market (LCM)
      1. Inventory will generally be presented on the balance sheet at cost, but if the (market) value of the inventory is less than cost, the market value will be used.
      2. **Market** is the key term in LCM.
         a. Generally, market is *replacement cost* (what you'd have to pay today to replace the inventory) except:
         b. Market cannot exceed the *net realizable value* (the amount of cash you'd expect to receive if you sold the inventory--which is the sales price less sales expenses).
            1) This is the **ceiling.**
         c. Market cannot be less than net realizable value less normal profit margin (the amount of gross profit you'd expect to realize on the sale of the inventory).
            1) This is the **floor.**
         d. Notice that LCM requires the integration of both *entry cost* and *exit values* (i.e., what the company paid for the inventory as well as what the company hopes to receive upon sale of the inventory).
         e. Notice also that while the market value is generally the replacement cost, the market value is bounded at the high end by the ceiling and at the low end by the floor.
      3. How to apply LCM
         a. Can apply to inventory in aggregate.
         b. Can apply to individual inventory items.
         c. Can apply to groups of inventory items.
      4. Steps used to apply LCM
         a. Define pertinent values: historical cost; floor; replacement cost; ceiling.
         b. Determine "market" (replacement cost constrained by ceiling and floor).
         c. Compare cost with market and select the lower amount.
      5. LCM valuation is normally done at year-end and is recorded as an adjusting entry to the inventory account.
         a. Example:
            Unadjusted balance in inventory account: $25,000
               (note: this is the "cost" number)
            Market valuation $22,500
            In this case, the market is lower than cost, so the inventory must be written down to market, thus:
            Loss from Decline in Value of Inventory   2,500
               Inventory   2,500
         Thinking question: What is the impact of this journal entry on (1) income statement, (2) balance sheet and (3) cash flow statement?
         (Answer: (1) net income is reduced by the loss of $2,500; the loss is usually reported on the income statement after gross profit, but occasionally companies will include the loss in cost of goods sold; (2) assets [inventory] are reduced by $2,500 and equity [due to decline in net income] is reduced by $2,500; (3) there is no direct cash flow impact of this adjusting entry this period)
         Thinking question: Why is there no direct cash flow impact of this adjusting entry this period?
         (answer: The cash paid for inventory is not affected by the write-down).
         b. Another example:
            Assume the same facts as above but now assume that the company wanted to maintain the inventory account strictly at cost. In this case, the journal entry to acknowledge the LCM adjustment would be:
            Loss from Decline in Value of Inventory   2,500
               Allowance for Decline in Value of Inventory   2,500

The allowance account in this case behaves just like the allowance for doubtful accounts with accounts receivable, namely, it is a valuation account which is used to absorb changes in market/cost relationships in inventory.

The advantage to using an allowance account is that companies can keep track of the impact of market value fluctuations from year to year and can easily account for recoveries in market value should they occur.

For example:

Let's assume the same facts as in the previous examples, but let's assume the following for next year:

Inventory (at cost)	$43,000
Market Value of inventory	$47,000

Notice that market is now greater than cost so the company must present the inventory at cost on the balance sheet. However, keep in mind that the company is carrying a valuation account with a credit balance of $2,500 at this time (remember valuation accounts are permanent accounts which do not close at year-end).

This means that if the company does nothing, inventory will be presented on the balance sheet thusly:

Inventory (at cost)	$43,000
Less: allowance for decline in market value	(2,500)
Net inventory	$40,500

Clearly, the company does not want to (or need to) report inventory at $40,500. Rather, the company should report inventory at the lower of cost or market, in this case, cost of $43,000. To do so, the company must make the following adjusting entry:

    Allowance for Decline in Value of Inventory 2,500
        Cost of Goods Sold   2,500

Thinking question: Why is the recovery only $2,500 when market is $4,000 greater than cost? (answer: inventory is stated at the *lower* of cost or market; in this case, cost is lower so that's the figure to use)

Thinking question: What is balance in the allowance account after the adjusting entry is made? (answer: $0)

Thinking question: What is the impact of the adjusting entry on (1) income statement, (2) balance sheet and (3) cash flow statement? (answer: (1) income increases by the amount of the recovery, $2,500; (2) assets increase by $2,500 as does equity; (3) there is still no direct cash flow impact as a result of the adjusting entry)

Thinking question: Why do you suppose inventory is stated at the *lower* of cost or market? (answer: the principle of conservatism motivates LCM)

II. Gross Profit Method
   A. Used to estimate inventory
   B. Why estimate inventory?
      1. Unable to take a physical count of inventory.
      2. Estimate the loss if inventory has been destroyed.
      3. Auditors often use estimation procedures to "test" the ending inventory balance reported by the company.
      4. Occasionally used internally as a check to perpetual inventory record.
   C. Basics of Gross Profit Method
      1. To understand this inventory estimation technique you MUST understand the relationships between sales, cost of goods sold, and ending inventory.
      2. Assumes a stable relationship between sales and costs.
      3. Since sales are known, apply estimated gross profit percentage to sales to determine cost of goods sold, and hence, ending inventory.
      4. To apply the gross profit method, you need four pieces of information about inventories:
         a. Sales
         b. Cost of beginning inventory

c. Cost of purchases during the period
d. Estimated gross profit margin
   1) as a percentage of sales or
   2) as a percentage of cost (or markup)
5. Example:
   a. Assume sales are $5,000 and gross profit is 20%. Therefore, cost of goods sold must be 80% of sales, or $4,000. Next, review inventory records to confirm beginning inventory and purchases of inventory during the period (the total of these two amounts is the total goods available for sale during the period). Let's say beginning inventory was $900 and purchases during the period were $5,100. Therefore, the total goods available for sale during the period must have been $6,000. If $4,000 of the total can be assumed to have been sold (using an estimate of gross profit), then the ending inventory must be $2,000.

III. Retail Inventory Method
  A. Retailers often use the retail inventory method to estimate inventory.
    1. High volume of low-cost transactions.
    2. More flexible than the gross profit method because it allows estimates based upon LIFO, FIFO, or average cost assumptions.
    3. Can use with LCM values.
    4. Can be used after physical inventory is taken to compute cost of inventory.
  B. Method is appealing to retailers because it uses sales price data to back into inventory valuation.
    1. Sales prices are easier for retailers to keep track of than cost numbers.
    2. Generally retail inventory method is applied on a departmental basis because markups (the difference between cost and initial sales price) tend to be similar within departments.
  C. Five pieces of information are necessary to apply retail inventory method:
    1. Sales
    2. Beginning inventory (at cost and retail)
    3. Purchases (at cost and retail)
    4. Original retail, markups, markdowns
       a. *Original retail*: initial sales price, including the original increase over cost referred to as *markup*.
       b. *Markup*: increase that raises sales price above original retail price.
       c. *Markdown*: decrease that reduces sales price below original retail price.
    5. Adjustment data (freight-in, purchase discounts, sales returns and allowances, inventory losses [due to damage, theft, etc])
  D. Examples:
    1. Let's begin with a very simple example:
       Assume the following data:

	Cost	Retail
Beginning inventory	$10,000	$20,000
Purchases	30,000	60,000
Goods available for sale	$40,000	$80,000
Cost percentage (40,000/80,000 = 50%)		
Sales		50,000
Ending inventory (retail)		$30,000
Ending inventory (estimated cost)	$15,000	

       Note: as you work through this example, keep in mind that the retail inventory method requires considerable data, and that the only piece of data not normally kept by the retailer is cost of goods sold data, which essentially we back into by estimating ending inventory.
    2. What if the retail business is more complicated (i.e., the retailers experiences markups and markdowns) Assume the following data:

	Cost	Retail
Beginning inventory	$10,000	$20,000
Purchases	30,000	60,000
Additional markups		4,000
Goods available for sale	$40,000	$84,000
Cost percentage (40,000/84,000 = 48%)		
Markdowns		5,000
Goods available for sale		$79,000
Deduct:		
Sales		52,000
Ending inventory: retail		$27,000
Ending inventory: estimated cost (.48 x 27,000)	$12,960	

- E. Freight, discounts, returns, and allowances
  1. Freight-in increases the cost of purchases.
  2. Discounts, returns, and allowances decrease cost.
  3. Consider these items *before* calculating cost percentage on goods available for sale.
  4. Ignore sales discounts and allowances in the retail inventory calculation.
     a. Why????
     b. Because the retail price used to determine the cost percentage is the gross price; gross sales price is used because estimates of discounts and allowances are generally not reliably possible. Since gross sales price is used to estimate inventory at retail, the gross sales price is used to estimate ending inventory [at retail] also.
  5. Sales returns ARE included because they represent physical flows of inventory--i.e., inventory that was previously considered sold is now once again available for sale.

IV. Effects of Errors in Recording Inventory
  A. Errors in accounting for inventory are common and impact both the income statement and the balance sheet.
  B. To assess the impact of inventory errors, keep in mind:
     Beginning inventory
     + Purchases
     = Goods available for sale
     − Cost of goods sold
     = Ending inventory
  C. So, if beginning inventory is misstated, then goods available for sale is also misstated, and that means cost of goods sold (and hence, net income) is also misstated.
  D. An error in beginning inventory will not necessarily affect ending inventory.
  E. If ending inventory is misstated, so is cost of goods sold (and hence, net income).
  F. If ending inventory this period is misstated, beginning inventory next period is also misstated. But also note, that over the two year period, the errors in inventory cancel each other out, and the end of the second year, retained earnings will be ok (this is called a counterbalancing error).
  G. "C." through "F." imply that only one aspect of inventory is misstated, but usually if one aspect of inventory is misstated, generally something else having to do with inventory (such as purchases, sales, or accounts receivable) is misstated, too.
     1. Hence, discovering and correcting inventory errors is quite a challenge.
     2. Because of the complexity of inventory errors, it is unwise to try to memorize the impact of a particular type of error. Rather, train yourself to analyze each situation individually and completely.

EXPANDED MATERIAL KEY POINTS

V. Dollar-Value LIFO Retail Method
  A. Essentially the same as the dollar-value LIFO method in Chapter 8, but with the adjustment from retail to cost.
  B. Dollar-value LIFO retail method is a cost method.

C. Beginning inventory is excluded from the cost-retail calculation (**Why?** because beginning inventory is in its own layer which has already been accounted for, so all we need to account for this period is this period's purchases, sales, and new ending inventory).
D. Net markups and markdowns are included.
E. Inventory layers are adjusted for changes in price levels.
   1. Ending inventory at retail is divided by the current year's price index to restate it at base-layer prices.
      a. **Think:** What does this computation tell you? (answer: whether a new layer of inventory has been added or whether layers have been invaded.)
   2. Each layer stated at retail in base-layer prices is then:
      a. Multiplied by the price index for its year to inflate it to the price level in effect during the year the layer was created.
   3. Use the inflated (restated) layer prices as the basis for application of the cost-retail percentage to determine cost of goods sold for the year.

VI. Purchase Commitments
   A. **Purchase commitments** are formal agreements to buy a specified product at a specified price over a specified period of time.
      1. Purchase commitments are executory contracts, indicating a promise to perform in the future.
      2. The purchaser uses purchase commitments to secure flow of inventory at a specified price.
      3. No journal entry is written at the time the purchase commitment is made (because no transaction has actually occurred at this point).
      4. What if the market value of the item in the purchase commitment declines over the life of the contract? The contract specifies that the contract price will be paid, which means the cost of the inventory (the contract price) is greater than market.
      5. A loss on purchase commitments is recognized when the items are purchased and the amount of the loss is equal to the difference between the contract price and the market value of the inventory.

VII. Foreign Currency Inventory Transactions
   A. Foreign currency transactions
      1. Transactions denominated (stated) in a currency other than the company's reporting currency. For a U.S. company, a transaction denominated in any currency other than the U.S. dollar is a foreign currency transaction.
      2. Foreign currency transactions are important because they are frequent and often involve huge amounts of money.
   B. Exchange rates
      1. The relationship between currencies.
      2. Exchanges rates measure the cost in one currency to purchase units of another currency.
      3. **Spot rate**: exchange rate for delivery of currency today, and the rate used for immediate trades.
   C. Accounting for transactions denominated in a foreign currency (this method is called the two-transaction approach) Assume that on December 1, a U.S. company purchased inventory from a Canadian supplier in the amount of C$10,000. Assume that the payable will be settled on January 15 and the U.S. company has a December 31 year-end. Spot rates: December 1: C$1 = US$.80; December 31: C$1 = US$.85; January 15: C$1 = US$ .90.
      1. On the date of the transaction, record the transaction in local currency (U.S. dollars) using the spot rate for that date.

Inventory	8,000	
Accounts Payable		8,000

      (C$10,000 x .80 = U.S. $8,000)

      2. At the balance sheet date, recognize any change in exchange rates via an exchange gain or loss; doing so will restate the receivable or payable to the current rate and will recognize in the current year the cost (risk or exposure) of doing business in another currency:

Exchange Loss	500	
Accounts Payable		500

      (C$10,000 X [.85 – .80] = 500)

152 Chapter 9

3. At the settlement date, recognize the cost in U.S. dollars of paying the foreign currency obligation.

   Exchange Loss   500
       Accounts Payable   500
         (C$10,000 x [.90 – .85] = 500)
       Accounts Payable   9,000
         Cash   9,000

4. Note: inventory is recorded at the exchange rate in effect on the date of transaction.
5. Note: the exchange rate loss is the cost of borrowing money in a foreign currency, and that this cost is NOT an operating item; rather it is recorded on the income statement as an "other" item.
6. Note: if a company enters into many foreign currency transactions, it faces considerable economic risks if the dollar weakens (as in the case of the example we just worked). To mitigate the possible effects of exchange rate changes, companies often *hedge* their foreign currency receivables and payables. *Hedging* means that the company enters into other financial instrument transactions to "lock in" the exchange rate.

TEST YOUR UNDERSTANDING

Fill-in-the-Blanks

Required: Fill in the blanks to complete the following sentences.

1. _____ _____ _____ _____ _____ (_____) is a generally accepted accounting method for the valuation of inventories which allows for the immediate recognition of all unrealized losses on inventory during the period.

2. The replacement cost of inventory adjusted for an upper and lower limit that reflects the estimated net realizable value of the inventory is the _____ _____.

3. _____ _____ is the cost that would be required to regenerate the existing asset.

4. The acquisition cost of an asset is also called the _____ _____.

5. The value received for an asset when it is sold is the _____ _____.

6. In the LCM calculation, the _____ represents the upper boundary of "market," and is the estimated selling price of the inventory less any normal selling costs.

7. In the LCM calculation, the _____ _____ _____ (_____) represents the expected amount of cash to be received from the conversion of assets in the normal course of business; it is equal to the selling price of the inventory less any normal selling costs.

8. In the LCM calculation, the _____ represents the lower boundary of "market," and is the estimated selling price of the inventory less any normal selling costs and less normal profit.

9. The inventory estimation technique based upon the relationship between gross profit and sales is the _____ _____ _____.

10. Gross profit divided by sales is the _____ _____ _____; it is a measure of profitability.

11. An inventory estimation procedure that converts the retail value of inventory to an estimate of cost by using a cost percentage reflecting the relationship of inventory available for sale at retail and cost is the _____ _____ _____.

Name: _____ **Chapter 9**   153

12. The _____ _____ is the percentage reflecting the relationship between cost values and retail values.

13. _____ _____ is the initial sales price, including the original increase over cost referred to as the initial markup.

14. _____ _____ is the difference between the initial retail price of merchandise and the original historical cost.

15. The increase that raises sales price above cost is the _____.

16. The decrease that reduces sales price is the _____.

17. If the beginning inventory is overstated, cost of goods available for sale will be _____, and even if the ending inventory is correctly stated, cost of goods sold will be _____, and net income will be _____.

18. Inventory as of December 31, 1997 (year-end) was overstated. Inventory as of January 1, 1998 is _____.

19. Assuming beginning inventory is correctly stated, if ending inventory is overstated, cost of goods sold will be _____, and net income will be _____.

Expanded material items:
20. In the _____-_____ _____ _____ _____ of inventory estimation, retail values are converted to base-year amounts by use of index numbers; LIFO incremental layers are determined based on incremental dollar changes; and the retail values are converted to cost using a cost percentage.

21. An executory contract representing an exchange of promises about future actions involving the purchase of inventory at specified prices is called a _____ _____.

22. An exchange of promises about future actions is an _____ _____.

23. A _____ _____ _____ is any transaction for a U.S. company that is denominated in a currency other than the U.S. dollar.

24. The exchange rate quoted today for immediate delivery of currency is the _____ _____.

Multiple Choice

Required: Circle the best answer.

1. Which pieces of information are necessary to apply the gross profit method of inventory estimation?
   A. Sales, beginning inventory [cost], purchases [cost], gross profit margins.
   B. Sales, beginning inventory [cost, retail], gross profit margin, purchases [cost, retail], markups, markdowns, cancellations.
   C. Sales, beginning inventory [cost, retail], gross profit margin, purchases [cost, retail], markups, markdowns, cancellations, adjustment data [freight-in, etc.].
   D. Sales, beginning inventory [cost, retail], purchases [cost, retail], markups, markdowns, cancellations, adjustment data [freight-in, etc].

Chapter 9

2. Which pieces of information are necessary to apply the retail inventory method of inventory estimation?
   A. Sales, beginning inventory [cost], purchases [cost], gross profit margins.
   B. Sales, beginning inventory [cost, retail], gross profit margin, purchases [cost, retail], markups, markdowns.
   C. Sales, beginning inventory [cost, retail], gross profit margin, purchases [cost, retail], markups, markdowns, adjustment data [freight-in, etc.].
   D. Sales, beginning inventory [cost, retail], purchases [cost, retail], markups, markdowns, adjustment data [freight-in, etc].

3. Lower of cost or market valuations can be applied to inventory:
   A. in aggregate.
   B. on a product line basis.
   C. on an individual inventory basis.
   D. either in aggregate, by product lines, or individually.

4. The ceiling in the lower of cost or market valuation is:
   A. net realizable value of the inventory.
   B. net realizable value of the inventory plus normal gross profit percentage.
   C. net realizable value of the inventory less normal gross profit percentage.
   D. replacement value.

5. The floor in the lower of cost or market valuation is:
   A. net realizable value of the inventory.
   B. net realizable value of the inventory plus normal gross profit percentage.
   C. net realizable value of the inventory less normal gross profit percentage.
   D. replacement value.

6. The replacement cost is:
   A. estimated cost to replace inventory today.
   B. net realizable value of the inventory.
   C. estimated sales price less net realizable value.
   D. esltimated sales price less actual costs.

7. Pepples Company mistakenly excluded $4,000 of goods from its 12/31/97 inventory. Assuming no other inventory errors existed:
   A. 1997 income is overstated by $4,000.
   B. 1997 income is understated by $4,000.
   C. shareholders' equity as of 12/31/97 is correctly stated.
   D. shareholders' equity as of 1/1/98 is correctly stated.

8. During its year-end 1997 physical inventory, Gordo's Gold Bricks Inc. mistakenly counted $8,000 of inventory twice. Inventory as of 12/31/98 is correct. Assuming no other inventory errors existed:
   A. 1998 income is understated by $8,000.
   B. 1998 cost of goods sold is understated by $8,000.
   C. shareholders' equity as of 12/31/98 is understated.
   D. shareholders' equity as of 12/31/98 is overstated.

9. The Tree Bar Company valued its beginning inventory as $1,000, its ending inventory at $6,000, and calculated cost of goods sold to be $40,000. An analysis of inventory valuations revealed that beginning inventory should have been $2,000 and ending inventory should have been $9,000. The adjusted cost of goods sold should be:
   A. $44,000.
   B. $36,000.
   C. $42,000.
   D. $38,000.

10. The use of the gross profit method assumes:
    A. the amount of gross profit is the same as in prior years.
    B. sales and cost of goods sold have not changed from previous years.
    C. inventory values have not increased from previous years.
    D. the relationship between selling price and cost of goods sold is similar to prior years.

11. Socks 'n' Ties, Inc. maintains a markup of 60% based on cost. The company's selling and administrative expenses average 30% of sales. Annual sales were $2,600,000. Socks 'n' Ties' cost of goods sold and operating profit for the year were:

	Cost of Goods Sold	Operating Profit
A.	$1,560,000	$1,040,000
B.	$1,560,000	$ 260,000
C.	$1,625,000	$ 195,000
D.	$1,625,000	$ 260,000

12. The following information is available for ABC Company for the quarter ended June 30, 1997:

Inventory, April 1	$ 900,000
Purchases	4,500,000
Freight-in	300,000
Sales	6,400,000

    The gross margin was 25% of sales. What is the estimated inventory balance at June 30?
    A. $880,000
    B. $1,600,000
    C. $900,000
    D. $1,200,000

    (AICPA adapted)

13. A December merchandise purchase was inadvertently not recorded in the purchases account, but it was appropriately included in the December 31 ending inventory. What effect will this error have on the company's assets, liabilities, and retained earnings at year-end?

	Assets	Liabilities	Retained Earnings
A.	No effect	Understated	Overstated
B.	No effect	No effect	Understated
C.	No effect	Understated	Understated
D.	Understated	Understated	Overstated

14. The Company estimates ending inventory for its month-end financial statements. All sales are made on account. The rate of markup is 50%. The following information relates to the month of August:

Accounts receivable, August 1	$20,000
Accounts receivable, August 31	30,000
Collections of accounts receivable during August	50,000
Inventory, August 1	36,000
Purchases of inventory during August	32,000

    The estimated cost of the August 31 inventory is:
    A. $24,000.
    B. $28,000.
    C. $38,000.
    D. $44,000.

    (AICPA adapted)

15. Under the retail inventory method, freight-in would be included in the cost of goods available for sale for which of the following?

	Cost	Retail
A.	No	No
B.	No	Yes
C.	Yes	No
D.	Yes	Yes

16. The retail inventory method would include which of the following in the calculation of goods available for sale at both cost and retail?
    A. Purchase returns
    B. Sales returns
    C. Markdowns
    D. Markups

17. Under generally accepted accounting principles, the lower of cost or market calculation for inventory valuation can be applied to:
    A. individual inventory items.
    B. groups of similar inventory items.
    C. total inventory.
    D. all of the above.

18. Under the lower of cost or market method of inventory valuation, the replacement cost of an inventory item would be used as the designated market value:
    A. when it is below the net realizable value minus the normal profit margin.
    B. when it is below the net realizable value and above the net realizable value minus the normal profit margin.
    C. when it is above the net realizable value.
    D. regardless of net realizable value. (AICPA adapted)

19. The original cost of an inventory item is below both the replacement cost and the net realizable value. The net realizable value minus normal profit margin is below the original cost. Under the lower of cost or market method for inventory valuation, the inventory item should be valued at:
    A. replacement cost.
    B. net realizable value.
    C. net realizable value minus normal profit margin.
    D. original cost. (AICPA adapted)

20. Lonesome Pine Company has determined its December 31, 1997 inventory on a FIFO basis to be $400,000. Information pertaining to that inventory follows:

Estimated selling price	$408,000
Estimated cost of disposal	20,000
Normal profit margin	60,000
Current replacement cost	360,000

    Lonesome Pine records losses that result from applying the lower of cost or market rule. At December 31, 1997, what should be the net carrying value of Lonesome Pine's inventory?
    A. $400,000
    B. $388,000
    C. $360,000
    D. $328,000 (AICPA adapted)

21. Based on a physical inventory taken on December 31, 1997, Charles Company determined its raw materials inventory on a FIFO basis at $26,000, with a replacement cost of $20,000. Charles estimated that, after further processing costs of $12,000, the inventory could be sold as finished goods for $40,000. Charles' normal profit margin is 10% of sales. Under the lower of cost or market rule, what amount should Charles report as raw materials inventory in its December 31, 1997 balance sheet?
    A. $28,000
    B. $26,000
    C. $24,000
    D. $20,000   (AICPA adapted)

22. The original cost of an inventory item is above the replacement cost and the net realizable value. The replacement cost is below the net realizable value less the normal profit margin. As a result, under the lower of cost or market method, the inventory should be reported at the:
    A. net realizable value.
    B. net realizable value less the normal profit margin.
    C. replacement cost.
    D. original cost.   (AICPA adapted)

23. Colorado Company uses the FIFO method of inventory valuation. The following information is available:

	Cost	Retail
Beginning inventory	$12,000	$ 30,000
Purchases	60,000	110,000
Markups		10,000
Markdowns		20,000
Sales revenue		90,000

    If the lower of cost or market rule is disregarded, what would be the estimated cost of the ending inventory?
    A. $24,000
    B. $20,800
    C. $20,000
    D. $19,200   (AICPA adapted)

24. (Expanded material) Purchase commitments are:
    A. formal promises to purchase product exclusively from one supplier.
    B. formal agreements to buy a specified product at a specified price over a specified period of time.
    C. formal agreements to sell a specified product at a specified price over a specified period of time.
    D. none of the above.

25. (Expanded material) On December 31, 1997, Bear Company adopted the dollar value LIFO retail inventory method. Inventory data for 1997:

	LIFO cost	Retail
Inventory, 12/31/96	$360,000	$500,000
Inventory, 12/31/97	????	660,000
Increase in price level for 1997		10%
Cost to retail ratio for 1997		70%

    Under the dollar-value LIFO retail inventory method, Bear's inventory at December 31, 1997 should be:
    A. $430,000.
    B. $462,000.
    C. $472,000.
    D. $483,200.   (AICPA adapted)

26. (Expanded material) During 1997, the DataMan Manufacturing Company signed a noncancellable contract to purchase 2,000 pounds of raw materials at $32 per pound during 1998. On December 31, 1997, the market price of the raw material is $26 per pound, and the selling price of the finished product is expected to decline accordingly. The financial statements for 1997 should report:
   A. a negative adjustment to inventory for $12,000.
   B. nothing regarding this matter.
   C. a footnote describing the expected loss on the purchase commitment.
   D. a loss of $12,000 on the income statement. (AICPA adapted)

27. (Expanded material) During 1997, Warbucks Coffee Company, a retailer of coffee and coffee products, contracted to purchase 200,000 pounds of coffee beans at $1.00 per pound, delivery to be made in the spring of 1998. Because a record harvest is predicted for 1998, the price per pound for coffee beans has fallen to $.80 by December 31, 1997. Of the following journal entries, the one that would properly reflect in 1997 the effect of the purchase commitment in Warbucks' financial statements is:

   A. Coffee Inventory   200,000
        Accounts Payable   200,000
   B. Coffee Inventory   160,000
      Loss on Purchase Commitments   40,000
        Accounts Payable   200,000
   C. Loss on Purchase Commitments   40,000
        Estimated Loss on Purchase Commitments   40,000
   D. No entry is required in 1997; disclosure of the potential loss on the purchase commitments is to be included in the footnotes. (AICPA adapted)

28. (Expanded material) The spot rate is the exchange rate:
   A. at which currencies can be traded immediately.
   B. in effect on the date of the specific transaction.
   C. in effect on the date the balance sheet is prepared.
   D. in effect on the date the invoice for the transaction is issued. (AICPA adapted)

29. (Expanded material) Blair Company purchased inventory from a Japanese distributing company for 1,000,000 yen on December 1, 1997 when the exchange rate for yen was $.004. On December 31, 1997, Blair's year-end, the exchange rate was $.0035. The invoice was paid by Blair in 1998 when the exchange rate was $.0038. How much exchange gain or loss would be recognized by Blair in 1997 relating to this transaction?
   A. $200 loss
   B. $200 gain
   C. $500 loss
   D. $500 gain (AICPA adapted)

30. (Expanded material) Blair Company purchased inventory from a Japanese distributing company for 1,000,000 yen on December 1, 1997 when the exchange rate for yen was $.004. On December 31, 1997, Blair's year-end, the exchange rate was $.0035. The invoice was paid by Blair in 1998 when the exchange rate was $.0038. How much exchange gain or loss would be recognized by Blair in 1998 relating to this transaction?
   A. $200 loss
   B. $200 gain
   C. $300 loss
   D. $300 gain (AICPA adapted)

31. (Expanded material) The dollar-value LIFO inventory method requires:
   A. use of a year-end price index.
   B. identification of inventory layers.
   C. computation of the incremental cost percentage.
   D. all of the above.

Chapter 9

Exercises and Problems

1. **Estimating inventory**
   The Las Crusas Company had its entire inventory destroyed on August 10 when a tornado swept through the company's warehouse. The following information for the period up to the date of the tornado was taken from the accounting records:

Net sales (Jan. 1 through August 10)	$458,000
Beginning inventory (Jan. 1)	71,200
Net purchases (Jan. 1 through August 10)	357,400

   The average gross profit in recent years has been 25 percent of cost.
   Required: Using the gross profit method, calculate the estimated value of the inventory destroyed by the tornado.

2. **Estimating inventory**
   On June 15, 1997 a freak snowstorm destroyed the entire inventory of Ollie's Store. The inventory was not insured. Using the following data, compute the approximate amount of inventory loss due to the snowstorm.

Beginning inventory	$ 80,000
Purchases (through June 15)	260,000
Sales (through June 15)	320,000
Approximate gross margin	30%

3. **Estimating inventory**
   Artie's Marina conducts a physical inventory annually. Inventories are estimated for quarterly financial statements. Use the following data to estimate inventory as of June 30, 1997.

Inventory (March 31)	$36,000
Sales (April, May, June)	88,000
Markup on cost	40%
Purchases (April, May, June)	$72,000

4. **Lower-of-cost-or-market calculations**
   Diskers, Inc. sells three products and uses the lower of cost or market to value inventory. Data relating to the three products as of 12/31/97 follows:

Item	Cost	Replacement Cost	Estimated Sales price	Selling Cost	Normal Profit
A	$11.00	$11.40	$16.00	$1.80	$3.00
B	12.00	12.00	19.00	1.60	2.00
C	6.00	4.00	8.50	1.25	2.00
D	14.00	13.50	16.00	1.75	1.00

   Required: Determine the lower of cost or market for each inventory item.

5. **Effects of inventory errors**
   Hillerman Enterprises reported income before taxes of $270,000 for 1998 and $360,000 for 1999. A later audit provided the following information:
   A. The ending inventory for 1998 erroneously included $10,000 of inventory on consignment from Barr Company.
   B. Merchandise costing $17,000 was shipped to Hillerman Enterprises, FOB shipping point, on December 28, 1998. The purchase was recorded in 1998 but the inventory was not included in the 1998 year-end inventory.

Chapter 9

C. On December 28, 1998, inventory costing $3,000 was sold to Doyle Company, FOB shipping point. Though the sale was properly recorded in December, 1998, the inventory was erroneously included in Hillerman's 1998 ending inventory.

Required: Compute the correct income before taxes for 1998 and 1999 for Hillerman Enterprises.

6. (Expanded material) Foreign currency transaction
   Texas Toys sold product to a customer in London on November 4, terms n/60. The sales price was £100,000 and cost of goods sold was $80,000. The sale was denominated in £, the British currency [pounds Sterling]. The customer paid on January 15. Texas Toys year end is December 31. Exchange rates during the period were: November 4: $1.00 = £.6322; December 31: $1.00 = £.6354; January 15: $1.00 = £.6566.

   Required: Record the relevant events of this sales transaction.

7. (Expanded material) Dollar-value LIFO
   Gottenburg Feed Store uses the dollar-value LIFO retail method. Information relating to inventory during 1998:

	Cost	Retail
Inventory, January 1, 1998	$104,400	$162,000
Purchases	468,000	799,200
Freight-in	72,000	
Sales		684,000
Markups		144,000
Markdowns		43,200

   There was no change in the price index during 1998.

   Required: Compute the inventory at December 31, 1998, using the dollar-value LIFO retail method.

SOLUTIONS TO TEST YOUR UNDERSTANDING

Fill-in-the-Blanks

1. Lower of cost or market (LCM)
2. market value
3. Replacement cost
4. entry cost
5. exit value
6. ceiling
7. net realizable value (NRV)
8. floor
9. gross profit method
10. gross profit percentage
11. retail inventory method
12. cost percentage
13. Original retail
14. Initial markup
15. markup
16. markdown
17. overstated; overstated; understated
18. overstated
19. understated; overstated
20. dollar-value LIFO retail method

21. purchase commitment
22. executory contract
23. foreign currency transaction
24. spot rate

Multiple Choice

1.	A	9.	D	17.	D	25.	A
2.	D	10.	D	18.	B	26.	D
3.	D	11.	C	19.	D	27.	C
4.	A	12.	C	20.	C	28.	A
5.	C	13.	A	21.	C	29.	C
6.	A	14.	C	22.	B	30.	D
7.	B	15.	C	23.	A	31.	D
8.	A	16.	A	24.	B		

Exercises and Problems

1. Estimating inventory
   $62,200
   Calculation:

Beginning inventory	$ 71,200
Add: Purchases	357,400
Goods available for sale	$428,600
Less: Estimated cost of goods sold	366,400 **
Estimated inventory loss	$ 62,200

   ** 458,000/1.25 = $366,400

2. Estimating inventory
   Estimated loss = $116,000
   Calculations:

Sales	$320,000
Cost of Sales	$224,000 (.70 X $320,000)
Beginning inventory	$ 80,000
Purchases	260,000
Less: Cost of sales	(224,000)
Estimated ending inventory	$116,000

3. Estimating inventory
   Estimated inventory as of June 30 = $45,143
   Calculations:

Sales	$88,000
Cost of Sales	$62,857 ($88,000 / 1.40)
Beginning inventory	$36,000
Purchases (cost)	72,000
Less: Cost of sales	(62,857)
Estimated ending inventory	$45,143

4. Lower-of-cost-or-market calculations

Item	Cost	Replacement Cost	Ceiling*	Floor**	Lower of Cost or Market
A	$11.00	$11.40	$14.20	$11.20	$11.00
B	12.00	12.00	17.40	15.40	12.00
C	6.00	4.00	7.25	5.25	5.25
D	14.00	13.50	14.25	13.25	13.50

* Ceiling is equal to selling price less selling costs.
** Floor is equal to selling price less selling costs less normal profit.

Explanation:
A: Cost is the lower of cost or market for this item.
B: Cost is the lower of cost or market for this item. In this case, the "market" number would be $15.40 because replacement cost is less than the floor. Coincidentally, replacement cost and actual cost happen to be equal, however.
C: Market is the lower of cost or market for this item. Note that the market number is the floor because the replacement cost is lower than the floor, which is, by definition the lowest value the market can be for this calculation.
D: Market is the lower of cost or market for this item. In this case, the replacement cost is the market. Generally, replacement cost is the market.

5. Effects of inventory errors
1998 errors:
A. Ending inventory overstated by $10,000
B. Ending inventory understated by $17,000
C. Ending inventory overstated by $3,000

Net errors: ending inventory understated by $4,000

Since ending inventory is understated by $4,000, cost of goods sold was overstated by $4,000; therefore, income before taxes was understated by $4,000. Corrected 1998 income before tax should be: $274,000 [calculation: $270,000 + $4,000].

1999:
Because 1998 ending inventory was understated by $4,000, 1999 beginning inventory was understated by $4,000. The understatement of beginning inventory causes goods available for sale for 1999 to be understated by $4,000. Though 1999 ending inventory is correctly stated, cost of goods sold for 1999 is understated by $4,000 so 1999 income is overstated by $4,000. Therefore, the corrected 1998 income before tax should be $356,000 [calculation: $360,000 - $4,000 = $356,000].

6. Foreign currency transaction
November 4   Cost of Goods Sold   80,000
                Inventory   80,000
               To record cost of inventory sold.
November 5   Accounts Receivable (International)   158,178
                Sales (International)   158,178
               To record sales to British customer.
               [Calculation: 100,000/.6322]

December 31	Exchange Rate Loss	797	
	Accounts Receivable (International)		797
	To record exchange rate loss on international receivables.		
	[Calculation: {100,000/.6354 - 100,000/.6322}]		
January 15	Exchange Rate Loss	5,081	
	Accounts Receivable (International)		5,081
	To record exchange rate loss on international receivables.		
	[Calculation: {100,000/.6566 - 100,000/.6354}]		
	Cash	152,300	
	Accounts Receivable (International)		152,300
	To record receipt of payment of international receivables.		

7. Dollar-value LIFO

	Cost	Retail
Purchases	$468,000	$799,200
Freight-in	72,000	
Markups		144,000
Markdowns		(43,200)
	$540,000	$900,000
Cost/retail [$540,000/$900,000]	60%	
Sales		$684,000
1998 layer at retail		$216,000
1998 layer at cost [$216,000 x .60]	$129,600	
Inventory, January 1, 1998	104,400	162,000
Inventory, December 31, 1998	$234,000	$378,000

CHAPTER 10

DEBT FINANCING

KEY POINTS

I. Classification and Measurement Issues Associated with Debt
   A. Definition of liabilities
      1. "Probable future sacrifices of economic benefits arising from present obligations of a particular entity to transfer assets or provide services to other entities in the future as a result of past transactions or events" (FASB, Concept Statement No. 6).
      2. *Past transactions or events*: liabilities are not recorded until they are incurred, so a liability is not recorded until the company enters into a transaction or is involved in an economic event.
      3. *Probable future transfer of assets or services:* to record a liability the company must be obligated to *do something* for another company, such as pay money or perform services.
      4. *Obligation of particular entity*: a liability does not exist for the company unless it individually is responsible for the "probable future economic sacrifice."
   B. Classification and Measurement of Liabilities
      1. Classification
         a. Generally, liabilities are classified by maturity.
         b. Liabilities due within a year or the company's operating cycle are **current**.
         c. Liabilities that mature after a year or extend beyond the company's operating cycle are **noncurrent**.
      2. Importance of classification by maturity
         a. The relationship between total debt and total assets or between total debt and total equity is an important measure of the company's liquidity.
         b. The ratios are often used by lending institutions and creditors in assessing credit worthiness. In addition to total debt, creditors look very carefully at current debt, because that is a measure of what must be paid quickly, and thus, affects solvency.
         c. Accordingly, companies are quite concerned about ratios that measure solvency, such as the current ratio and working capital.)
         d. **Review question:** Do you remember how to calculate the current ratio? (hint: current ratio = current assets divided by current liabilities).
   C. Measurement of Liabilities
      1. Generally, the amount recorded on the balance sheet is the *present value of the future cash flows* (i.e., the cash that must be paid out).
      2. For measurement purposes, three categories of liabilities:
         a. Liabilities that are definite in amount (such as rent, insurance, payroll, etc.) are recorded at face value, i.e., the amount of cash that is required to be paid.
         b. Liabilities that are estimated (such as warranties) are recorded at the *estimated* face value, or cash outflow.
         c. Contingent liabilities (liabilities whose occurrence is dependent upon factors outside the company's control) are generally not recorded in the books, but rather, are disclosed in the footnotes.

II. Accounting for Short-Term Debt Obligations
   A. Accounts Payable
      1. Amount due for the purchases of materials by a manufacturing company or merchandise by a wholesaler or retailer.
      2. Record at the amount due for the obligation.
      3. Generally, no interest is recognized as payment terms are short.
   B. Short-Term Debt
      1. Record at the principal amount, as stated in the *promissory note*.

2. Recorded as *notes payable*.
   a. Notes issued to creditors for goods and services: *trade notes payable*.
   b. Notes issued to banks, officers and shareholders: *nontrade notes payable*.
3. Interest on notes payable is generally recorded as "interest expense" (income statement, expense) and "interest payable" (balance sheet, current liability).
4. Short-Term Obligations Expected to be Refinanced
   a. Classify as noncurrent only if both of the following conditions are met:
      1) Management must intend to refinance the debt to a long-term basis.
      2) Management must demonstrate that it *can* refinance the debt.

III. Financing with Bonds
   A. Long-term financing is accomplished with either long-term debt or equity (issuance of additional stock).
   B. *Long-term debt* as a means of financing has the following characteristics:
      1. Creditors are not owners, and thus, do not normally participate in running the corporation (either directly as management or indirectly as voting shareholders).
      2. Interest paid on long-term debt is tax deductible.
      3. Interest cost of debt is likely to be less in the long run than the dividend and capital return cost to shareholders.
      4. Charge against earnings for interest may be less, in the long run, than the amount of dividends demanded by shareholders.
   C. Some types of financing are hybrids between debt and equity. This chapter discusses a few of these. Accounting is instrument specific, and is based upon characteristics of debt and equity.
   D. Accounting for Bonds
      1. Bonds and long-term notes are similar concepts, but differ technically.
         a. Trust indenture with bonds provides extensive detail about the bond contract.
         b. Bonds generally have a longer maturity than long-term notes.
      2. Three main issues to consider in accounting for bonds:
         a. Record issuance or purchase.
         b. Record applicable interest during the life of the bonds.
         c. Account for the retirement of the bonds, either at maturity or before.
   E. Nature of Bonds
      1. *Face value = maturity value = par value*, and is generally $1,000.
      2. Contract between bond issuer and bondholder = *bond indenture*.
         a. Specifies terms: interest, payment dates, recall provisions, etc.
      3. Bonds may be sold directly to investors or they may be underwritten by investment bankers or syndicates.
      4. Bonds are issued by most major corporations, the U.S. government, school districts, government sponsored agencies and state and local governments.
         a. Total bond issues in the U.S. is greater than $1 trillion.
   F. Types of bonds:
      1. *Term bonds*: bonds that mature on a single date.
      2. *Serial bonds*: bonds that mature in installments.
      3. *Secured bonds:* bonds for which assets are pledged as collateral.
      4. *Unsecured bonds*: also known as debentures, these are bonds for which no collateral other than the good credit of the issuing company is offered.
      5. *Collateral trust bond*: bond secured by stocks and bonds of other corporations which are owned by the corporation issuing the collateral trust bond.
      6. *Registered bonds*: bonds for which the holder's name and address is kept on file by the issuing company.
      7. *Bearer or Coupon bonds:* bonds for which the holder's name and address are not recorded by the issuing company; interest is paid to whomever presents the bond for payment.
      8. *Zero-interest bonds*: also called deep-discount bonds, these are bonds that have no stated interest rate and on which no regular interest payments are made.
      9. *Junk bonds*: high-risk, high yield bonds issued by companies that are already heavily in debt or otherwise in weak financial condition.

10. *Convertible bonds:* bonds that provide for the conversion into common stock at the option of the bondholder.
11. *Commodity-backed bonds:* bonds that may be redeemed in something other than cash or common stock, generally commodities such as oil or precious metals.
12. *Callable bonds:* bonds for which the issuer reserves the right to early retire the bond instrument.

G. Market price of bonds
1. Depends upon the safety of the investment and the prevailing market rate of interest for an alternative investment with similar risk.
   a. As the riskiness of investment increases the rate of interest increases to attract investors.
2. Amount of interest paid on bonds is a specified percentage of the face value (called the *stated or contract rate*).
3. Market rate of interest: rate of interest for a similar instrument with a similar riskiness.
4. Bonds sell at a price to yield the market rate of interest, which becomes the effective interest rate of the bond.
   a. To accomplish market yield, bonds may sell at:
      1) *premium*: implying market interest rate is greater than stated interest rate.
      2) *discount*: implying market interest rate is less than stated interest rate.
      3) *par*: implying market and stated interest rates are equal.
5. Computation of the market price of bonds: two components which must be added together to equal the issue price:
   a. Part I: Present value of the principal
      1) present value of a single sum, discounted at the market interest rate (per interest period) for number of periods over which interest will be paid.
   b. Part II: Present value of the interest payments:
      1) present value of the annuity (the amount of each interest payment as specified in the bond contract), discounted at the market interest rate (per interest period), over the number of interest payments.

H. Issuance of Bonds
1. Process of issuing bonds
   a. Sold by brokers on behalf of borrowers (brokers charge a substantial fee for this service).
   b. Most bond issues are privately placed with large investors.
2. Bonds issued at par on interest date; record entries for issuance and first interest payment as follows:
   a. Issuer
Date	Cash	CCC	
	Bonds Payable		BBB

      [CCC = proceeds; BBB = Face value of bonds; therefore, when bonds are issued at par, the proceeds equal the face value of the bonds]

Date	Interest Expense	III	
	Cash		III

      [III = interest stated on bond; note when bonds are issued at par, interest expense and cash paid for interest are the same]
   b. Investor
Date	Bond Investment	BBB	
	Cash		BBB
Date	Cash	III	
	Interest Revenue		III
3. Bonds issued at a discount on interest date; record entries for issuance
   a. Issuer
Date	Cash	CCC	
	Discount on Bonds Payable	DDD	
	Bonds Payable		BBB

      [CCC= proceeds; DDD = discount; BBB = face value of bonds; note that when bonds sell at a discount, the proceeds are less than the face value of the bonds]

b. Investor
   Date   Bond Investment   CCC
               Cash   CCC
4. Bonds issued at a premium on an interest date; record entries for issuance as follows:
   a. Issuer
      Date   Cash   CCC
                 Premium on Bonds Payable   PPP
                 Bonds Payable   BBB
      [CCC = proceeds; PPP = premium; BBB = face value of bonds; note when bonds sell at a premium, the proceeds exceed the face value of the bonds]
   b. Investor:
      Date   Bond Investment   CCC
                 Cash   CCC
5. Bonds issued at par between interest dates
   a. Adjust for the interest accrued between the last interest payment date and the date of issuance.
   b. Buyer pays the accrued interest along with the purchase price because he will receive the total interest payment on the next interest payment date.
6. Bond issuance costs
   a. Costs incurred by the borrower to issue the bonds (includes legal services, taxes, underwriting costs, printing costs, and so on).
   b. Bond issuance costs are not trivial.
   c. APB Opinion No. 21 says bond issuance costs should be reported on balance sheet as deferred charges, which are amortized over the life of the bond issue.

I. Accounting for bond interest
   1. Interest expense each period is equal to:
      a. Stated rate of interest (annual rate divided by the number of payments per year) times the face value of the bonds **PLUS**
      b. Pro-rata amortization of bond discount **OR MINUS**
      c. Pro-rata amortization of bond premium.
   2. Amortization of premium or discount
      a. Amortization of premium reduces interest expense but not cash paid out.
      b. Amortization of discount increases interest expense but not cash paid out.
      c. **Thinking question**: How does the amortization of premium and discount affect the cash flow statement? (Answer: actual cash paid out is the amount to report on cash flow statement as operating cash item.)
   3. Two acceptable methods to amortize premium and discount
      a. *Straight-line method*: Calculate amortization amount.
         Calculation: amount of amortization per month = amount of premium or discount divided by number of months to maturity.
      b. *Effective-interest method*: Calculate interest expense and use that number to calculate the amortization amount, thusly:
         Interest expense = effective rate of interest (at the time of issuance) times the carrying value of the bond issue at the beginning of the period*
         Interest expense less cash paid for interest (**) = discount amortization this period
         (*carrying value = investment balance, which is gross liability in bonds payable account less balance in discount on bonds payable account)
         (**cash paid for interest = stated rate (for this period) times the principal or face value of the bonds)
      c. APB Opinion No. 21 recommends effective interest method, but straight-line method can be used if the amount calculated with straight-line is not materially different per period than the amount calculated by effective-interest method.

J. Cash flow effects of amortizing bond premium and discounts
   1. Amortization of discount or premium does not involve receipt or payment of cash

2. Using indirect method to report cash flow from operating activities, adjustment to net income is necessary:
   a. Add back amount of discount amortization.
   b. Deduct amount of premium amortization.
K. Retirement of bonds at maturity
   1. Easy accounting situation:
      a. The carrying value of the bond liability will be equal to the face value at maturity (if discounts and premiums were amortized correctly), so the journal entry to retire is:
      Date   Bonds Payable   BBB
                   Cash   BBB
L. Extinguishment of debt prior to maturity
   1. "Early extinguishment of debt"
      a. FASB Statement No. 4 classifies gain on or loss on early retirement as extraordinary.
      b. Gain or loss is equal to the difference between the price paid to retire the debt and the carrying value (investment value) of the debt.
   2. How to early retire:
      a. *Redeemed*: issuer purchases the bonds in the open market or exercises the call provision on the bonds.
      b. *Converted*: bonds may be exchanged for a different security, such as stock.
      c. *Refinanced* (also known as "refunded") : issue a new set of bonds and use the proceeds to retire an older set of bonds.
      d. *In-substance defeasance*: although bonds are not actually retired in an in-substance defeasance, "risk free" assets are set aside to pay the bond obligation, and thus, the bond issue can be treated as, in essence, retired. [see expanded material for more on in-substance defeasance]
   3. Redemption by purchase of bonds on the market
      a. Remember, this will result in a gain or loss.
      b. Upon redemption, must clear the following accounts:
      Bonds Payable (face value of debt)
      Discount on Bond Payable (unamortized portion) OR
      Premium on Bond Payable (unamortized portion)
      c. If redemption occurs between interest dates, need to accrue interest expense and amortize discount (premium).
   4. Redemption by exercise of call provision
      a. Remember, a gain or loss will result.
      b. If called between interest dates, interest expense must be accrued.
      c. The call provision may provide for payment of cash to the bondholder or it may include a conversion provision.
   5. Convertible bonds
      a. Securities whose terms permit holder to convert the bond instrument into common stock.
      b. Features:
         1) Interest rate is generally lower than issuer could attain for nonconvertible debt.
         2) Instrument conversion price if generally higher than market value of common stock at the time of issuance.
         3) Call option is retained by issuer.
      c. If the call provision is a conversion, accounting for the call depends upon how the original bond issue was recorded.
         1) Two possible treatments:
            a) Record the original issue as debt only.
            b) Record the original issue as debt and equity.
         2) Which one is "right?"
            a) Both are ok.
            b) Debt only is common, especially when the convertible bond sells for a price that is quite close to a bond without the conversion feature.
            c) Theory suggests that recorded debt and equity portions is best, but measurement of the components is difficult.

6. Bond refinancing
    a. Definition: issue new bonds and use the proceeds to retire old bond issue.
    b. Remember, a gain or loss will result.
    c. What to do with unamortized premium or discount????
        1) FASB requires immediate recognition of the gain or loss (which will be magnified by the amount of the unamortized discount or premium).

IV. Off-Balance-Sheet Financing
    A. What is off-balance-sheet financing (OBS)?
        1. Techniques to borrow money while keeping the debt off the balance sheet.
    B. Techniques:
        1. Sale of receivables with recourse
        2. Unconsolidated entities
            a. Companies used to form subsidiaries, load them up with debt, let the parent use the debt, and report all the debt on the sub's books only.
            b. FASB Statement No. 94 deals with this issue and requires consolidation of these types of entities.
        3. Research and development arrangements
            a. Form another entity to conduct R&D or contract R&D with unrelated sub.
            b. No accounting problem unless the company bears the risk of the outcome of the R&D effort.
        4. Project financing arrangements
            a. Often accomplished via joint ventures, in which two (or more) companies jointly form another company to develop a product or project.
            b. None of the partners or investors owns more than 50% and so consolidation is generally not required.
            c. The newly formed entity borrows money, usually on the good name of the investors, but the debt is reported on the new entity's books only.
    C. Why do OBS?
        1. Primarily to strengthen balance sheet.
    D. Problems with OBS
        1. Difficult for investors to see how much a company may actually be liable for.
        2. Experience with the leveraged buy-outs and hostile takeovers of the 1980's makes investors leery of debt-ridden companies, but if there's a means of keeping this debt off the balance sheet, the investors aren't so leery.

V. Analyzing a Firm's Debt Position
    A. Leverage: relationship between a firm's debt and assets or its debt and stockholders' equity.
    B. Ratios:
        1. Debt/equity = total debt/total equity
        2. Debt/assets = total debt/total assets
        3. Times interest earned = income before taxes and interest expense/interest expense

VI. Disclosing Debt in the Financial Statements
    A. Required disclosures include:
        1. Nature of liabilities
        2. Maturity dates
        3. Interest rates
        4. Methods of liquidation
        5. Conversion privileges
        6. Sinking fund requirements
        7. Borrowing restrictions
        8. Assets pledged
        9. Dividend limitations

Name: _____   **Chapter 10**   171

EXPANDED MATERIAL KEY POINTS

VII. Understanding and Accounting for In-Substance Defeasance
  A. In-substance defeasance = economic defeasance: process involving the transfer of assets (generally cash and securities) to a trust which uses those assets and their earnings to satisfy long-term obligations as they come due.
    1. Generally, a gain or loss arises from an in-substance defeasance.
    2. After an in-substance defeasance, both the debt and the assets placed in trust are removed from the debtor's balance sheet.
  B. Transfer improves both earnings per share (EPS) and key financial ratios.
  C. FASB Statement No. 76 sets forth conditions which must be met for in-substance defeasance.
    1. Primary goal of FASB Statement No. 76: prevent manipulation of earnings or balance sheet.
    2. Therefore, assets transferred must be sufficient to cover interest and principal payments of debt defeased, and assets transferred must be essentially risk-free.

VIII. Accounting for Troubled Debt Restructuring
  A. Troubled debt restructuring: revision of debt terms to allow debtors to eliminate or significantly modify debt obligations; arises because debt is in financial difficulty.
  B. Authoritative literature: FASB Statement No. 15, issued in 1977.
    1. Key concept: concession on the part of the creditor, implying that the creditor foregoes some economic wealth to restructure the borrower's debt.
    2. Major issue: should the restructuring be viewed as a significant economic event?
      a. If "yes," a gain or loss is reflected on the issuer's books.
      b. If "no," no gain or loss.
  C. Three major types of troubled debt restructurings:
    1. Transfer of assets in full settlement: asset swap
      a. Significant economic event ➔ gain or loss.
      b. Gain or loss on disposal = carrying value of assets transferred less market value of assets transferred.
      c. Gain or loss on restructuring = market value of assets transferred less carrying value of debt liquidated.
      d. Investor always recognizes a loss on restructuring due to concessions granted unless the investor already has written down the debt.
    2. Transfer of equity in full settlement: equity swap
      a. Significant economic event ➔ gain or loss.
      b. Debtor recognizes extraordinary gain = fair market value of equity interest less carrying value of debt liquidated.
      c. Creditor recognizes loss in same amount.
    3. Modification of debt terms
      a. Total payment under new terms exceeds debt carrying value = NOT significant economic event, and therefore, no gain or loss.
      b. Total payment under new terms less than debt carrying value = significant economic event, and therefore, gain or loss is recognized.
      c. Modifications can involve interest, principal, or both.
      d. Most modifications do not result in a gain or loss because they are usually an extension of time over which debt is repaid.

TEST YOUR UNDERSTANDING

Fill-in-the-Blanks

Required: Fill in the blanks to complete the following sentences.

1. The claims of creditors against an entity's resources are referred to as _____.

2. The analytical measure of a firm's liquidity which is calculated by dividing current liabilities into current assets is the _____ _____.

3. The amount due for the purchase of materials by a manufacturing company or merchandise by a wholesaler or retailer is referred to as _____ _____.

4. A _____ _____ is a formal written promise to pay a certain amount of money at a specified future date in time.

5. _____ _____ represents the amount due from formal written promises to pay a specified amount at specified dates in the future.

6. A note issued to trade creditors for the purchase of goods or services is recorded in the account entitled _____ _____ _____.

7. _____ _____ _____ is a note issued to nontrade creditors for purposes other than the purchase of goods or services.

8. Obligations that are not expected to be settled in cash during the current year or operating cycle are _____-_____ _____.

9. A _____ _____ is a legal agreement specifying how a fund will be administered by the trustees.

10. The amount that will be paid on a bond at the maturity date is referred to as one of three different terms, all of which mean the same thing; the terms are _____ _____, _____ _____, and _____ _____.

11. Bond certificates are generally issued in denominations of $_____.

12. The contract between the issuing entity and the bondholders which specifies the terms, rights, and obligations of the contracting parties is the _____ _____.

13. Debt securities issued by state, county, and local governments and agencies is _____ _____.

14. _____ _____ mature in one lump sum at a specified future date.

15. _____ _____ mature in installments over future dates.

16. _____ _____ have assets pledged to guarantee payment.

17. Bonds for which no specific collateral has been pledged are _____ (_____) _____.

18. Bonds for which the bondholders' names and addresses are kept on file by the issuing company are _____ _____.

19. _____ (_____) _____ are not recorded in the name of the owner, but rather have attached to them coupons which are detached and presented on bond interest dates for payment.

20. Also referred to as deep-discount bonds, _____ _____ _____ do not bear interest, but rather are issued at deep discount, thus providing the investor with an interest yield upon maturity of the bond.

21. High-risk, high-yield bonds issued by companies with weak financial condition are called _____ _____.

22. Bonds that provide for conversion into common stock at the option of the bondholder are _____ _____.

23. Bonds that may be redeemed in terms of commodities, such as oil or precious metals are _____-_____ _____.

24. _____ _____ are characterized by a call feature, which allows the issuer to retire the bonds prior to maturity.

25. _____ _____ _____ are costs incurred by the issuer of bonds for legal services, printing costs, engraving costs, taxes, and underwriting.

26. An adjustment to interest expense for either the premium or discount to reflect the effective rate of interest being incurred on bonds is called _____.

27. The method of amortization of bond premium or discount which provides recognition in equal installments over the life of the bond is the _____-_____ _____.

28. The method of amortization of bond premium or discount which provides recognition in an equal rate of amortization over the life of the bonds is the _____-_____ _____.

29. _____ _____ involves issuing new bonds and using the proceeds to retire existing outstanding bonds.

30. A _____ _____-_____ (_____) is an acquisition of a company in which a substantial amount of the purchase price (generally, more than 90%) is debt-financed.

31. The relationship between a firm's debt and its assets or between a firm's debt and shareholders' equity is called _____; a firm that is _____ _____ has a large amount of debt relative to either assets or equity.

32. A common measure of leverage is the _____-to-_____ ratio, calculated by dividing _____ _____ by _____ _____.

33. The _____ _____ is an indicator of the company's overall ability to repay its debts; it is calculated by dividing _____ _____ by _____ _____.

34. An indicator of a company's ability to service its debt is the ratio computed by dividing interest expense into income before interest and taxes; this indicator is called _____ _____ _____.

Expanded material items:
35. _____-_____ _____ is a process involving the transfer of assets, generally cash and securities, to a trust which uses the assets and their earnings to satisfy the terms of long-term debt obligations; upon completion of the _____-_____ _____, both the assets transferred to the trust and the long-term debt are removed from the balance sheet.

36. In a _____ _____ _____, the lender approves certain concessions to the borrower whereby debt is either eliminated or the terms of the debt are significantly modified.

Chapter 10

Multiple Choice

Required: Circle the best answer.

1. Interest payable is normally classified as a:
    A. current liability.
    B. noncurrent liability.
    C. current or noncurrent liability, depending upon the maturity of the debt on which the interest is calculated.
    D. estimated liability.

2. If the market rate of interest is 10% and the stated rate on the bond is 8%, the bond will sell at:
    A. par.
    B. discount.
    C. premium.
    D. cannot determine from the information given.

3. If the market rate of interest is 10%, and the stated rate on the bond is 8%, the bond will sell to yield:
    A. 8%.
    B. 10%.
    C. 9%.
    D. cannot determine from the information given.

4. If the market rate of interest is 10%, and the stated rate on the bond is 12%, the bond will sell at:
    A. par.
    B. discount.
    C. premium.
    D. cannot determine from the information given.

5. Bonds sell at a premium because:
    A. investors like the prospects of the company issuing the bond.
    B. investors are willing to pay more money to obtain higher interest payments.
    C. investors are willing to pay less money because interest payments they will receive from the bond will be less than the market.
    D. the bonds are less risky than others in the market.

6. Bond issuance costs should be:
    A. netted (co-mingled) with bond discount (or premium) and amortized over the life of the bond issue.
    B. expensed in the year the bonds are issued.
    C. netted (co-mingled) with bond discount (or premium) and expensed in the year the bonds are retired.
    D. reported on the balance sheet as a deferred charge and amortized over the life of the bond issue.

7. During 1998, Smarton Company issued $20,000,000 in ten-year 10% bonds. In conjunction with the issuance, the following bond issue costs were incurred:

Printing and engraving	$ 20,000
Legal fees	220,000
Fees paid to independent accountants	40,000
Underwriting fees	350,000
Overtime pay for in-house accountants involved in the bond issue	10,000

    What amount should be recorded as a deferred charge to be amortized over the life of the bond issue?
    A. $630,000
    B. $640,000
    C. $590,000
    D. $610,000

8. ABC Corporation issued bonds at a premium and amortizes the premium using the effective-interest method. Interest is paid quarterly. Interest expense is:
   A. equal to the amount of cash paid to bondholders.
   B. less than the amount of cash paid to bondholders.
   C. greater than the amount of cash paid to bondholders.
   D. equal to the amount of cash paid plus the amortization of the premium plus the amortization of the bond issuance costs.

9. A 10-year bond was issued on January 1, 1994 at a discount. The carrying value (investment balance) of the bond on December 31, 1996 will be:
   A. lower than the carrying value at December 31, 1994.
   B. the same as the carrying value at January 1, 1994.
   C. higher than the carrying value at December 31, 1997.
   D. higher than the carrying value at December 31, 1994.

10. How will the amortization of bond discount be reported on the cash flow statement if the indirect method is used?
    A. Subtracted from net income as an adjustment in the operating section of the statement.
    B. Reported in the financing activities section of the cash flow statement.
    C. Added to net income as an adjustment in the operating section of the statement.
    D. Added to net income in the operating section and reported as a financing activity.

11. What will be the impact on interest expense as a result of amortization of:

	Discount	Premium
A.	Increase	Increase
B.	Increase	Decrease
C.	Decrease	Decrease
D.	Decrease	Increase

12. A bond issue is being retired prior to maturity by refinancing (refunding). The call provision, unamortized discount (premium) and issue costs relating to the retired bond issue will be:
    A. deferred and amortized over the life of the original bond issue.
    B. deferred and amortized over the life of the new bond issue.
    C. booked currently as a loss on retirement of debt.
    D. netted against the call provision, discount (premium) and issue costs of the new issue.

13. A 15-year bond was issued in 1990 at a discount. During 1995, a 10-year bond was issued at par and the proceeds were used to retire the 1990 bond at its face amount. As a result of this transaction, the long-term liabilities on the company's balance sheet will:
    A. increase by the excess of the 10-year bond's face amount over the 15-year bond's carrying value.
    B. increase by the excess of the 10-year bond's face amount over the 15-year bond's face amount.
    C. decrease by the excess of the 10-year bond's face amount over the 15-year bond's face amount.
    D. decrease by the excess of the 10-year bond's face amount over the 15-year bond's carrying value.

14. Bonds payable issued with scheduled maturities at various dates are called:

	Serial bonds	Term bonds
A.	No	Yes
B.	No	No
C.	Yes	No
D.	Yes	Yes

    (AICPA adapted)

15. The market price of a bond issued at a discount is the present value of its principal amount at the market rate of interest:
   A. less the present value of all future interest payments at the market rate of interest.
   B. less the present value of all future interest payments at the rate of interest stated on the bond.
   C. plus the present value of all future interest payments at the market rate of interest.
   D. plus the present value of all future interest payments at the rate of interest stated on the bond.

   (AICPA adapted)

16. On March 1, 1998, Sea Corporation issued at 103 plus accrued interest, two hundred of its 9%, $1,000 bonds. The bonds are dated January 1, 1998 and mature on January 1, 2008. Interest is payable semiannually on January 1 and July 1. Sea paid bond issue costs of $10,000. Sea should realize net cash receipts from the bond issue in the amount of:
   A. $216,000.
   B. $209,000.
   C. $206,000.
   D. $199,000.

   (AICPA adapted)

17. On November 1, 1998, Martin Company issued $800,000 of its 10-year, 8% term bonds dated October 1, 1998. The bonds were sold to yield 10%, with total proceeds of $700,000 plus accrued interest. Interest is paid every April 1 and October 1. What amount should Martin report for interest payable on its December 31, 1998 balance sheet?
   A. $17,500
   B. $16,000
   C. $11,667
   D. $10,667

   (AICPA adapted)

18. On July 1, 1997, Wally Ham Company received $103,288 for $100,000 face value, 12% bonds, a price that yields 10%. Interest expense for the six months ended December 1, 1997 should be:
   A. $6,197.
   B. $6,000.
   C. $5,164.
   D. $5,000.

   (AICPA adapted)

19. For the issuer of a ten-year term bond, the amount of amortization using the effective-interest method would increase each year if the bond was sold at a:

	Discount	Premium
A.	No	No
B.	Yes	Yes
C.	No	Yes
D.	Yes	No

   (AICPA adapted)

20. In 1998, Enrod acquired, at a premium, 10-year bonds of Faraway Company. At December 31, 1999, Faraway's bonds were quoted at a small discount. Which of the following situations is the most likely cause of the decline in the bonds' market value?
   A. Faraway issued a stock dividend.
   B. Faraway is expected to call the bonds at a premium, which is less than Enrod's carrying amount.
   C. Interest rates have declined since Enrod purchased the bonds.
   D. Interest rates have increased since Enrod purchased the bonds.

   (AICPA adapted)

21. An investor purchased a bond as a long-term investment on January 1. Annual interest was received on December 31. The investor's interest income for the year would be highest if the bond was purchased at:
   A. par.
   B. face value.
   C. a discount.
   D. a premium.

   (AICPA adapted)

22. On January 2, 1994, Swiss Company issued 10-year convertible bonds at 105. During 1998, these bonds were converted into common stock having an aggregate par value equal to the total face amount of the bonds. At conversion, the market price of Swiss's common stock was 50 percent above its par value. On January 2, 1994, cash proceeds from the issuance of the convertible bonds should be reported as:
    A. contributed capital for the entire proceeds.
    B. contributed capital for the portion of the proceeds attributable to the conversion feature and as a liability for the balance.
    C. a liability for the face amount of the bonds and contributed capital for the premium over the face amount.
    D. a liability for the entire proceeds. (AICPA adapted)

23. On March 1, 1997, HiFi Company issued bonds at a discount. HiFi incorrectly used the straight-line method instead of the effective-interest method to amortize the discount. How were the following items, as of December 31, 1997, affected by the error?

	Bond carrying amount	Retained earnings
A.	Overstated	Overstated
B.	Understated	Understated
C.	Overstated	Understated
D.	Understated	Overstated

    (AICPA adapted)

24. On June 30, 1997, Keller Compay had outstanding 9%, $5,000,000 face value bonds maturing on June 30, 2002. Interest was payable semiannually every June 30 and December 31. On June 30, 1997, after amortization was recorded for the period, the unamortized bond premium and bond issue costs were $30,000 and $50,000 respectively. On that date, Keller acquired all its outstanding bonds in the open market at 98 and retired them. At June 30, 1997, what amount should Keller recognize as a gain before income taxes on the retirement of the bonds?
    A. $ 20,000
    B. $ 80,000
    C. $120,000
    D. $180,000 (AICPA adapted)

25. Gains and losses from early retirement of debt, if material, should be:
    A. recognized in income before taxes in the period of retirement.
    B. recognized as an extraordinary item in the period of retirement.
    C. amortized over the life of any new bonds issued to retire the outstanding bonds.
    D. amortized over the remaining life of the bonds. (AICPA adapted)

26. Harold purchased bonds at a discount of $10,000. Subsequently, Harold sold these bonds at a premium of $14,000. During the period that Harold held this investment, amortization of the discount amounted to $2,000. What amount should Harold report as a gain on the sale of the bonds?
    A. $12,000
    B. $22,000
    C. $24,000
    D. $26,000 (AICPA adapted)

27. (Expanded material) An in-substance defeasance:
    A. has no impact on the balance sheet but affects the income statement.
    B. affects only the liability section of the balance sheet and does not affect the income statement.
    C. generally, reduces current assets and long-term debt on the balance sheet but has no impact on the income statement.
    D. generally, reduces current assets and long-term debt on the balance sheet and affects the income statement as well.

178 *Chapter 10*

28. (Expanded material) Which of the following statements describes in-substance defeasance?
    A. If a gain results from an in-substance defeasance, the gain would not be recognized until the debt's original maturity date.
    B. If a gain results from an in-substance defeasance, the gain would be amortized over the remaining life of the bonds defeased.
    C. If a gain results from an in-substance defeasance, the gain would be recognized immediately in income from continuing operations.
    D. If a gain results from an in-substance defeasance, the gain would be recognized immediately as an extraordinary item.

29. (Expanded material) In a troubled debt restructuring in which the borrower settles the debt by an asset swap, the borrower's gain on the restructuring is equal to:
    A. the difference between the book value of the debt and the book value of the assets transferred.
    B. the difference between the book value of the debt and the fair value of the assets transferred.
    C. zero; there will never be a gain for the borrower.
    D. the difference between the book value of the assets transferred and the fair value of the assets transferred.

30. (Expanded material) In a troubled debt restructuring in which the borrower settles the debt by an equity swap, the borrower *normally* recognizes an:
    A. extraordinary gain on the debt restructuring.
    B. extraordinary loss on the debt restructuring.
    C. ordinary gain on the debt restructuring.
    D. ordinary loss on the debt restructuring.

31. (Expanded material) In a troubled debt restructuring in which the creditor agrees to modify the original terms of the debt agreement, an extraordinary gain will be recognized by the borrower if:
    A. the book value of the debt exceeds the present value of the restructured cash flows.
    B. the present value of the restructured cash flows exceeds the book value of the debt.
    C. the book value of the debt exceeds the restructured cash flows.
    D. the restructured cash flows exceed the book value of the debt.

32. (Expanded material) In a troubled debt restructuring in which the debtor settles the debt obligation by a modification of terms, the creditor normally recognizes:
    A. an extraordinary gain on the restructuring.
    B. an extraordinary loss on the restructuring.
    C. no gain or loss, since the modification is generally an extension of terms, rather than a concession.
    D. an ordinary gain.

33. (Expanded material) The extinguishment of debt prior to the maturity date by an in-substance defeasance meets which following conditions?
    A. Assets, generally cash or risk-free securities, are transferred to an irrevocable trust, and the trust services, and eventually retires the debt.
    B. The debt extinguished must have no more than 10 years remaining until maturity.
    C. Both the extinguished debt and the assets placed in trust continue to appear on the balance sheet of the entity which originally issued the debt.
    D. Creditors must be notified of the transfer prior to the in-substance defeasance.

Name: *Chapter 10*

Exercises and Problems

1. Bond interest amortization
   On January 2, 1997, Rally Company issued bonds payable with a face value of $480,000 at a discount. The stated rate on the bonds was 6%, and the market rate was 10%. The bonds are due in 10 years and interest is payable semiannually every June 30 and December 31. On June 30, 1997, and on December 31, 1997, Rally made the required semiannual interest payments and recorded interest expense and the amortization of the bond discount.

   Required: Complete the partially-complete amortization table below:

	Cash	Interest Expense	Amortization	Discount	Carrying Value
1/2/97	n/a	n/a	n/a		
6/30/97			$3,600		$363,600
12/31/97	$14,400				

   (AICPA adapted)

2. Computing bond issue prices
   Assume 10-year, 10% bonds of $500,000 are to be sold in the marketplace. Interest will be paid quarterly. Calculate the market price of the bonds in each of the following situations:
   a. Market rate of interest is 8%.
   b. Market rate of interest is 12%.
   c. Market rate of interest is 10%.

3. Bond financing
   Smethetic, Inc. is planning the construction of a new production facility. Construction and outfitting the facility will cost approximately $6,500,000. Smethetic plans to issue bonds to finance the facility. However, the company has limited cash flow at this time and would like to issue zero-coupon, 10-year bonds. If the market rate of interest is currently 10%, how many bonds (in terms of dollars) will Smethetic have to issue to received $6,500,000 in proceeds?

4. Bond interest
   On January 1, 1997, THE Corp. issued 10%, 10-year bonds with a face value of $400,000. The bonds were issued to yield 12%. THE Corp. uses the effective-interest method to amortize discounts and premiums. Interest is accrued and paid semiannually on July 1 and January 1. Write the journal entries necessary on July 1, 1997.

5. Bond retirement
   On March 6, 1987, XYZ Corp. issued $1,000,000 in 10-year, 10% bonds to yield 8%. Interest was paid semiannually on July 1 and January 1. The bonds were retired at maturity on January 1, 1997. All interest payments were made on a timely basis. Write the January 1, 1997 journal entry to retire the bonds.

6. Impact of bond retirement
   On December 31, 1997, Eagle Corp. reported bonds payable of $10,000,000 and related unamortized bond issue costs of $520,000. The bonds had been issued at par. On January 10, 1998, Eagle retired $5,000,000 of the bonds and paid a call premium of $100,000. What amount should Eagle report on its 1998 income statement as a result of the early extinguishment of debt?

7. Leverage ratio
   Required: Complete the following table:

Ratio	Calculation	What does it mean?
Debt/equity		
Debt/assets		
Times interest earned		

8. (Expanded material) Troubled debt restructuring

Complete the following table, being careful to explain how each type of restructuring is or is not a significant economic event.

ACCOUNTING FOR TROUBLED DEBT RESTRUCTURE ON BORROWER'S BOOKS		
Type	Significant economic event: Recognize gain or loss	No significant economic event: No gain or loss
Asset swap (transfer assets in full settlement)		
Equity swap (grant equity interest in full settlement)		
Modify terms: total payment under new terms exceeds debt carrying value		
Modify terms: total payment under new terms is less than debt carrying value		

SOLUTIONS TO TEST YOUR UNDERSTANDING

Fill-in-the-Blanks

1. liabilities
2. current ratio
3. accounts payable
4. promissory note
5. Notes payable
6. trade notes payable
7. Nontrade notes payable
8. long-term debt
9. trust indenture
10. face value, par value, maturity value
11. $1,000
12. bond indenture
13. municipal debt
14. Term bonds
15. Serial bonds
16. Secured bonds
17. unsecured (debenture) bonds
18. registered bonds
19. Bearer (coupon) bonds
20. zero-interest bonds
21. junk bonds
22. convertible bonds
23. commodity-backed bonds (or asset-linked bonds)
24. Callable bonds
25. Bond issuance costs
26. amortization
27. straight-line method
28. effective-interest method
29. Bond refinancing
30. leveraged buy-out (LBO)
31. leverage; highly leveraged
32. debt-to-equity; total liabilities; total stockholders' equity
33. debt ratio; total liabilities; total assets
34. times interest earned
35. In-substance defeasance; in-substance defeasance
36. troubled debt restructuring

Multiple Choice

1.	A	9.	D	17.	B	25.	B
2.	B	10.	C	18.	C	26.	B
3.	B	11.	B	19.	B	27.	D
4.	C	12.	C	20.	D	28.	D
5.	B	13.	A	21.	C	29.	B
6.	D	14.	C	22.	D	30.	A
7.	A	15.	C	23.	C	31.	C
8.	B	16.	D	24.	B	32.	C
						33.	A

Name: **Chapter 10**   183

Exercises and Problems

1. Bond interest amortization

	Cash	Interest Expense	Amortization	Discount	Carrying Value
1/2/97	n/a	n/a	n/a	$120,000^d	$360,000^c
6/30/97	$14,400^a	$18,000^b	$3,600	$116,400	$363,600
12/31/97	$14,400	$18,180	$3,780	$112,620	$367,380

^{a}$480,000 × .06 × ½
^{b}$14,400 + $3,600
^{c}$18,000 ÷ .05
^{d}$480,000 − $360,000

2. Computing bond issue prices
   a. Part 1: Present value of principal (maturity value):
   Maturity value, after 10 years, 40 quarterly payments $500,000
   Effective interest rate = 8% per year, or 2% per quarter
       (Table II, present value factor)   x   .4529
   Present value of $500,000 discounted at 2% for 40 periods $226,450

   Part 2: Present value of interest payments:
   Quarterly payment, 2.5% of $500,000 $ 12,500
   Effective interest rate = 8% per year or 2% per quarter,
       present value of annuity (Table IV)   x 27.3555
   Present value of 40, $12,500 payments, discounted at 2% $341,938

   Total present value (market price) of bond $568,388

   Note: Bond sells at a premium. Why? (Because the market rate is less than the stated rate, and investors are willing to pay a premium to receive higher interest payments over the life of the bond.)

   b. Part 1: Present value of principal (maturity value):
   Maturity value of bonds after 10 years, or 40 quarterly periods $500,000
   Effective interest rate = 12% per year, or 3% per quarter,
       present value factor, (Table II)   x   .3066
   Present value of lump-sum payment of $500,000,
       discounted at 3% for 40 periods $153,300

   Part 2: Present value of interest payments:
   Quarterly payment, 2.5% of $500,000 $ 12,500
   Effective interest rate = 12% per year, 3% per quarter,
       present value of annuity (Table IV)   x 23.1148
   Present value of 40, $12,500 payments, discounted at 3% $288,935

   Total present value (market price) of bond $442,235

   Note: Bonds sell at a discount. Why? (Because the borrower is offering a lower rate of interest than investors could earn on a similar investment; in order to entice the investor, the bond will be priced below par.)

c. Part 1: Present value of principal:

Maturity value of bonds after 10 years, or 40 quarterly payments	$500,000	
Effective interest rate = 10% per year, or 2.5% per quarter, present value factor (interpolate from Table II)	x .3700	(rounded)
Present value of lump-sum payment	$185,500	

Part 2: Present value of interest payments:

Quarterly payment, 2.5% of $500,000	$ 12,500
Effective interest rate = 2.5% per quarter, present value of annuity (interpolate Table IV)	x 25.2400
Present value of 40, $12,500 payments, discounted at 2.5%	$315,500
Total present value of bond issue	$501,000

Note: The difference is due to rounding, but this issue sells at par. Why? (Because stated rate and market rate of interest are the same.) Since you knew that the stated rate and the market rate were the same, you could calculate the proceeds from the bond issue immediately (i.e., par).

3. Bond financing
   $16,859,050

   Calculation:

Present value required	$ 6,500,000
Effective interest = 10%, for 10 years, future value (Table I)	x 2.5937
Amount to borrow	$16,859,050

   This seems like a lot of money to borrow to receive proceeds of $6,500,000, doesn't it? Let's check our calculations then:
   Remember, the company is not making any interest payments, so, in essence the interest is embedded in the price of the bonds. Since investors could earn 10% on similar investments, they will demand 10% on this one, too. Since they won't receive any periodic interest payments, they will discount the principal even further:

Future value (or principal to repay)	$16,859,050
Effective interest = 10%, for 10 years (Table II)	x .3855
Present value of $16,859,050, discounted at 10% for 10 years	$ 6,500,000

4. Bond interest
   Before you can write the journal entries on July 1, 1997, you need to calculate the balances in the Bonds Payable and Discount on Bonds Payable accounts. The bonds were issued at a discount on January 1. How do you know that? (Answer: the stated interest rate on the bonds was 10% and the market rate was 12%; thus, the bonds will sell at a discount). How much is the discount? (Answer: $46,000). Thus, the journal entry written on the date of issuance would be:

Jan. 1	Cash	354,000	
	Discount on Bonds Payable	46,000	
	Bonds Payable		400,000

   Next step: How much interest will be accrued on these bonds? Amortization of the discount will increase interest expense. Using the effective-interest method, interest expense for the first six months will be:

Investment balance	x	Yield interest rate	x	6/12	OR	
$354,000	x	12%	x	6/12	=	$21,240

How much cash will be paid to bondholders? The bondholders have $400,000 of bonds, with a stated interest rate of 10% and they've held the bonds for 6 months, so they will receive:

$400,000 x 10% x 6/12 = $20,000

The difference between interest expense accrued and cash paid for interest ($1,240) represents the amortization of the discount for the period, so the journal entry at 7/1/97 will be:

```
July 1   Interest Expense              21,240
              Cash                              20,000
              Discount on Bonds Payable          1,240
```

5. Bond retirement

```
Jan. 1   Bonds Payable              1,000,000
              Cash                           1,000,000
```

[Explanation: Since the bonds were held to maturity and all interest payments have been made, the premium has been completely amortized at the time the bonds mature. Thus, the entry to retire the bonds simply eliminates the bond liability.]

6. Impact of bond retirement
   $360,000 loss on extinguishment of debt

   Calculation:
   First, there is no premium or discount to worry about, since the bonds were issued at par.
   Second, half the bonds were retired, so we can assume that half the bond issue costs relate to those bonds: $520,000 /2 = $260,000. This half of the unamortized bond issue costs must be charged to the income statement during 1995.
   Third, the company paid a call premium of $100,000 to retire these bonds, and this cost must be expensed in 1995 also.
   So, the total loss associated with the retirement is $260,000 + $100,000 or $360,000.

7. Leverage ratio

Ratio	Calculation	What does it mean?
Debt/equity	Total debt/ total equity	measure of leverage; means the proportional funding of assets from debt versus equity; though there is no "magic" ratio here, industry trends do tend to measure riskiness of the company's capital structure
Debt/assets	Total debt/ total assets	measure of leverage; measure of the proportion of assets funded by debt; though there is no "magic" ratio here, industry trends do tend to measure riskiness of the company's capital structure
Times interest earned	[income before taxes and interest expense] / interest expense	measures the company's ability to service its debt (i.e., make the interest payments on debt).

8. Troubled debt restructuring

ACCOUNTING FOR TROUBLED DEBT RESTRUCTURE ON BORROWER'S BOOKS		
Type	**Significant economic event: Recognize gain or loss**	**No significant economic event: No gain or loss**
Asset swap (transfer assets in full settlement)	The borrower is required to give up assets to settle the liability. To the extent that these assets' fair value exceeds the carrying value of the debt, the borrower has given up more than it planned, and thus, a loss results.	
Equity swap (grant equity interest in full settlement)	In this case, the borrower has changed the nature of the relationship with the creditor, and the creditor now becomes an (partial) owner. This change in relationship is an economic event because the borrower now owes the creditor/owner something different than that which was owed prior to the TDR.	
Modify terms: total payment under new terms exceeds debt carrying value		Since the debt still exists and will now be paid in full, the borrower is not, effectively, better or worse off as a result of the TDR.
Modify terms: total payment under new terms is less than debt carrying value	The borrower will repay less than planned, and thus, has "gained" on the TDR	

CHAPTER 11

EQUITY FINANCING

KEY POINTS

I. Nature and Classifications of Paid-In Capital
   A. Corporate form of organization
      1. Treated under the law as an entity, a legal person.
      2. Large amounts of resources assembled under one management.
      3. Corporation issues stock certificates, which are evidence of ownership interest.
      4. Stockholders elect board of directors who oversee strategic and long-term planning for the corporation.
      5. Stock is issued by corporations.
         a. Two types: common stock and preferred stock.
         b. All corporations issue common stock.
         c. Some also issue preferred stock.
   B. Common stock
      1. True owners of corporation are the common shareholders.
      2. Share in dividends, although dividends are not necessarily guaranteed at all.
      3. Voting (elect board of directors and determine corporate policy).
         a. Not all shares vote equally.
            Example: Ben and Jerry's class B common stock [which is held mostly by insiders] has 10 votes to every one vote of class A stock, which is publicly traded.
      4. Pre-emptive rights: right to maintain proportional ownership interest.
      5. Share in proceeds upon liquidation of the company.
      6. Par or stated value
         a. Assigned at the time of incorporation.
         b. Generally the amount is nominal, such as $1 per share or $10 per share; also could be zero.
         c. Stock with zero par value is sometimes also called no par stock; no par stock often has a stated value, however; the stated value acts like par value.
         d. Par value has little significance from either an economic substance standpoint or an accounting standpoint.
   C. Preferred stock
      1. "Preferred" means preference in receiving dividends.
      2. Preferred shareholders forego some rights of common shareholders for dividend preference, including:
         a. Limited voting rights (no voting for board of directors).
         b. Limited or fixed amount of dividends.
         c. Often preferred stock has many classes, each with different characteristics and rights.
      3. Preferred stock generally has a par value.
      4. Common features of preferred stock may include:
         a. *Cumulative*: dividends, in essence, accrue.
         b. *Noncumulative*: it is not necessary to provide for passed dividends.
         c. *Participating*: after regular preferred dividends and common dividends are paid, participating shares get another round of dividends.
         d. *Convertible*: can be exchanged for some other security.
         e. *Callable*: can be called or redeemed by the corporation.
         f. *Redeemable*: can be redeemed at the option of the holder.
      5. **Thinking question**: Review the different types of preferred stock described above. Don't the features of some of them sound more like debt instruments than equity?

II. Issuance of Capital Stock
   A. Capital stock issued for cash
      1. Example: XYX Corporation issues 100 shares of $10 par value stock for $1,500:

Cash	1,500	
Common Stock		1,000
Paid-In Capital in Excess of Par		500

2. Paid-In Capital in Excess of Par represents the investment by shareholders in excess of the amount assigned to capital stock.
- B. Capital stock sold on subscription
    1. *Subscription* means that the buyer of the stock has promised to pay a fixed price for a certain number of shares on a certain date (i.e., a contract).
    2. Subscribed shareholders generally have the same rights as "paid up" shareholders, although some charters limit subscriber's powers.
    3. Although the corporation has the legal right to receive the money from the subscriber, the money isn't here yet, so a receivable must be established.
        a. This receivable is NOT an asset, but rather is an offset to equity.
    4. Likewise, the subscribed stock is reported separately from common stock, though still in the equity section.
    5. What to do with defaults is established by corporate policy. Options:
        a. Refund any partial payments made.
        b. Refund part of partial payments made.
        c. Issue shares in proportion to the amount paid.
        d. Do not refund any partial payments.
- C. Capital stock issued for consideration other than cash
    1. Contributed capital increases by the fair market value of the consideration received.
- D. Issuance of capital stock in a business combination
    1. APB Opinion No. 16 deals with business combinations.
    2. Two common types: pooling-of-interests or purchase method.
    3. Accounting for both is quite complicated, and generally addressed in advanced accounting classes.

III. Stock Repurchases
(Note to student: the text illustrates the reacquisition of preferred stock; this study guide illustrates the same principle using common stock. Note that while the types of stock involved are different, the accounting treatment is identical.)
- A. Stock reacquired for immediate retirement
    1. Reacquire at par or stated value:

Common Stock	CCC	
Cash		CCC

    2. Reacquired at price greater than par or stated value: Several options (see APB Opinion No. 6):
        a.

Common Stock	CCC	
Paid-In Capital in Excess of Par	XXX	
Cash		CXCX

        b.

Common Stock	CCC	
Retained Earnings	XXX	
Cash		CXCX

        Note: CCC = par value of stock; XXX= difference between par and cash paid; CXCX = cash paid
    3. Reacquired at price less than par value:

Common Stock	CCC	
Paid-In Capital from Stock Reacquisition		XXX
Cash		CXCX

    4. **IMPORTANT NOTE:** Reacquisition of shares may *reduce* retained earnings, but it will NEVER *increase* retained earnings.
- B. Treasury stock
    1. Stock reacquired by the issuing company that is held rather than retired.
    2. Why do this?
        a. Employee stock purchase plans.
        b. Executive compensation (stock options).
        c. Discourage takeovers.
    3. General important rules about treasury stock:
        a. NOT an asset; rather a contra to equity.
        b. Legal capital is not affected by acquisition or reissuance of treasury stock.

        c. Receives no dividends.
        d. No gain or loss on acquisition, reissuance or retirement of treasury stock.
        e. Retained earnings *can* be decreased by treasury stock transactions, but cannot be increased.
    4. Two methods to account for treasury stock:
        a. Cost method
        b. Par (or stated) value method
    5. Cost method
        a. Assumes the entire realm of transactions associated with treasury stock relates; thus, impact of transactions are aggregated.
        b. Debit treasury stock account for total purchase price of stock (credit Cash).
        c. If treasury stock is reissued at a price greater than purchase price, difference increases an additional paid-in capital account.
        d. If treasury stock is reissued at a price less than purchase price:
           1) Debit additional paid-in capital account in an amount equal to the additional paid-in capital credited by prior sales of treasury stock, *then*
           2) remaining difference is debited to Retained Earnings.
    6. Par (stated) value method
        a. Assumes acquisition of treasury stock liquidates a group of shareholders and reissuance creates new shareholders; thus, the transactions of treasury stock are not related to each other.
        b. Acquisition of treasury stock:
        Debit Treasury Stock for par value of stock; difference between par and price paid debited (to the extent possible) to additional paid-in capital account, and then to Retained Earnings; credit to Cash.
        c. Reissue
        Debit Cash for proceeds; credit Treasury Stock for par value; difference credited to additional paid-in capital account.
    7. Which method to use?
        a. Both are GAAP.
        b. Most companies use the cost method because it is simpler.

IV. Stock Rights, Warrants, and Options
    A. Company may issue *rights, warrants,* and/or *options*, all of which are financial instruments that permit the purchase of the company's stock at a specified price for a specified period of time.
        1. *Exercise period*: period of time during which the purchase of the company's stock may be purchased under the terms of the instrument.
        2. *Exercise price:* price per share as specified in the instrument.
        3. *Stock rights*: issued to existing shareholders to permit them to retain their proportionate share of stock ownership; also known as preemptive rights.
        4. *Stock warrants*: sold by the company for cash or other consideration, and usually attached to another security, such as long-term debt.
        5. *Stock options*: granted to officers and other employees as part of compensation.
    B. Stock rights
        1. Also known as preemptive rights.
        2. Rights of existing shareholders to purchase enough shares to maintain their proportional ownership in the company when new stock issues are created.
        3. Accounting by the issuer:
        No journal entry; memorandum entry only.
    C. Stock warrants
        1. Warrants are generally included with other securities as an incentive to investors.
        2. Warrants that can be traded separately from the original instrument are "detachable." "Nondetachable" warrants are inexorably linked to the original instrument.

3. APB Opinion No. 14 is used to account for the valuation of warrants and requires allocation of the issue price between the underlying instrument and the warrant.
   a. Value assigned to warrant is equal to

   $$\text{Total issue price} \times \frac{\text{Market value of warrants}}{\text{Market value of security without warrants} + \text{Market value of warrants}}$$

V. Accounting for Stock-Based Compensation
   A. VERY controversial accounting issue.
      1. Issue: should fair value of stock options granted to employees be estimated and recognized as compensation expense?
      2. FASB said "yes."
      3. Most major U.S. corporations' executives said "no."
      4. Why the disagreement?
         a. The recognition of compensation expense reduces reported earnings, which was not desirable from the perspective of corporate managers--especially because the amount of expense would be VERY large.
   B. Vigor of corporation opposition led the FASB to compromise with the issuance of FASB Statement No. 123:
      1. Under the provisions of FASB Statement No. 123, companies can continue to the use the *intrinsic value* method to account for stock option plans.
         a. The intrinsic value method dates back to APB Opinion No. 25.
         b. For most companies, application of the intrinsic value method results in no compensation expense recognition.
      2. Companies are encouraged, but not required, to adopt the *fair value* method to account for stock options.
         a. For most plans, the fair value method results in compensation expense.
      3. All companies are required to disclose details of options outstanding, exercise prices, contract periods, and fair value of options.
      4. Companies using the intrinsic value method (which is most companies) are also required to disclose what net income would have been had the fair value method been adopted.
   C. Three main issues relating to stock-based compensation:
      1. Valuation: how to value stock options and similar instruments used in the plans?
      2. Measurement: how much compensation expense should be recorded and when should it be recognized?
      3. Disclosure: what information should be disclosed in the annual report relating to the stock-based plan?
   D. Intrinsic value method (APB Opinion No. 25)
      1. Valuation
         a. Value of a fixed stock option (one with a fixed exercise price) = difference between option price and market price on the grant date.
      2. Measurement
         a. At grant date:
            1) The options are assumed to have no value and thus, no compensation expense is recorded.
         b. At exercise date:
            1) Still no compensation expense.
            2) Rather, debit cash for assets received and credit common stock for stock issued.
      3. Disclosure
         a. Information regarding details of the plan or plans.
         b. What net income would have been had the fair value method been used (this is a requirement of FASB Statement No. 123).
   E. Fair value method
      1. Valuation
         a. There is value to the option at the grant date because there is a chance that stock price will increase during the contract period, but employee will have the right to buy the stock at a fixed (and presumably, lower than market) price, so.....
         b. There is compensation expense.
         c. Valuation is based upon the expected volatility of stock price and the length of time options are valid.
            1) Would the value of the option increase if the option period were lengthened? Yes. Why? Because there is more time for the stock price to increase, yet the option price remains fixed.

2) Would the value of the option increase if the volatility of the stock increased? Yes. Why? Because there is more volatility associated with the investment, and thus, the possibility of increased returns to the shareholder exists, so the value of fixed options increases accordingly.

3) Would the value of the option increase if the stock price increased? Yes. Why? An increase in the stock price indicates an increased value of the firm, and thus, the fixed option becomes more valuable because it gives the holder the right to earn a greater return.

2. Measurement
 a. At grant date:
  1) Use an option pricing model, which impounds the elements of time, volatility, and risk. (Computer spreadsheets can do this calculation easily.)
  2) Compensation Expense   XXX
      Additional Paid-In Capital—Stock Options   XXX
 b. At exercise date:
  1) Cash   XXX
      Additional Paid-In Capital—Stock Options XXX
        Common Stock   XXX
3. Disclosures
 a. Information regarding the details of the plan.

VI. Stock Conversions
 A. Convert one type of security into another.
 B. Generally convert preferred stock to common or debt to common stock.
 C. Accounting issue: is there a gain or loss on the conversion?
  1. For the company? No gain, but maybe a loss; if so, debit Retained Earnings for the amount.
  2. For the investor? Generally, no.

VII. Factors Affecting Retained Earnings
 A. Account reconciliation
  1. Account increased (credited) by:
   a. Prior period adjustments for understatements of past earnings.
   b. Certain changes in accounting principles.
   c. Current net income.
   d. Quasi-reorganizations.
  2. Account decreased (debited) by:
   a. Prior period adjustments for overstatements of past earnings.
   b. Certain changes in accounting principles.
   c. Current net loss.
   d. Cash dividends.
   e. Stock dividends.
   f. Treasury stock transactions.
 B. Earnings
  1. Positive earnings increase retained earnings.
  2. Negative earnings (losses) decrease retained earnings.
  Thinking question: If losses persist and retained earnings become negative (deficit), what does this mean in terms of the accounting equation? [Answer: While the company may still have equity in the form of contributed capital, in all likelihood, the liabilities of the company either exceed or are close to exceeding the assets of the company, which is, of course, undesirable.]
 C. Prior-period adjustments
  1. Errors made in prior periods that are discovered and corrected this period.
  2. Many such errors are counterbalancing, such as inventory errors discussed in earlier chapters.
   a. Counterbalancing errors require no correction as they will self-correct.
  3. Noncounterbalancing errors will be corrected and the adjustment made to retained earnings.

D. Restrictions on retained earnings
   1. Appropriated retained earnings are 'set aside' or earmarked for some special purpose and therefore are not available for dividends.
   2. Generally transfer to special equity account, "Appropriated Retained Earnings."

VIII. Accounting for Dividends
   A. Dividends can generally only be paid if enough free or unrestricted retained earnings exist (or if company is liquidating—see H. Liquidating dividends).
   B. Recognition and payment of dividends
      1. Date of declaration: date board of directors announces the dividend.
      2. Date of record: cut-off date for dividends; on this date a listing of shareholders is made, and those are the people/institutions to whom the dividends are sent.
      3. Date of payment: date dividends are paid.
      4. Stocks trade during the period between the date of declaration and the date of record with the value of the dividends impounded into the price.
      5. After the date of record, stocks trade ex-dividend, that is, without the value of the dividends included in the price because the new owner is not entitled to the dividends.
   C. Cash dividends
      1. Journalize dividends on date of declaration and payment date.
      2. No entry on date of record.
   D. Property Dividends
      1. Journal entries similar to cash dividends.
      2. Record at fair market value of property given, if the fair market value is readily determinable.
      3. If FMV not readily determinable, use book value.
      4. Thus, there can be a gain or loss on property dividend distribution.
   E. Stock dividends
      1. Accounting by issuer
         a. Company must have sufficient retained earnings to absorb the increase in contributed capital.
         b. Distinction made between large and small stock dividends.
         c. Small dividend: less than 20-25% of outstanding stock.
         d. Record small dividend at fair market value of existing shares, with debit to Retained Earnings in this amount and credits to common stock and additional paid in capital accounts.
         e. Large stock dividends, transfer only par or stated value of newly issued shares from retained earnings.
   F. Fractional share warrants
      1. Share warrants issued in conjunction with stock dividends to shareholders who hold an irregular number of shares; share warrants entitle these shareholders to receive an exact number of shares in the stock dividend.
   G. Stock split
      1. Reduction in the par or stated value of stock accompanied by a proportional increase in the number of shares outstanding.
   H. Liquidating dividends
      1. Dividends, whose declaration decimates retained earnings and requires debit to contributed capital.
      2. These dividends, in essence, represent a return to shareholders of their original investment, noting that the company did not earn enough from which to dividend.
      3. They are called, "liquidating," because they seriously weaken the company's capital position.

IX. Other Equity Items
   A. Foreign currency translation adjustment
      1. Change in equity of foreign subsidiaries that occurs because exchange rates change.
   B. Minimum pension liability adjustment
      1. Negative equity item resulting from the adjustment to pension liability to ensure that a required minimum pension liability is recorded.
   C. Unrealized gain or loss on available-for-sale securities
      1. Arises due to fair value accounting for investments in securities of other corporations.

D. International accounting: equity reserves
    1. In other countries, the equity section of the balance sheet is divided into nondistributable and distributable reserves.
        a. Nondistributable
            1) Par value of shares.
            2) Share premium (similar to additional paid-in capital).
            3) Capital redemption reserve (this is a concept not commonly found in U.S. accounting).
            4) Asset revaluation reserve (another concept not found in U.S. accounting).
        b. Distributable
            1) Retained earnings.
            2) General and special reserves (U.S. accounting generally does not define the concept of reserves, but the concept is similar to that of appropriations).

X. Disclosures Related to the Equity Section
    A. Must disclose separately:
        1. Contributed capital and its components.
        2. Retained earnings.

EXPANDED MATERIAL KEY POINTS

XI. Quasi-Reorganizations
    A. Reorganization of company's capital structure such that a deficit or zero retained earnings balance can be handled.
    B. The economic process indicates that the company is actively adopting a new business strategy in the face of difficult financial times.
    C. Since deficit is eliminated, the company, in essence, starts over.
    D. Assets are generally written down to fair market value and any losses are debited to Retained Earnings.
        1. Since Retained Earnings is likely zero or negative anyway, the effect of this write-down is to reduce additional paid-in capital even further.

Thinking question: What if the write-down is so huge that it more than eliminates all of additional paid-in capital? [Answer: think about the financial condition the company must be in for this to occur. Do you think such a company *could* do a quasi-reorganization?]

XII. Accounting for Stock-Based Compensation
    A. Fixed stock option plan
        1. Plan in which exercise price and the number of shares granted are fixed on the grant date.
        2. Accounting issues associated with fixed plans have been discussed in Section V of this outline.
    B. Performance-based stock option plan
        1. Plan in which exercise price and number of options depends upon how well the company performs during the contract period.
        2. Performance-based plans are complex, so valuation and measurement issues are more complicated.
        3. Fair value method:
            a. Compensation expense = value of options on grant date with an estimate of the number of options expected to vest.
            b. As the estimates of the number of options change, the amount of compensation expense changes, so "catch-up" may be required in any one period such that cumulatively, the total of amount of expected compensation expense is recorded.
        4. Intrinsic value method
            a. Total compensation expense for a service period is remeasured at the end of each year in response to changes in the variables used to measure the initial value.
            b. Thus, compensation expense may exist (unlike the case of the fixed plan).
            c. A 'catch-up' may be required in any one year of the contract period.

C. Stock appreciation rights (SARs)
  1. The right of a holder, typically an employee, to receive an amount equal to the excess of the market value of the issuing company's common stock above a specified price.
  2. From the employee's standpoint, this is very much like a fixed option plan.
  3. From the company's standpoint, SARs create liabilities to transfer cash.
  4. Recognize compensation expense equal to the forecasted amount of cash to be transferred.
  5. "Catch-up" may be required as the estimates of the amount of cash to be transferred change.

TEST YOUR UNDERSTANDING

Fill-in-the-Blanks

Required: Fill in the blanks to complete the following sentences.

1. The portion of corporate capital that represents investments by the stockholders is _____ (_____-_____) _____.

2. _____ _____ is the portion of owners' equity that represents the net accumulated earnings of the corporation.

3. A _____ is a legal, artificial entity with an existence separate and distinct from its owners and which engages in business as if it were a real person.

4. The group of people elected by the shareholders of a corporation to oversee the strategic and long-run planning of the corporation is the _____ _____ _____.

5. _____ _____ is the class of stock that represents the basic ownership of the corporation.

6. _____ _____ is the nominal value assigned to stock by the terms of the corporate charter.

7. The nominal value assigned to no-par stock is its _____ _____.

8. Holders of _____ _____ receive dividends and liquidation proceeds before the common shareholders do, but these shareholders generally give up the right to vote for their dividend preferences.

9. When a corporation fails to declare dividends on _____ _____ _____, such dividends accrue and require payment in the future before any dividends can be paid to common shareholders.

10. Dividends on cumulative preferred stock that have been passed or not paid are said to be "_____ _____."

11. Preferred stock that has no claim on any prior year dividends not paid is _____ _____ _____.

12. Dividends on preferred stock are generally fixed in amount; however, one class of preferred stock, _____ _____ _____, provides for additional dividends to be paid to the preferred shareholders after dividends of a specified amount are paid to the common shareholders.

13. Preferred stock is _____ when it can be exchanged by its owner for some other security of the issuing corporation.

14. Preferred stock that is _____ may be redeemed and canceled at the option of the issuing corporation.

Name: _____   Chapter 11   195

15. _____ _____ _____ differs from callable preferred stock in that it can be returned to the issuing corporation for consideration at the option of the holder.

16. _____ _____-_____ _____ is the investment by shareholders in excess of the amounts assigned to capital stock as par or stated value.

17. A contract between the purchaser of common stock and the issuer in which the purchaser promises to buy a specified number of shares at a specified price within a specified amount of time is recorded as _____ _____ _____, a contributed capital account.

18. Stock issued by a corporation but subsequently reacquired by the corporation is _____ _____.

19. The method of accounting for treasury stock in which the entire amount of the repurchase price is debited to the treasury stock account is the _____ _____.

20. In the _____ _____ _____ of accounting for treasury stock, the treasury stock account is debited only for the par value of the stock repurchased, with the additional repurchase price being debited to the additional paid-in capital account.

21. Rights issued to existing shareholders entitling them to maintain their proportionate ownership interest are _____ _____.

22. _____ _____ are rights to purchase shares of stock that are often issued in conjunction with other securities, such as long-term debt.

23. _____ _____ are rights granted to officers and employees enabling them to purchase shares of stock at a specified price over a specified period of time.

24. The major issue in accounting for employee stock option plans is whether the granting of stock options brings about _____ _____.

25. In the _____ _____ _____ of accounting for employee stock option plans, compensation is calculated as the difference between the exercise price and the market price of the stock on the grant date; this method is the method set forth in _____ _____.

26. In the _____ _____ _____ of accounting for employee stock option plans, compensation is calculated as the fair value of the options granted on the grant date.

27. The method of accounting for employee stock option plans that is most likely to recognize compensation expense in the year the options are granted is the _____ _____ _____.

28. An excess of dividend payments and losses over a period of time will bring about a _____ (or debit balance) in the retained earnings account.

29. An adjustment made to the beginning retained earnings to correct errors made in prior years is a _____-_____ _____.

30. A cash return on investment made directly to shareholders is a _____ _____.

31. A dividend paid in the form of something other than cash is a _____ _____.

Chapter 11

32. A stock dividend of less than _____-_____ percent of the number of shares previously outstanding is classified as a small stock dividend; conversely, a large stock dividend is more than _____-_____ percent.

33. In a _____ _____, the par value of stock is reduced and the number of shares outstanding is proportionately increased.

34. In a _____ _____, a distribution is made to shareholders that represents a portion of their contributed capital.

Expanded material items:

35. In a _____ _____ _____ _____, the option price, exercise price, and number of options granted are fixed on the grant date.

36. In a _____-_____ _____ _____ _____, the number of options granted, the exercise price, or the exercise period vary depending on how well the company performs after the grant date.

37. _____ _____ _____ (_____) are awards granted to employees entitling the employee to receive, in cash, the excess of the market price of the company's stock on a specified date over a specified price.

Multiple Choice

Required: Circle the best answer.

1. Which of the following is NOT normally a right associated with common stock ownership?
   A. Voting
   B. Share in proceeds upon liquidation and after settlement of all debts
   C. Preemptive rights
   D. Receive regular dividends

2. The "par value" of common stock represents:
   A. the liquidation value of the stock.
   B. the book value of the stock.
   C. the legal nominal value assigned to the stock.
   D. the amount on which dividends are based.

3. BarZ Company has not declared or paid dividends on its cumulative preferred stock in the last three years. These dividends should be reported:
   A. in a footnote to the financial statements.
   B. as a current liability on the balance sheet.
   C. as an expense on the income statement.
   D. as a noncurrent liability.

4. On July 15, SSS Company issued 10,000 shares of $10 par value common stock in exchange for a tract of land. The land was appraised at $150,000. The stock of SSS Company was publicly traded and closed at $17 per share on July 14. SSS Company should record an increase in additional paid-in capital of:
   A. $150,000.
   B. $170,000.
   C. $50,000.
   D. $70,000.

5. On February 15, 1998, THE Company was formed by issuing:
   - Common stock, no par, $1 stated value, 12,000 shares issued at $16 per share.
   - Preferred stock, $20 par, 5,000 shares, issued at $21 per share.

   As of February 16, 1998, the statement of stockholders' equity for THE Company should contain the following balances:

	Common Stock	Preferred Stock	Additional Paid-In Capital
A.	$ 12,000	$100,000	$180,000
B.	$ 12,000	$100,000	$185,000
C.	$192,000	$100,000	$ 5,000
D.	$192,000	$105,000	$ 0

6. Midway Corporation issued 100,000 shares of common stock when it began operations in 1992. In 1994, it issued an additional 50,000 shares of common stock. In 1994, Midway Corporation also issued 60,000 shares of cumulative preferred stock. In 1997, Midway purchased 25,000 shares of common stock and held it in Treasury. At December 31, 1997, how many shares of common stock were:

	Issued	Outstanding
A.	210,000	210,000
B.	150,000	150,000
C.	210,000	150,000
D.	150,000	125,000

7. MicroDisk began operations in 1995 and issued 10,000 shares of $10 par value common stock at $15 per share. In 1997, MicroDisk reacquired 2,000 shares at $18 per share and placed the shares in Treasury. As a result of the 1997 stock transaction, using the par value method,:
   A. MicroDisk's 1997 net income decreased by $36,000.
   B. MicroDisk's 1997 net income decreased by $6,000.
   C. MicroDisk's additional paid-in capital decreased.
   D. MicroDisk's retained earnings increased.

8. MicroDisk began operations in 1995 and issued 10,000 shares of $10 par value common stock at $15 per share. On July 1, 1997, MicroDisk reacquired 2,000 shares at $18 per share and placed the shares in Treasury. On September 30, 1997, MicroDisk declared and paid its first dividend, in the amount of $5 per share. Dividends paid during 1997 total:
   A. $50,000.
   B. $40,000.
   C. $45,000.
   D. $0.

9. Treasury Stock is presented:
   A. on the balance sheet as a deduction at cost from total stockholders' equity.
   B. on the balance sheet as a deduction at par from total stockholders' equity.
   C. on the balance sheet as an asset, carried at the lower of cost or market.
   D. on the income statement as a current period cost.

10. Gains (losses) on the sale of treasury stock:
    A. increase (decrease) current period income.
    B. increase (decrease) additional paid-in capital and increase (decrease) in retained earnings.
    C. increase (decrease) additional paid-in capital and decrease in retained earnings.
    D. increase (decrease) current period income, additional paid-in capital, and retained earnings.

11. Common stock issued will exceed common stock outstanding if:
    A. stock splits have been declared.
    B. stock dividends have been declared.
    C. convertible preferred stock has been converted to common stock.
    D. treasury stock has been purchased.

12. When treasury stock is purchased for more than its par value, treasury stock is debited for the purchase price under which of the following methods?

	Cost Method	Par Value Method
A.	Yes	Yes
B.	No	No
C.	Yes	No
D.	No	Yes

    (AICPA adapted)

13. Treasury stock was acquired for cash at a price in excess of its par value. The cost method was used to account for the transaction. The stock was subsequently reissued at a price in excess of the acquisition price. What is the effect on retained earnings?

	Acquisition of Treasury Stock	Reissuance of Treasury Stock
A.	no effect	increase
B.	increase	no effect
C.	no effect	no effect
D.	increase	decrease

    (AICPA adapted)

14. 5,000 shares of common stock with a par value of $10 per share were issued at $12 per share. Subsequently, 1,000 of these shares were acquired as treasury stock at $15 per share. The par value method was used to account for the transaction. What is the effect of the acquisition on the following accounts:

	Additional Paid-In Capital	Retained Earnings
A.	increase	no effect
B.	increase	decrease
C.	decrease	increase
D.	decrease	decrease

    (AICPA adapted)

15. Which of the following is issued to shareholders by a corporation as evidence of ownership of rights to acquire its unissued or treasury stock?
    A. Stock options
    B. Stock rights
    C. Stock dividends
    D. Stock splits

    (AICPA adapted)

16. Stock warrants should be classified as:
    A. liabilities.
    B. reductions in additional paid-in capital.
    C. capital stock.
    D. additions to contributed capital.

    (AICPA adapted)

17. Toller Industries grants all its full-time employees rights to purchase common stock in the company in the amount up to 2% of their annual compensation . The option price is 90% of the market price on the grant date. The exercise period begins one year hence and extends for a period of 18 months. This plan is an example of a:
    A. fixed stock option plan.
    B. performance-based plan.
    C. broad-based plan.
    D. stock appreciation rights plan.

18. On December 10, D Corporation split its stock 5-for-2 when the market value was $85 per share. Prior to the split, D Corporation has 400,000 shares of $10 par value stock. After the split, the par value of the stock was:
    A. $10.
    B. $4.
    C. $2.
    D. $50.

19. A company declared a cash dividend to be paid at a later date. How would retained be affected on:

	Date of Declaration	Date of Record	Date of Payment
A.	Increase	Increase	Increase
B.	Decrease	Decrease	Decrease
C.	Decrease	No effect	No effect
D.	Decrease	No effect	Decrease

20. When a property dividend is declared, and the market value of the property is greater than its book value, the difference is credited to:
    A. Gain on Distribution of Property Dividends.
    B. Retained Earnings.
    C. Additional Paid-In Capital.
    D. Miscellaneous Assets.

21. How would retained earnings be affected by:

	Stock Dividends	Stock Split
A.	Decrease	Decrease
B.	No effect	No effect
C.	No effect	Decrease
D.	Decrease	No effect

    (AICPA adapted)

22. How would the declaration of a 15% stock dividend affect:

	Retained Earnings	Total Shareholders' Equity
A.	Decrease	No effect
B.	Decrease	Decrease
C.	No effect	Decrease
D.	No effect	No effect

23. Retained Earnings is increased by:
    A. net income and prior-period adjustments for understatements of prior earnings.
    B. net income and prior-period adjustments for overstatements of prior earnings.
    C. net income and treasury stock transactions.
    D. net income and liquidating dividends.

24. Appropriated retained earnings are transferred to a:
    A. current asset account.
    B. current liability account.
    C. special equity account.
    D. noncurrent asset account.

25. On March 1, 1998, Walton Corporation issued 1,000 shares of $20 par value common stock and 2,000 shares of $20 par value convertible preferred stock for a total of $80,000. At this date, Walton's common stock was selling for $36 per share, and the convertible preferred stock was selling for $27 per share. What amount of the proceeds should be allocated to Walton's convertible preferred stock?
    A. $60,000
    B. $50,000
    C. $48,000
    D. $44,000

    (AICPA adapted)

26. During 1997, Eagle Computing issued for $110 per share, 5,000 shares of $100 par value convertible preferred stock. One share of preferred stock can be converted into three shares of Eagle's $25 par value common stock at the option of the shareholder. On December 31, 1997 all of the preferred stock was converted into common stock. The market value of the common stock on the conversion date was $40 per share. What amount should be credited to the common stock account on December 31, 1997?
    A. $375,000
    B. $500,000
    C. $550,000
    D. $600,000

    (AICPA adapted)

27. Alfred Incorporated issued preferred stock with stock warrants. The issue price exceeded the sum of the warrants' fair value and the preferred stocks' par value. The preferred stocks' fair value was not readily determinable. What amount should be assigned to the warrants?
    A. Total proceeds
    B. Excess of the proceeds over the par value of the preferred stock
    C. The proportion of the proceeds that the warrants' fair value bears to the preferred stocks' value
    D. The fair value of the warrants

    (AICPA adapted)

28. Kearney Company issued preferred stock with warrants at a price which exceeded both the par value and the market value of the preferred stock. At the time the warrants were exercised, Kearney's total stockholders' equity is increased by the:

	Cash received upon exercise of the warrants	Carrying amount of the warrants
A.	Yes	No
B.	Yes	Yes
C.	No	No
D.	No	Yes

    (AICPA adapted)

29. Assuming collectibility is reasonably assured, the excess of the subscription price over the par value of common stock subscribed should be recorded as:
    A. common stock.
    B. additional paid-in capital when the subscription is recorded.
    C. additional paid-in capital when the subscription is collected.
    D. additional paid-in capital when the common stock is issued.

    (AICPA adapted)

30. In 1998, Dallas Company acquired 6,000 shares of its $1 par value common stock at $36 per share. During 1999, Dallas issued 3,000 of these shares at $50 per share. Dallas uses the cost method to account for treasury stock. What accounts and amounts should Dallas credit to record the issuance of the 3,000 shares?

	Treasury Stock	Additional Paid-In Capital	Retained Earnings	Common Stock
A.		$102,000	$42,000	$6,000
B.		$144,000		$6,000
C.	$108,000	$ 42,000		
D.	$108,000		$42,000	

    (AICPA adapted)

31. On incorporation, Sema Corporation issued common stock at a price in excess of the par value. No other stock transactions occurred except treasury stock was acquired for an amount exceeding the issue price. If Sema uses the par value method of accounting for treasury stock, what affect will the acquisition of treasury stock have on the following accounts?

	Outstanding Common Stock	Additional Paid-In Capital	Retained Earnings	
A.	No effect	Decrease	No effect	
B.	Decrease	Decrease	Decrease	
C.	Decrease	No effect	Decrease	
D.	No effect	Decrease	Decrease	(AICPA adapted)

32. At December 31, 1997 and 1998, Waverly Company has outstanding 2,000 shares of $100 par value 6% cumulative preferred stock and 10,000 shares of $10 par value common stock. At December 31,1997, dividends in arrears on the preferred stock were $6,000. Cash dividends declared in 1998 totaled $22,000. What amounts are payable to each class of stock?

	Preferred Stock	Common Stock	
A.	$12,000	$10,000	
B.	$16,000	$ 6,000	
C.	$18,000	$ 4,000	
D.	$22,000	$ 0	(AICPA adapted)

33. (Expanded material) Eaton's Company granted 30,000 stock appreciation rights to key employees. The SARs enable the employees to receive cash equal to the difference between $20 and the market price of the stock on the date the SAR is exercised. The service period is 1995 through 1997, and the rights are exercisable in 1998 and 1999. The market price of the stock was $25 on December 31, 1996. The market price was $28 on December 31, 1997. What amount should Eaton report as the liability for SARs on its December 31, 1997 balance sheet?
    A. $0
    B. $130,000
    C. $160,000
    D. $240,000   (AICPA adapted)

Exercises and Problems

1. Prior-period adjustment
   During the preparation of the 1997 financial statements, an error in the calculation of depreciation expense for 1995 and 1996 was discovered. As a result of the error, depreciation expense had been overstated by $20,000 (net of taxes) each year. Previously issued financial statements revealed the following:

	1995	1996
Beginning retained earnings	$800,000	$ 950,000
Net income	150,000	160,000
Ending retained earnings	950,000	1,110,000

   Income for 1997 was correctly calculated at $200,000.

   Required: Calculate the prior period adjustment for 1997.

2. Cash and property dividends
   During 1997, The X Company declared a cash dividend of $2,000 on January 6 to shareholders of record on March 6 and payable on April 6. The X Company also distributed machinery and equipment with a fair market value of $10,000 to its shareholders. The property dividend was declared on May 15 to shareholders of record on June 1 and payable on June 15. The machinery and equipment had an original acquisition cost of $20,000 and a book value of $8,000.

   Required: Prepare, in good form, the necessary journal entries for the abovementioned transactions.

Chapter 11

3. Stock subscriptions
   The following transactions occurred during 1997
   - Jan. 1 5,000 shares authorized common stock (par value $1) sold on a subscription basis for $7,500; subscribers paid 20% of the purchase price on Jan. 1
   - Mar. 1 Subscribers paid $1,500
   - June 1 Subscribers paid the remaining subscription contract costs, and common stock was issued.

   Required: Prepare, in good form, the journal entries for the transactions above.

4. Reacquisition and reissuance of stock
   On July 1, 1997 Bennet Corporation reacquired 8,000 shares of its $100 par value common stock at $134. The stock was originally issued at $110. The shares were reissued on November 15, 1997 for $145.

   Required: Provide the necessary journal entries to record the re-acquisition and reissuance of the stock using:
   1) par value method
   2) cost method

SOLUTIONS TO TEST YOUR UNDERSTANDING

Fill-in-the-Blanks

1. Contributed (paid-in) capital
2. Retained earnings
3. corporation
4. board of directors
5. Common stock
6. Par value
7. stated value
8. preferred stock
9. cumulative preferred stock
10. "in arrears"
11. noncumulative preferred stock
12. participating preferred stock
13. convertible
14. callable
15. Redeemable preferred stock
16. Additional paid-in capital
17. common stock subscribed
18. treasury stock
19. cost method
20. par value method
21. Stock rights
22. Stock warrants
23. Stock options
24. compensation expense
25. intrinsic value method; APB Opinion No. 25
26. fair value method
27. fair value method
28. deficit
29. prior-period adjustment
30. cash dividend

31. property dividend
32. 20-25; 20-25
33. stock split
34. liquidating dividend
35. fixed stock option plan
36. performance-based stock option plan
37. stock appreciation rights (SARs)

Multiple Choice

1.	D	9.	A	17.	C	25.	C
2.	C	10.	C	18.	B	26.	A
3.	A	11.	D	19.	C	27.	D
4.	D	12.	C	20.	A	28.	A
5.	B	13.	C	21.	D	29.	B
6.	D	14.	D	22.	A	30.	C
7.	C	15.	B	23.	A	31.	B
8.	B	16.	D	24.	C	32.	C
						33.	C

Exercises and Problems

1. Prior-period adjustment
   Since depreciation expense has been overstated, net income for 1995 and 1996 was understated by $20,000 each year. In the year the error is discovered, the beginning retained earnings should be adjusted to reflect the total impact of the errors, in this case, $40,000. Accordingly, 1997 beginning retained earnings should be increased by $40,000 to $1,150,000.
   Thinking question: What if comparative financial statements are presented in 1997 and the 1996 financial statements are included for comparative purposes in the 1997 annual report? [Answer: restate 1996 to reflect the correction of the error, namely increase income by $20,000 to $180,000 and include the effect of correcting the error in 1996 beginning retained earnings. Note that ending retained earnings in 1996 will still be $1,150,000 but beginning retained earnings will be $970,000.]

2. Cash and property dividends

Jan. 6	Retained Earnings		2,000	
	Dividends Payable			2,000
Mar. 6	No entry			
Apr. 6	Dividends Payable		2,000	
	Cash			2,000
May 15	Retained Earnings		10,000	
	Property Dividends Payable			8,000
	Gain on Distribution of Property Dividends			2,000
Jun. 1	No entry			
Jun. 15	Property Dividends Payable		8,000	
	Accumulated Depreciation		12,000	
	Machinery & Equipment			20,000

3. Stock subscriptions

Jan. 1	Cash		1,500	
	Common Stock Subscriptions Receivable		6,000	
	Common Stock Subscribed			5,000
	Paid-In Capital in Excess of Par			2,500
Mar. 1	Cash		1,500	
	Common Stock Subscriptions Receivable			1,500
June 1	Cash		4,500	
	Common Stock Subscriptions Receivable			4,500
	Common Stock Subscribed		5,000	
	Common Stock			5,000

4. Reacquisition and reissuance of stock

   1) Par Value Method

July 1	Treasury Stock	800,000	
	Paid-In Capital from Treasury Stock	80,000	
	Retained Earnings	192,000	
	Cash		1,072,000

[Calculations: Treasury Stock: 8,000 x $100; Paid-In Capital from Treasury Stock: 8,000 x $10; Retained Earnings: 8,000 x $24; Cash: 8,000 x $134]

Nov. 15	Cash	1,160,000	
	Treasury Stock		800,000
	Paid-In Capital from Treasury Stock		360,000

   2) Cost Method

July 1	Treasury Stock	1,072,000	
	Cash		1,072,000
Nov. 15	Cash	1,160,000	
	Treasury Stock		1,072,000
	Paid-In Capital from Treasury Stock		88,000

CHAPTER 12

INVESTMENTS IN NONCURRENT OPERATING ASSETS—ACQUISITION

KEY POINTS

I. What Costs Are Included in Acquisition Cost?
   A. *Noncurrent operating assets* are: probable future economic benefits owned or controlled by the entity and used in the production (either directly or tangentially) of revenue over a period greater than one year or an operating cycle.
      1. *Tangible*: land, buildings, and equipment used in the production of revenue.
      2. *Intangible*: goodwill, patents, licenses, copyrights, franchises, trademarks, organization costs, development costs, and other difficult to observe (or touch) noncurrent assets which are used indirectly in the production of revenue.
   B. General rule: Capitalize all costs necessary to purchase the asset and to get it ready for productive use.
      1. Generally, most such costs will occur at the time of acquisition or shortly thereafter.
      2. Note that virtually all the costs which are capitalized relate directly to the acquisition, installation, testing, or make-ready activities of the asset.
      3. Decision rule: if the company must expend the cost to either acquire title to the asset or to put the asset into productive use, the cost should normally be capitalized.
   C. Review Exhibit 12-2 on page 671 for definitions and costs associated with various tangible noncurrent operating assets.
   D. Review Exhibit 12-3 on page 672 for definitions and costs associated with various intangible noncurrent operating assets.

II. Acquisitions Other Than Simple Cash Transactions
   A. Assets acquired in a basket purchase for one lump sum price
      1. Often a group of separate assets is acquired in one transaction with only one stated purchase price.
         a. For example, as stated in the example in the text, when Jerry Jones purchased the Dallas Cowboys, he acquired numerous assets in the transaction, but only one purchase price was quoted.
      2. Assets must be recorded in books individually.
      3. So, accountant must allocate the purchase price to individual assets:
         a. If fair market values can be determined, use them.
         b. Appraisals can also be used.
         c. Allocate costs to individual assets based upon proportion of appraised value to total acquisition cost.
   B. Purchase on deferred payment plan
      1. Acquisition of (existing) assets by incurring debt for all or part of the purchase price.
      2. Original acquisition cost of the asset is still the purchase price plus all costs necessary to place the asset in service.
      3. Interest on the debt incurred to purchase the asset is generally expensed in the period incurred.
      4. If interest is not explicitly stated in the debt agreement, then the stated purchase price may include interest.
         a. To exclude the interest included in the stated purchase price, and thus, record the correct original acquisition cost of the asset:
            1) Determine the fair market value of the asset acquired, which is the original acquisition cost.
            2) The difference between the fair market value of the asset and the present value of the total debt represents the interest inherent in the contract.
            3) This interest is booked as a Discount on Notes Payable, and is amortized over the life of the debt by debiting Interest Expense and crediting Discount on Notes Payable.
   C. Acquisition via capital lease
      1. A *lease* is a contract whereby the *lessee* is granted the right to use and control the asset by the owner (*lessor*) for a specified period of time.
      2. Some leases are structured such that the lessee has all the rights and responsibilities of ownership except legal title. These are *capital leases*.

3. Assets acquired via capital leases should be recorded as assets at the present value of the future lease payments--this represents the original acquisition cost.
4. More about capital leases in Chapter 15.
D. Acquisition by exchange of nonmonetary assets
   1. The new asset should generally be recorded at its fair market value or the fair market value of the asset given up, whichever is more readily determinable.
E. Acquisition by issuance of securities
   1. When the market value of the securities issued (either bonds or stocks) can be readily determined, use that as the original acquisition cost of the newly acquired asset.
   2. If the securities issued are not regularly traded, and thus, a reliable market measure cannot be determined, the asset acquired should be appraised, and the appraised value should be used as the original acquisition cost of the asset.
F. Acquisition by self-construction
   1. Self-constructed assets are recorded at cost, including all costs necessary to construct the asset and to place it into service.
   2. Certain costs incurred during construction can be confusing, so there are special accounting rules for them. Such costs include:
      a. Overhead chargeable to self-construction.
      b. Difference between self-construction costs and what the costs would have been if someone else had done the construction.
      c. Interest incurred on money borrowed to fund construction.
   3. Overhead costs
      a. Although there is no hard and fast rule for determining the portion of overhead costs that can be allocated to self-constructed assets, the general criterion is:
         1) Capitalize as part of the cost of the self-constructed asset those overhead costs which have "discernable future benefits."
   4. Savings or loss due to self-construction
      a. Sometimes the company saves money by self-constructing assets; sometimes it doesn't.
      b. Nonetheless, the *cost* of the self-constructed asset is still how much money the company spent acquiring it.
   5. Interest during construction period (FASB Statement No. 34)
      a. Interest incurred on money borrowed specifically for the purpose of constructing an asset can be capitalized.
      b. Only the interest incurred during the period of construction can be capitalized.
      c. Although there is also an implicit "interest" cost associated with equity funding, current accounting practices do not allow computation and capitalization of such an amount.
      d. The maximum amount of interest that can be capitalized is the amount actually incurred or paid during the construction period.
      e. Capitalizable interest is based upon the *average amount of accumulated expenditures* for the self-construction.
      f. Interest rate to use is either the *nominal rate on specific debt* or *weighted average interest rate* from all outstanding debt.
      g. Capitalized interest reduces the amount of interest expense on the income statement.
      h. Cash paid for capitalized interest is generally recorded on the cash flow statement as an investing activity.
G. Assets acquired by donation or discovery (FASB Statement No. 116)
   1. Fair market value of assets donated is used as the original acquisition cost of the assets.
   2. Since no assets were given up and no liabilities were incurred to acquire donated assets, the company incurs a gain at the time of the donation.
      a. The amount of the gain is equal to the fair market value of the assets received.
H. Acquisition of an entire company
   1. Purchase of an entire company is a "business combination."

2. Accounting for business combinations depends upon the economic substance of the transaction.
   a. Combinations in which two companies essentially merge and proceed together as a merged entity are accounted for using the *pooling-of-interests* method:
      1) Book values of assets and liabilities from both prior companies' records are used in the new merged entity.
   b. Business combinations in which one entity essentially takes over the other entity are accounted for using the *purchase* method:
      1) Fair values of the assets and liabilities acquired in the purchase transaction are the bases for recording acquisition cost in the new entity.
3. Goodwill
   a. When the purchase price of the entity exceeds the sum of the fair values of the net assets acquired, the difference is assumed to be goodwill, an intangible asset.
   b. Goodwill is recognized and amortized over 40 years.
4. Negative goodwill
   a. If the purchase price of the entity is less than the total fair value of all net assets, negative goodwill exists.
   b. A (negative) asset, "negative goodwill," is not recorded.
   c. Rather, negative goodwill is used to reduce the recorded amounts of the net assets acquired.

III. Capitalize or Expense?
   A. General rule: a significant (material) expenditure is capitalized if it provides future economic benefits that extend beyond the current period, including expenditures which:
      1. Extend the productive life of the asset and/or
      2. Enhance the productive capability of the asset.
   B. Post-acquisition expenditures
      1. Maintenance and repairs: expenditures necessary to keep plant assets productive or in good operating condition.
         a. Examples: lubricating, changing the oil, painting.
         b. Since these expenditures do NOT extend the asset's life or enhance its productivity, they are expensed.
      2. Renewals and replacements: overhauling plant assets or substituting new parts.
         a. Examples: replace old tires on auto with new tires; overhaul motor in lawn tractor.
         b. If renewal or replacement does not extend the asset's life beyond the original estimated useful economic life or does not enhance productivity of the asset, the cost of renewal or replacement is expensed.
      3. Additions and betterments: enlargements and improvements
         a. Examples: build a new structure attached to old structure to house additional productive capabilities; replace existing heating and air conditioning units with larger capacity, more efficient units.
         b. Generally, additions and betterments are designed to extend productive life or enhance productivity, so the cost is usually capitalized.
   C. Some types of expenditures are confusing:
      1. Research and development
      2. Software development
      3. Oil and gas exploration costs
   D. Research and development (R&D) costs (FASB Statement No.2, 1974)
      1. Expenditures undertaken to discover new knowledge and to develop new processes or products.
      2. FASB (refer to FASB Statement No. 2) decided that such costs should be expensed in the period incurred.
         a. Why? uncertainty with respect to measurability or existence of future economic benefits.
   E. Computer software development costs (FASB Statement No. 86, 1985)
      1. Expenditures undertaken to create, develop, and test computer software.
      2. Similar to R&D, but FASB considered separately because of the intensity of computer software development activity during the mid-1980's.
      3. Created a new threshold: *technological feasibility*.
         a. Technological feasibility means essentially that the software exists and works as planned.

208   **Chapter 12**

      b. Technological feasibility requires:
         1) detail program design or
         2) working prototype or model.
    4. All costs expended up to the point of technological feasibility are expensed when incurred.
  F. Oil and gas exploration costs
    1. Considerable exploration effort is expended to locate oil reserves.
    2. Accounting question: how to account for exploration costs?
    3. Two methods:
      a. *Full Cost*: capitalize all exploration costs and amortize over life of productive wells.
         1) Popular with small oil companies.
         2) FASB proposed elimination of full cost method in 1977, but small companies lobbied Congress and the SEC to keep the method in tact; spurred a VERY heated debate.
         3) **Thinking question**: does this remind you of the debate regarding employee stock option plans?
      b. *Successful Efforts*: expense exploration costs for dry wells in the period incurred; capitalize only costs associated with producing wells.
         1) Popular with large oil companies.

IV. Valuation of Assets at Current Values
  A. Noncurrent operating assets are generally recorded at cost and remain at cost throughout their productive lives.
  B. Accounting question: is it appropriate to continue to account for long-term assets at costs when their current market values may be very different than historical cost?
  C. Many countries, for example the U. K., allow companies to periodically assess the relationship between historical cost and fair value of their noncurrent assets and if a large difference exists, "write-up" the carrying value of the long-term assets.
  D. The issue of current value accounting for noncurrent assets will likely be an issue addressed by the FASB in the future.

EXPANDED MATERIAL KEY POINTS

V. Capitalized Interest: Complexities
  A. Basic method to capitalize interest introduced in the text is the *avoidable interest method*.
  B. Another method commonly used: *average accumulated expenditure method*.
    1. Based on the assumption that the average expenditures amount was outstanding during the entire year.
    2. Thus, interest capitalized is based upon that number.
    3. Generally, use of this method increases the amount of interest capitalized.
    4. Caution: be careful not to try to capitalize more interest than actually incurred.

TEST YOUR UNDERSTANDING

Fill-in-the-Blanks

Required: Fill in the blanks to complete the following sentences.

1. _____ is realty used for business purposes.

2. A _____ is an exclusive right granted by the U.S. government enabling the inventor of a product or process to control its manufacture, sale, or use for 17 years.

3. A _____ is an exclusive right granted by the U.S. government enabling an author to sell, license, or control his or her own work for a period extending 50 years after his/her death.

4. A lease that is economically equivalent to the rental of a leased asset is a(n) _____ _____.

5. A(n) _____ _____ is a lease which is economically equivalent to the purchase of the leased asset.

6. The joining of two separate companies into one company is a _____ _____.

7. In the _____ - _____ - _____ method of business combinations, the book values of both companies form the carrying basis for the new entity's assets.

8. The method of accounting for a business combination in which the assets of the acquired company are recorded at the fair values is the _____ _____.

9. _____ is the measure of the company's ability to earn above normal income.

10. _____ is the normal cost of keeping property in good operating condition.

11. Expenditures made to restore operating assets to operating condition are called _____.

12. The cost of major overhaul of an asset is a _____.

13. _____ is the process of substituting new parts or components in existing assets.

14. Enlargements or extensions of existing assets are _____.

15. Expenditures designed to improve or increase productive capability of existing assets are called _____.

16. Activities to discover, refine, and develop new knowledge that will result in new or improved products or process are called _____ _____ _____ (_____).

17. _____ is the search for new knowledge.

18. _____ is the application of research findings to the planning or designing of new products or processes.

19. Research has reached _____ _____ when it has progressed far enough that the firm's ultimate ability to economically produce a new product is reasonably assured.

20. In the _____ _____ method of accounting of oil exploration costs, the costs of all exploration efforts are initially capitalized and then expensed over the life of productive ventures.

21. In the _____ _____ method of accounting for oil exploration costs, the costs of dry holes are expensed currently.

Expanded material items:

22. The method of computing the amount of capitalized interest which uses the assumption that the average expenditure amount was outstanding all during the year is the _____ _____ _____ _____.

23. In the _____ _____ method of accounting for capitalized interest, the amount of interest capitalized is that which is estimated to have been avoidable had the asset construction project not begun.

Chapter 12

Multiple Choice

Required: Circle the best answer.

1. Land was purchased to be the site of a new office building. An existing building was sold and removed by the buyer to make room for the new office building. The proceeds from the sale of the existing building should be:
   A. recognized as other revenue.
   B. deferred and amortized over the life of the new building.
   C. deducted from the cost of the land.
   D. netted against the costs to construct the new office building.

2. Land was purchased to create a wildlife refuge. Several small buildings, which were on the land at the time of purchase, were razed. The cost of razing the buildings should be:
   A. deducted from the cost of the land.
   B. added to the cost of the land.
   C. expensed in the current period.
   D. netted against the costs to develop the wildlife refuge.

3. Valuable artwork was donated to the Springson Company. The transaction should be recorded by Springson as:
   A. extraordinary income equal to the fair market value of the art.
   B. gain equal to fair market value of the art.
   C. additional paid-in capital equal to the fair market value of the art.
   D. Since Springson paid nothing for the art, it does not need to record its acquisition at all.

4. Which of the following assets is "intangible?"
   A. Drilling rights
   B. Intellectual capital
   C. Retained earnings
   D. Franchise

5. Which of the following assets would not normally be listed on the balance sheet?
   A. Purchased goodwill
   B. Donated assets
   C. Internally generated goodwill
   D. Patents

6. Which of the following expenditures would NOT normally be included in the original acquisition cost of a noncurrent operating asset?
   A. Purchase price
   B. Current year property taxes
   C. Past due property taxes
   D. Real estate brokerage fees

7. In which of the following instances would interest normally be capitalized?
   A. Actual interest incurred during construction of an asset that will eventually be used by the business.
   B. Imputed interest during construction of an asset that will eventually be used in the business.
   C. Interest incurred to purchase land.
   D. Actual interest incurred during construction and after completion of a self-constructed asset.

8. Research and development costs:
   A. should be capitalized if the company believes the costs will generate future revenues.
   B. should be capitalized if the company purchased research from other companies to aid in its own development efforts.
   C. should be expensed in the period incurred.
   D. can be expensed or capitalized, depending upon the company's preferences.

9. Computer software development costs:
   A. are expensed up to the point of technological feasibility.
   B. are expensed as incurred.
   C. should be capitalized if the company believes the costs will generate future revenues.
   D. should be capitalized if the software will be used internally.

10. Ted owns a rental house. When tenants move out, Ted routinely replaces the carpet in the house. The cost of the new carpet:
    A. should be capitalized.
    B. should be expensed currently.
    C. should be capitalized only if the carpet provides future economic benefit that extends beyond the current period.
    D. can be expensed or capitalized depending upon Ted's preference.

11. Carter Company began construction of a warehouse on January 1, 1996. Construction was completed in June, 1997, and Carter put the warehouse into service as of July 1, 1997. The total cost of the warehouse was $2,500,000. Of the total cost, $2,000,000 was incurred during 1996 evenly throughout the year. Carter's incremental borrowing rate was 12% during 1996, and the total amount of interest incurred by Carter was $102,000. What amount of interest should Carter capitalize during 1996?
    A. $102,000
    B. $120,000
    C. $150,000
    D. $240,000   (AICPA adapted)

12. Elmwood Murdock incurred costs to modify its building and rearrange its production line. The modification and rearrangement is expected to significantly reduce production costs. However, the modifications did not increase the building's market value, and the rearrangement did not extend the life of the production assets. Should the building modification costs and the production line rearrangement costs be capitalized?

	Building modification costs	Production line rearrangement cost
A.	Yes	No
B.	Yes	Yes
C.	No	No
D.	No	Yes (AICPA adapted)

13. Artworks Inc., began construction of a building for its own use in January, 1997. During 1997, Artworks incurred interest of $50,000 on specific construction debt, and $20,000 on other borrowings. Interest computed on the weighted-average amount of accumulated expenditures for the building during 1997 was $40,000. What amount of interest should Artworks capitalize?
    A. $20,000
    B. $40,000
    C. $50,000
    D. $70,000   (AICPA adapted)

14. Which of the following statements concerning patents is correct?
    A. Legal costs incurred to successfully defend an internally developed patent should be capitalized and amortized over the patent's remaining economic life.
    B. Legal fees and other direct costs incurred in registering a patent should be capitalized and amortized on a straight-line basis over a five-year period.
    C. Research and development contract services purchased from others and used to develop a patented manufacturing process should be capitalized and amortized over the patent's economic life.
    D. Research and development costs incurred to develop a patented item should be capitalized and amortized on a straight-line basis over 17 years. (AICPA adapted)

15. During 1997, Cheetah Manufacturing constructed machinery for its own use and for sale to customers. Bank loans financed these assets both during construction and after construction was complete. How much of the interest incurred should be reported as interest expense on the 1997 income statement?

	Interest incurred for machinery for own use	Interest incurred for machinery held for sale
A.	All interest incurred	All interest incurred
B.	All interest incurred	Interest incurred after completion
C.	Interest incurred after completion	Interest incurred after completion
D.	Interest incurred after completion	All interest incurred

    (AICPA adapted)

16. A building was damaged during a tornado. The damage was not covered by insurance. The damaged portion of the building was refurbished with higher quality materials. The cost and related accumulated depreciation of the damaged portion of the building are identifiable. To account for these events, the owner should:
    A. reduce accumulated depreciation equal to the cost of refurbishing.
    B. record a loss in the current period equal to the sum of the cost of refurbishing and the carrying amount of the damaged portion of the building.
    C. capitalize the cost of refurbishing and record a loss in the current period equal to the carrying value of the damaged portion of the building.
    D. capitalize the cost of refurbishing by adding the cost to the carrying value of the building.
    (AICPA adapted)

17. On July 1, 1997, Lincoln Company purchased for $540,000 a warehouse building and the land on which it is located. The following data are available about the property:

	Current appraised value	Seller's original cost
Land	$200,000	$140,000
Warehouse	300,000	280,000
Total	$500,000	$420,000

    Lincoln should record the land at:
    A. $140,000.
    B. $180,000.
    C. $200,000.
    D. $216,000. (AICPA adapted)

18. Which of the following costs would normally NOT be capitalized as part of the original acquisition cost of land?
    A. Clearing and grading costs
    B. Legal fees to clear title to the land
    C. Government assessments for sewer and water lines
    D. Costs associated with installation of sidewalks

19. Which of the following companies would be likely to have a larger portion of its total assets invested in land than the others on the list?
    A. Waste Management, a waste disposal and sanitary landfill provider
    B. Merrill Lynch, a securities broker
    C. Haroldson and Company, a law firm
    D. UPS, a freight delivery service

20. Which of the following expenditures would generally be capitalized?
    A. Replacement of air conditioning filters in manufacturing facility. The new filters have an expected useful life of about 6 months.
    B. Painting of the dining room in a restaurant.
    C. Cost of construction of a temporary road necessary to facilitate construction of a shopping mall.
    D. Cost of employee training to maintain employees' professional certifications.

Exercises and Problems

1. Acquisition cost
   Mi Casa Steak House purchased a piece of land on which it planned to build another restaurant. Purchase price was $150,000. Mi Casa also paid brokerage fees, surveying costs, title policy fees, and other incidental legal fees in the amount of $8,000. Property taxes had not been paid on the land in several years, and Mi Casa had to pay back taxes in the amount of $12,000. Current year taxes will be $1,100. Included on the land was a ramshackle building which Mi Casa contracted to have razed at a cost of $9,200. Mi Casa's owners were concerned about prior use of the land, so they paid a special contractor/inspector $5,000 to inspect the land for hazardous waste. No hazardous waste or other toxic materials were found.

   Required: Calculate the original acquisition cost of the land.

2. Acquisition cost
   Mark owns and operates a mobile home park. Although most of his tenants own their own mobile homes, Mark owns and rents several units in the park. On December 1, 1997, Mark purchased a mobile home at an auction for $3,500. He hired a transport to deliver the mobile home to his trailer park at a cost of $350. Insurance cost during the transportation phase was $60. Mark also purchased an insurance policy on the mobile home for the upcoming year at a cost of $300. Mark replaced all the appliances, including heating and air conditioning units in the mobile home at a cost of $2,800. He repaired all the sub-flooring and installed new carpeting and flooring throughout the mobile home at a cost of $3,200. Mark did all the work himself, but he estimated that had he hired a contractor to replace the sub-flooring and install the carpeting and flooring, he would have spent $6,500. He painted the entire mobile home for $200. He estimated that a contractor would have charged $1,200 for the job. Mark purchased and installed miniblinds throughout the mobile home at a cost of $200.

   Required: Calculate the original acquisition cost of the mobile home.

3. Classifying expenditures
   Bart and Bret developed a device to safely and efficiently remove snow from roofs and roof gutters of homes. Because the product worked so well, Bart and Bret decided to incorporate and market the product, Roof Clear, nationally. Bart and Bret paid a lawyer $5,000 to do the legal work associated with forming and registering the corporation. State incorporation fees were $500. In addition, Bart and Bret paid a graphic artist to develop a logo for the Roof Clear; cost was $1,200. To market the product, Bart and Bret acquired an 800-telephone number, and advertised the product on late night television; cost was $8,900 for the first six months of operation.

   Required: Calculate the amounts which can be capitalized and determine how the costs will be classified.

4. Purchase of a company for cash

   Don Leaton acquired all the assets of Bryan Brothers Orchards for $1,000,000 in cash. Included in the assets of the Orchard were land, trees, farming machinery, processing equipment, a building in which sorting and processing was done, the company name and logo, and miscellaneous office equipment and furniture. The land and trees were appraised at $500,000. Fair market values for the farming equipment, based upon replacement costs were $100,000; $100,000 for the processing equipment; $80,000 for the building; and $20,000 for the office equipment and furniture.

   Required: Write the journal entry to record the purchase of Bryan Brothers Orchards.

5. Purchase of a company in installments

   Assume the same facts as in Problem 4 except that instead of paying $1,000,000 in cash, assume that Don Leaton paid $50,000 in cash and agreed to pay the balance in quarterly installments over a five-year period at an annual interest rate of 12%.

   Required: Write the journal entry to record the purchase of Bryan Brothers Orchards.

6. Purchase of a company by note payable

   Assume the same facts as in Problem 5, except assume that Don Leaton paid no cash but agreed to make ten annual payments of $175,000. Recall that total fair market value of the assets acquired is $800,000. Current market interest rate is 12%.

   Required: Write the journal entry to record the purchase of Bryan Brothers Orchards. Write the journal entry to record the first payment on the note. Hint: first calculate the present value of the debt agreement.

7. Capital lease

   Soland Distributing entered into a capital lease on a warehouse. The present value of the future lease payments is $800,000. The fair market value of the warehouse is $900,000.

   Required: Write the journal entry on Soland Distributing's books to record the acquisition of the warehouse.

8. Acquisition of land for stock

   Northern Lights Drilling acquired 2,000 acres of land in exchange for 10,000 shares of its $10 par value common stock.

   Required: Write the journal entry to record the acquisition of the land:
   a) Assume the common stock of Northern Lights Drilling is publicly traded at $47 a share.
   b) Assume the common stock of Northern Lights Drilling is not publicly traded, but an independent appraisal of the land values it at $450,000.

9. Donation of land and building

   To encourage the relocation of a semi-professional baseball team to Anytown, USA, John Johnson, a wealthy resident of Anytown donated 15 acres of land to the team as a site for the baseball stadium field. Mr. Johnson had owned the land for over twenty years and had paid $20,000 for it. Tom Johnson, John's brother, built the stadium and donated it to the team. Tom Johnson spent $2,500,000 to construct the stadium, and upon completion the stadium was appraised at $2,500,000. The land was appraised at $500,000.

   Required: Write the journal entry on the books of the baseball team to record the receipt of the land and stadium.

10. Goodwill
   Smetz Beverage Company is listed for sale for $2,500,000. Net assets were appraised at $1,600,000. Smetz Beverage has achieved stable earnings over the past 10 years, averaging $180,000 per year.

   Required: Calculate the amount of goodwill inherent in the asking price based upon appraisal of net assets.

11. Discovery of oil reserves
   Padlock Ranch consists of 10,000 acres of pasture and grazing land. The Ranch acquired the land over a period of thirty years at a total cost of $200,000. The land is currently listed on the Ranch's books at its original acquisition cost of $200,000. On June 30 of the current year, seismic exploration discovered a huge underground oil reservoir on the Ranch's land. Estimated present value of the oil reserves ranges from a low of $40,000,000 to a high of $100,000,000.

   Required: Assume the owners of Padlock Ranch have asked you to advise them regarding the accounting treatment of the discovery. Prepare an analysis of the accounting treatment, including issues to consider, applicable professional literature and economic consequences. Recommend action.

12. Acquisition and post-acquisition costs
   Prospector Development Company purchased 500 acres of land on which to build a golf course and surrounding residential neighborhood. Included in the purchase was an existing building, which Prospector planned to remodel and use as the club house for the golf course. The building presently housed several offices and businesses. Total purchase price was $2,800,000.

   As Prospector began construction of the golf course, it discovered that approximately 200 acres of the land were contaminated with old mine tailings. The Department of Environmental Quality examined the site and declared that the land could be reclaimed if Prospector "blanketed" the entire site with at least six inches of pure topsoil. The cost of reclamation was estimated to be $1,400,000.

   The businesses and offices housed in the existing building were relocated at Prospector's expense. The cost of relocation was $40,000.

   As remodeling of the building progressed, the contractor discovered asbestos in the building. To proceed with the remodeling, Prospector was required to have the asbestos removed at a cost of $82,000.

   Required: Determine the accounting treatment(s) relating to the acquisition and postacquisition costs of the land and building. Present your recommendations and your justifications for such recommendations.

SOLUTIONS TO TEST YOUR UNDERSTANDING

Fill-in-the-Blanks

1. Land
2. patent
3. copyright
4. operating lease
5. capital lease
6. business combination
7. pooling-of-interests
8. purchase method
9. Goodwill
10. Maintenance
11. repairs
12. renewal

13. Replacement
14. additions
15. betterments
16. research and development (R&D)
17. Research
18. Development
19. technological feasibility
20. full cost
21. successful efforts
22. average accumulated expenditures method
23. avoidable interest

Multiple Choice

1. C
2. B
3. B
4. D
5. C
6. B
7. A
8. C
9. A
10. C
11. A
12. B
13. B
14. A
15. D
16. C
17. D
18. D
19. A
20. C

Exercises and Problems

1. Acquisition cost
   Original acquisition cost: $184,200
   Calculations:

purchase price	$150,000
fees	8,000
back taxes	12,000
razing fees	9,200
inspection	5,000

2. Acquisition cost
   Original acquisition cost: $10,310
   Calculations:

purchase price	$3,500
transport	350
insurance	60
appliances	2,800
carpet	3,200
paint	200
blinds	200

   Note: all costs were considered to be necessary to put the asset into service. Use only actual costs incurred, not estimated costs.

3. Classifying expenditures
   Organization costs: $6,700
   Calculations:
legal fees	$5,000
other fees	500
logo development	1,200

   Note: the costs of the telephone and advertising are period expenses and will expensed in the year incurred.

4. Purchase of a company for cash

Land	500,000	
Farm Equipment	100,000	
Process Equipment	100,000	
Building	80,000	
Office Equipment	20,000	
Goodwill	200,000	
Cash		1,000,000

5. Purchase of a company in installments

Land	500,000	
Farm Equipment	100,000	
Process Equipment	100,000	
Building	80,000	
Office Equipment	20,000	
Goodwill	200,000	
Cash		50,000
Note Payable		950,000

6. Purchase of a company by note payable

Land	500,000	
Farm Equipment	100,000	
Process Equipment	100,000	
Building	80,000	
Office Equipment	20,000	
Discount on Note Payable	188,785	
Note Payable*		988,785

   *Calculation:
   PV of an ordinary annuity at 12% for 10 periods = 5.6502 factor
   $175,000 x 5.6502 = $988,785

Note Payable	175,000	
Interest Expense*	118,654	
Cash		175,000
Discount on Note Payable		118,654

   *Calculation:
   988,785 x .12 = $118,654

7. Capital lease

Leased Assets	800,000	
Lease Obligations		800,000

8. Acquisition of land for stock

a)	Land	470,000	
	Common Stock		100,000
	Paid-In Capital		370,000
b)	Land	450,000	
	Common Stock		100,000
	Paid-In Capital		350,000

9. Donation of land and building

Land	500,000	
Stadium	2,500,000	
Gain from Donated Assets		3,000,000

10. Goodwill

Goodwill = $900,000
[asking price less total appraised value]
[$2,500,000 - 1,600,000 = $900,000]

11. Discovery of oil reserves

This problem highlights the issue of the validity and decision usefulness of historical cost data for certain noncurrent operating assets. In the case of Padlock Ranch's grazing land, the historical cost is significantly below the current market value of the land, primarily due to the discovery of oil under the land. According to current U.S. GAAP, however, the increase in market value cannot be recognized on Padlock's books until a specific transaction occurs, most likely the sale of the land.

12. Acquisition and post-acquisition costs

There are three specific postacquisition costs to consider in this case: (1) $1,400,000 to blanket the contaminated soil; (2) $40,000 to temporarily relocate the present tenants; and (3) $82,000 to remove asbestos. Each of the costs must be incurred to proceed with construction of the golf course and clubhouse, so each cost is unavoidable, and therefore contributes to the long-term economic benefit of the asset. Accordingly, each cost will be capitalized. The cost incurred to blanket the contaminated soil will be added to the construction cost of the golf course. Though there may be some justification to expensing the cost of tenant relocation (on the theory that the cost does not extend the life of the building or enhance its productivity), the requirement to relocate the tenants was probably known at the time the sale was negotiated, and is, thus, a cost of purchasing the building and getting it ready for service. As such, the cost is capitalized. Finally, the cost of asbestos removal can also be capitalized in that it is a cost necessary to put the asset into service, albeit in its modified form.

CHAPTER 13

INVESTMENTS IN NONCURRENT OPERATING ASSETS—UTILIZATION AND RETIREMENT

KEY POINTS

I. Depreciation
   A. Definitions
      1. *Depreciation*: systematic and rational allocation of tangible asset cost over the periods benefited by the use of the asset.
      2. *Depletion*: cost allocation process relating to mineral and other natural resources.
      3. *Amortization*: cost allocation process relating to intangible assets.
      4. Depreciation (amortization and depletion) is calculated to match revenues and expense.
   B. Four factors must be considered to calculate depreciation:
      1. Asset cost
      2. Residual or salvage value of asset
      3. Useful life of the asset
      4. Pattern of use of the asset
   C. Asset cost
      1. Depreciable cost is the original acquisition cost less any residual or salvage value (if residual value is material).
      2. Review Chapter 12 if you are uncertain about the costs included in original acquisition cost.
   D. Residual or salvage value
      1. Definition: estimate of the amount that can be realized upon retirement of the asset.
      2. If material, the residual value is subtracted from the original acquisition cost of the asset to determine depreciable base.
      3. If not material, ignore residual value in the depreciation calculation.
      4. **Point:** Keep in mind that since depreciation is an *estimate*, it's ok to ignore nonmaterial salvage values.
   E. Useful life
      1. Definition: How long the company plans to use the asset. "How long" may be a function of *time, usage, or both*.
      2. Determination of useful life is determined by *physical factors* (such as wear and tear, deterioration and decay, and damage or destruction) and *functional factors* (such as obsolescence and inadequacy).
   F. Pattern of use
      1. To match revenues and expenses, depreciation expense should be estimated based upon the asset's pattern of use, implying that assets which are used more extensively in the early years of service should be depreciated proportionately more during those years than other years.
   G. Recording periodic depreciation
      1. Two alternate journal entries:
         a. Depreciation Expense   XXX
              Accumulated Depreciation   XXX
            (This entry charges depreciation as a period cost. Accumulated depreciation is a contra asset account, the balance of which is presented on the balance sheet concurrently with the related asset account.)
         b. Inventory   XXX
              Accumulated Depreciation   XXX
            (This entry allocates depreciation to the cost of producing inventory, thereby deferring the expense until the inventory is sold. Accumulated depreciation is the same as in the prior example.)
   H. Methods of depreciation
      1. Method selected must be systematic and rational. Alternative assumptions regarding the pattern of use of assets leads to alternative types of depreciation methods including:
         a. Time factor methods
            1) Straight-line

Chapter 13

   2) Accelerated methods (decreasing charge methods):
      a) Declining-balance methods
      b) Sum-of-the-years'-digits
  b. Use-factor methods
      1) Service-hours depreciation
      2) Productive-output (units of production)
  c. Group rate and composite rate methods
      1) Group depreciation
      2) Composite depreciation

We will review the calculation of depreciation using each method using an example similar to that in the text (see page 731). We will also use the same symbols as those in the text, namely:

C = Asset cost
R = Estimated residual value
n = Estimated life in years, hours of service or units of output
r = Depreciation rate per period, hour of service, or unit of output
D = Periodic depreciation charge
BV = Asset book value (cost less accumulated depreciation)

Example Data
Brandywick Farms purchased a new tractor on January 2, 1995 at a cost of $75,000, with an estimated salvage value of $10,000. Average life = 5 years, or 10,000 hours. C = $75,000 R = $10,000 Depreciable cost: $75,000 - $10,000 = $65,000

DEPRECIATION METHODS ILLUSTRATED	
Time-Factor Methods	
Straight-line	D = (C – R)/ n ($75,000 - $10,000) /5 = $13,000 per year
Sum-of-the-Years'-Digits (SYD)	D = (FACTOR) x (C – R) FACTOR = denominator = [(n + 1) /2] x n; numerator changes annually and corresponds to the asset life years' digits in reverse order. Year 1 D = (75,000 – 10,000) X 5/15 = $21,667 (rounded) Year 2 D = (75,000 – 10,000) X 4/15 = $17,333 Year 3 D = (75,000 – 10,000) X 3/15 = $13,000 Year 4 D = (75,000 – 10,000) X 2/15 = $8,667 Year 5 D = (75,000 – 10,000) X 1/15 = $4,333 Note: SYD depreciates the asset fully over its estimated useful life, down to its salvage value.
Double-Declining-Balance (DDB)	D = (Straight-line rate x 2.0) x BV See text page 733 for straight-line and declining balance rates Note: depreciation charge changes from year to year using this method: Year 1 D = (.20 x 2.0) x $75,000 = $30,000 Year 2 D = (.20 x 2.0) x (75,000 - 30,000) = 18,000 Year 3 D = (.20 x 2.0) x (45,000 - 18,000) = 10,800* * Most companies will switch to straight-line at this point because the annual depreciation charge using straight-line ($13,000) exceeds DDB at this time. Year 4 D = (.20 x 2.0) x (45,000-18,000-10,800) = $6,480** ** If the company incurs a depreciation expense of $6,480 during year 4, the book value of the asset will be $9,720, which is less than salvage and thus, not reasonable. Accordingly, the company (assuming it did NOT switch to straight-line during year 3) would incur depreciation expense of $6,200 during year 4.

150% Declining Balance	D = (Straight-line rate x 1.5) x BV Calculation is the same as for DDB, but with a smaller factor. **Thinking question:** will the company depreciate the asset to salvage prior to the end of its estimated useful life using 150% DB?

Use-Factor Methods	
Service-Hours Method	r (per hour) = (C – R)/ n r = ($75,000 - 10,000)/10,000 = $6.50 per hour of use
Productive Output	r (per unit) = (C – R)/n Note: we won't calculate depreciation for the tractor using productive output because the method doesn't make sense in this case as the tractor doesn't "produce" anything directly.

Group or Composite Methods (also known as Unit Depreciation)
Treat a collection of similar assets (such as furniture and fixtures) as single group. Based upon average useful life of the assets in the group, calculate depreciation expense for the entire group in one calculation.
Same depreciation rate is applied to all assets in the group that are still in service.
Generally a straight-line method is used.
When an asset in the group is retired, no gain or loss is recorded; the asset account is credited for the cost of the asset, and the accumulated depreciation account is debited for the difference between cost and any proceeds from the retirement (i.e., salvage).

II. Amortization of Intangible Assets
  A. APB Opinion No. 17 (1970) requires that all intangible assets be amortized over their estimated useful lives, not to exceed 40 years.
  B. Generally the straight-line method is used.

III. Depletion of Natural Resources
  A. The mining or removal of "wasting assets," such as oil, gas, timber, coal, copper, gold, silver, and iron, deplete the land of its ability to generate revenue.
    1. Accordingly, land used for these purposes is "depleted," and the expense is charged periodically to the income statement.
  B. In addition to acquisition costs, certain development costs, such as drilling, mining, and site road construction, are capitalized and depleted during production.
  C. Generally, a units of production method is used.
    1. Example:
    Facts: Land containing mineral deposits is purchased for $4,000,000. Additional exploration and development costs of $1,000,000 are incurred. Estimated cost to restore land after production is $600,000. After restoration, land can be sold for $800,000. Thus, the net salvage value is $200,000 [$800,000 - $600,000]. Total mineral deposits are estimated to be 2,000,000 tons. In the first year of production, 50,000 tons were mined, of which 30,000 tons were sold.
    Calculation:
      a. Depletion charge per ton:
      [($4,000,000 + 1,000,000) - $200,000]/2,000,000 = $2.40 per ton
      b. Depletion charge for first year:
      50,000 tons x $2.40 per ton = $120,000
      c. Record depletion:
      Because only 30,000 of the 50,000 tons mined were sold, depletion expense on the income statement will relate only to those tons sold. The remainder of depletion will be charged to mineral inventory, as follows:

Depletion Expense	72,000	
Inventory	48,000	
Accumulated Depletion		120,000

IV. Changes in Estimates of Cost Allocation Variables
    A. Change in estimated life
        1. The remaining depreciable cost is depreciated over the new estimated useful life.
    B. Change in estimated units of production
        1. The remaining depreciable cost is depreciated at the new rate per unit times the actual units produced during the period.
    C. Generally, B and C arise because of betterments. (Do you recall betterments from Chapter 12?)
        1. In these cases, the remaining depreciable cost of the asset changes also, so the company is now depreciating a new cost amount over a new estimated useful life.

**Example with change in estimated life
and change in estimated units of production**
(Use the earlier data regarding the tractor purchase)

At the end of year 3, the tractor is overhauled at a cost of $4,000. The overhaul will enhance the tractor's productivity, and will increase the tractor's estimated life by two years (so the tractor is expected to be productive four more years after the overhaul), and will increase hours of production by 3,000 hours.

Straight-line depreciation
At the end of year 3, the BV of the tractor is $36,000.
[Calculation: 3 years of depreciation at $13,000 per year subtracted from the asset's cost of $75,000]
The betterment of $4,000 will be added to the asset account, and now the BV of the tractor is $40,000.
The tractor will have a remaining useful life of 4 years.
Assuming no change in salvage value:
D = (C – R)/n
D = ([$75,000 – $39,000 + $4,000] – $10,000)/4
D = $7,500 per year

Double-Declining-Balance
At the end of year 3, the BV of the tractor is $16,200.
[Calculations: see example on page 220.]
The betterment of $4,000 will be added to the asset account, and now the BV of the tractor is $20,200.
The tractor will have a remaining useful life of 4 years, so the straight-line rate is 25%. The DDB rate will be 50%.
D (year 4) = .50 X $20,200 = $10,100
D (year 5) = .50 X $20,200 - $10,100 = $5,050, but incurring depreciation expense this great would take BV below salvage, so **D (year 4)** = $100.

Service Hours
Assume the tractor incurred 5,800 service hours during years 1-3. Thus, BV at the end of year 3 = Cost - Accumulated Depreciation, or $75,000 - $37,700 = $37,300.
The betterment would be added to the asset cost, and now BV of the tractor is $41,300.
Total remaining estimated hours = 3,000 + (10,000 - 5,800) = 7,200.
r (per hour) = (C – R)/n = (37,700 – 10,000)/7,200 = $3.85 per hour

---

V. Impairment
    A. Definition: reduction in the expected cash flow to be generated by a long-term asset sufficient to warrant reducing the carrying value of the asset.
    B. Authoritative literature regarding impaired assets: FASB Statement No. 121, issued during 1995.
    C. Consider four questions when assessing impairment:
        1. When should an asset be reviewed for possible impairment?
        2. When is an asset impaired?

3. How should an impairment loss be measured?
4. What information should be disclosed about an impairment?
- D. When should assets be reviewed for possible impairment?
  1. Whenever there has been a material change in the way the asset is used or in the general business environment.
- E. When is an asset impaired?
  1. *Undiscounted* sum of future cash flows are less than current book value of the asset.
  2. Add goodwill from acquisition of asset to book value of asset when computing impairment.
  3. Note: use of *undiscounted* cash flows ignores the time value of money, suggesting that only in very extreme cases will an asset be impaired under the provisions of FASB Statement No. 121.
- F. How should an impairment loss be measured?
  1. Difference between book value and fair value, which is present value of estimated future cash flows from asset.
  2. When impairment is indicated, first reduce goodwill, then reduce carrying value of asset.
- G. What information should be disclosed about an impairment?
  1. Description of impaired asset, explanation of impairment, measurement assumptions, and business segments affected.

VI. Asset Retirements
- A. Assets retired by sale
  1. First, record depreciation up to the date of sale (depending upon the company's policy, depreciation in the year of sale may be allocated at 1/2 the annual rate, or may be calculated to the nearest whole month or may be foregone altogether).
  2. Balances relating to the asset sold in the asset account and balance in the accumulated depreciation account will be taken to zero.
  3. If the sale involves cash, a **gain** or **loss** will be recognized as the difference between the amount of cash received and the BV of the asset sold.
- B. Assets retired by exchange for other nonmonetary assets
  1. First, record depreciation up to the date of the exchange.
  2. The balances in the asset and accumulated depreciation accounts relating to the asset given up will be taken to zero.
  3. Generally, the new asset will be recorded at its fair market value.
  4. Thus, a gain or loss may occur.
- C. Assets retired by exchange of similar assets
  1. Similar assets, cash given, no cash received, companies involved are in the same line of business.
     a. Exchange does not directly make the company better off (i.e., the transaction is not an earnings transaction).
     b. Cash given up is less than 25% of the market value of the asset received.
     c. No gain results from this transaction.
     d. Loss can result if the book value of the asset given exceeds the market value of the asset received.
     e. Asset received assumes the book value of the asset(s) surrendered.
  2. Similar assets, cash received
     a. This transaction actually makes the company better off economically because it has cash (a liquid asset).
     b. So, gain *may* be recognized to the extent of the cash received.
     c. Computation of recognized gain:
        Recognized gain = [cash received / (cash received + market value of asset acquired)] x total indicated gain.
  3. Exchange of assets can be quite complicated; review Exhibit 13-4 on page 750 in text.

EXPANDED MATERIAL KEY POINTS

VII. Depreciation for Partial Periods
   A. Often companies compute depreciation by month or some other period less than one year to recognize that not all asset acquisitions and dispositions occur on the first day of the fiscal year.
   B. The level of detail is more a planning tool than a measure of precision because depreciation is an estimate anyway.

VIII. Income Tax Depreciation
   A. Economic Recovery Tax Act (ERTA) of 1981 introduced a special form of accelerated depreciation, Accelerated Cost Recovery System (ACRS).
      1. ACRS was modified in the Tax Reform Act of 1986 to become the Modified Accelerated Cost Recovery System (MACRS).
   B. Note: term is *cost recovery* as opposed to depreciation, indicating that the system is not based strictly on asset life or usage.
   C. Though modified with subsequent tax law changes, MACRS still tends to lead to a more rapid write-off of assets than conventional financial reporting methods of depreciation.
   D. Firms can elect MACRS for tax purposes and a different method for financial reporting purposes.
   E. MACRS requires use of the *half-year convention*, which means that one-half year's depreciation will be taken in both the year of acquisition and the year of disposition, regardless of the actual dates of acquisition or disposition within the year.

TEST YOUR UNDERSTANDING

Fill-in-the-Blanks

Required: Fill in the blanks to complete the following sentences.

1. _____ is the process of allocating the cost of tangible long-term assets to periodic expense.

2. _____ is the process of allocating the cost of mineral and other natural resource assets to periodic expense.

3. _____ is the process of allocating the cost of intangible assets to periodic expense.

4. Historical cost less accumulated depreciation is _____ _____.

5. The _____ (_____) _____ is the estimate of the value for which an asset can be sold at the end of its productive life.

6. The length of time over which an asset is forecasted to provide economic benefit is its _____ _____.

7. Three time-factor methods of computing depreciation are used in the U.S.; they are _____-_____, _____-_____-_____ _____, and _____-_____.

8. Two use-factor methods are commonly used in the U.S.; they are _____-_____, and _____-_____.

9. The reduction in the expected cash flow of an asset sufficient to warrant reducing the carrying value of the asset is an _____.

10. The amount by which the proceeds from disposing of an asset exceed the asset's book value is the _____. If the proceeds from the sale of an asset are less than the book value of the asset at the time of the sale, a _____ results.

11. Assets that differ in their physical nature and use are _____ _____.

12. Assets that are the same in their physical nature and use are _____ _____.

13. The excess of the market value over the book value of an asset given up in an exchange of assets is the _____ _____.

14. The excess of the book value over the market value of an asset given up in an exchange of assets is the _____ _____.

15. A gain for which accounting recognition is delayed until future periods is a _____ _____.

Expanded material items:

16. The adaptation of the accelerated depreciation method introduced in the 1981 tax law is the _____ _____ _____ _____ (_____).

17. The modification to the cost recovery system referenced in #16, which was introduced in Tax Reform Act of 1986 is the _____ _____ _____ _____ _____ (_____).

Multiple Choice

Required: Circle the best answer from those given.

1. In which of the following situations is the declining-balance method of depreciation most appropriate?
    A. The asset's potential usefulness declines with usage.
    B. The asset's potential usefulness declines with the passage of time.
    C. The asset is subject to rapid obsolescence.
    D. The asset's potential usefulness is not affected by either the passage of time or usage.

2. In which of the following situations is the straight-line method of depreciation most appropriate?
    A. The asset's potential usefulness declines with usage.
    B. The asset's potential usefulness declines with the passage of time.
    C. The asset is subject to rapid obsolescence.
    D. The asset's potential usefulness is not affected by either the passage of time or usage.

3. In which of the following situations is the service-hours (or units of production) method of depreciation most appropriate?
    A. The asset's potential usefulness declines with usage.
    B. The asset's potential usefulness declines with the passage of time.
    C. The asset is subject to rapid obsolescence.
    D. The asset's potential usefulness is not affected by either the passage of time or usage.

4. Which depreciation method must be used so that at the end of an asset's estimated useful life, the net book value of the asset will equal the estimated salvage value of the asset?
    A. Straight-line
    B. Service-hours
    C. Sum-of-the-years'-digits
    D. All of the above

5. The composite or group methods of depreciation would be appropriate when:
   A. calculating depreciation on individuals assets is tedious.
   B. a collection of similar assets is acquired and used concurrently and without particular distinction between individual assets within the collection.
   C. the company owns many similar assets.
   D. the composite or group methods are never appropriate.

6. On January 1, 1995, XYZ Company purchased an asset with a salvage value of 10% of its original cost and an estimated useful life of 6 years. The asset was sold on December 31, 1997 at 50% of its original acquisition cost. A loss resulted and was recorded on the transaction. Which depreciation method was used?
   A. MACRS
   B. Double-declining-balance
   C. Straight-line
   D. Sum-of-the-years'-digits

7. An asset was purchased on January 1, 1995 for $500,000 with an estimated salvage value of $50,000 and an estimated useful life of 10 years. If the asset is depreciated using the double-declining-balance method, the net book value of the asset at the end of year 3 will be:
   A. $256,000.
   B. $320,000.
   C. $206,000.
   D. $230,400.

8. An asset was purchased for $500,000 with an estimated salvage value of $50,000. The asset had an estimated useful life of 10 years or 20,000 (2,000 per year) hours. Which method of depreciation will result in the largest net book value at the end of year 3, assuming production of the asset is constant over the three year period?
   A. Sum-of-the-years'-digits
   B. Service hours (units of production)
   C. Double-declining-balance
   D. MACRS

9. XYZ purchased an asset on January 1, 1995 for $800,000 with an estimated salvage value of $80,000 and an estimated useful life of 10 years, or 20,000 hours. The asset was sold for cash of $400,000 on December 31, 1997 for a loss of $9,600. What method of depreciation was used for this asset?
   A. Sum-of-the-years'-digits
   B. Straight-line
   C. Units of production
   D. Double-declining-balance

10. XYZ purchased an asset on January 1, 1995 for $800,000 with an estimated salvage value of $80,000 and an estimated useful life of 10 years, or 20,000 hours. The asset was depreciated using the straight-line method. The asset was sold for cash on December 31, 1997 for a loss of $9,600. How much cash was received?
    A. $9,600
    B. $720,000
    C. $400,000
    D. $524,000

11. A method which does not directly consider salvage value in calculating depreciation is:
    A. straight-line.
    B. sum-of-the-years'-digits.
    C. service-hours (units of production).
    D. double-declining-balance.

12. What is generally the maximum number of years over which goodwill can be amortized?
    A. Forty years
    B. Seventeen years
    C. Fifty years
    D. The average expected useful life of the tangible assets acquired in the transaction

13. Which method of amortization is generally recommended for intangible assets?
    A. Declining-balance
    B. Group or composite
    C. Straight-line
    D. MACRS

14. During 1995, XIX Company developed a new product at a cost of $500,000. The product was patented during 1996. Costs associated with receiving the patent were $300 and were expensed when incurred. The patent has a legal life of 17 years, but the estimated useful economic life is 5 years. During January, 1997, the company spent $56,000 defending the patent. Amortization expense for 1997 should be:
    A. $111,260.
    B. $11,200.
    C. $14,000.
    D. $14,060.

15. The sale of a noncurrent asset results in a gain when:
    A. proceeds received from the sale exceed the net book value of the asset sold.
    B. proceeds received from the sale exceed the fair market value of the asset sold.
    C. proceeds received from the sale are less than the book value of the asset sold.
    D. proceeds are received from the sale of the asset.

16. Starline Manufacturing traded an old machine (original acquisition cost of $120,000, 60% depreciated) for a new machine. The machines do not perform the same function. As part of the transaction, Starline paid $30,000 in cash. The new machine had a list price of $160,000. At what amount should the new machine be recorded on Starline's books?
    A. $68,000
    B. $160,000
    C. $120,000
    D. $150,000

17. Starfire exchanged an old machine (book value of $190,000, and a fair market value of $120,000) and $40,000 cash for a new similar machine. The new machine has a list price of $180,000. At what amount should the new machine be recorded in Starfire's books?
    A. $190,000
    B. $120,000
    C. $180,000
    D. $160,000

18. StarWind did business in the country of Klingon. As of December 31, 1994 StarWind's assets located in Klingon had net book value of $200,000. The assets were subject to $20,000 of annual depreciation. On June 30, 1995, the government of Klingon expropriated the assets of StarWind and compensated StarWind $100,000 for the expropriation. What amount of gain or loss should StarWind recognize on its 1995 income statement (ignore income taxes)?
    A. $90,000 loss
    B. $100,000 gain
    C. $100,000 loss
    D. No gain or loss

19. Eagle Farms exchanged a tractor for a computer system to be used as a long-term asset. The following information relates to this exchange which took place during 1997:

Book value of tractor	$30,000
Fair value of tractor	45,000
Fair value of computer system	43,000
Cash paid by Eagle Farms	5,000

    During 1997, what amount of gain should Eagle Farms recognize on the exchange?
    A. $0
    B. $ 8,000
    C. $10,000
    D. $13,000 (AICPA adapted)

20. On March 1, 1997, Partners Company traded in an old machine with a book value of $16,800 and paid cash difference of $6,000 for a new machine having a total cash price of $20,500. On March 31, 1997, what amount of loss would Partners recognize on this exchange?
    A. $0
    B. $2,300
    C. $3,700
    D. $6,000 (AICPA adapted)

21. Mart and Bart exchanged nonmonetary assets. The exchange did not culminate an earning process for either Mart or Bart. Mart paid cash to Bart in conjunction with the exchange. To the extent that the amount of cash exceeds a proportionate share of the carrying value of the asset surrendered, a realized gain on the exchange should be recognized by:

	Mart	Bart
A.	Yes	Yes
B.	Yes	No
C.	No	Yes
D.	No	No

    (AICPA adapted)

22. A depreciable asset has an estimated 15% salvage value. At the end of its estimated useful life, the accumulated depreciation would equal the original acquisition cost of the asset under which of the following depreciation methods?

	Straight-line	Productive output
A.	Yes	No
B.	Yes	Yes
C.	No	Yes
D.	No	No

    (AICPA adapted)

Exercises and Problems

1. Depreciation methods
   PC Construction purchased a dump truck on July 1, 1995:
   Cost = $90,000
   Residual Value = $8,000
   Estimated Useful Life = 8 years
   Estimated Service Hours = 18,000
   1995 activity: 1,100 hours
   1996 activity: 2,300 hours
   1997 activity: 2,400 hours

Required: Compute depreciation expense and net book value for 1995, 1996, and 1997 under each of the following methods:
1) straight-line
2) double-declining-balance
3) service-hours

2. Impaired assets and subsequent retirement

   In 1990, Dayton's Thoroughbreds, a professional Thoroughbred horse breeding, training, and racing company, purchased Lady Gillian, a four-year-old mare for $65,000. Because of her conformation and breeding, Dayton's used Lady Gillian as a brood mare (a horse that is used for breeding purposes rather than for show or racing). Dayton's estimated that Lady Gillian would serve as a brood mare until she was 20, at which time she would be donated to charity or to a 4-H horse club. Between 1990 and 1995, Lady Gillian produced five champion foals (baby horses), each of whom sold as yearlings for at least $25,000. Lady Gillian did not foal in 1996. Although unexpected, Dayton's was not too concerned about Lady Gillian in 1996. However, when she failed to produce a foal in 1997, Dayton's became concerned because as a brood mare, Lady Gillian's job was to foal every couple of years. Further, she produced champion foals, so Dayton's was anxious to successfully breed her for several more years. When Lady Gillian failed to foal in 1997, Dayton's became concerned that Lady Gillian's foaling days were over—several years prior to expectations.

   Required: a. Discuss the concept of impairment as it relates to Lady Gillian (ignore any special tax rules relating to livestock and racehorses). Consider specifically (1) is Lady Gillian an impaired asset? Why? (2) When should Dayton's Thoroughbreds perform an impairment analysis on Lady Gillian? (3) If Lady Gillian is an impaired asset, at what point did the asset become impaired? Into which period should the write-down for impairment occur? (4) To what amount should the mare be written down?

   b. If Dayton's concludes that Lady Gillian will not foal again (i.e., the expected useful life of the asset is over), and if Dayton's donates the horse to a 4-H club (charity), will Dayton's recognize a loss on its income statement? If so, how much?

3. Amortization of goodwill

   In the spring of 1997, Folton Development and Management Company purchased an aging apartment complex for $4,200,000. An independent appraisal of all the assets acquired in the transaction rendered the fair market value of the individual assets at $3,600,000. Folton plans to renovate the apartment complex at an estimated cost of $2,000,000. It will then manage the complex. Folton estimates that after the renovation the estimated useful life of the complex is about 15 years.

   Required: What is the amount of amortization that should be recorded annually on the goodwill acquired in the purchase of the apartment complex?

4. Depletion

   Jackson Mountain Mining Corporation purchased a mineral mine for $8,400,000 with removable ore estimated by geological surveys at 6,570,000 tons. The property has an estimated value of $840,000 after the ore has been mined. Jackson incurred $4,824,000 in development costs preparing the property for mining. During the first year of mining, 640,000 tons of ore were mined, and 580,000 tons were sold.

   Required: Calculate the amount of depletion charged to cost of goods sold during the first year of operation.

5. Exchanges of Assets

   Winkin exchanged an asset costing $500,000 with accumulated depreciation of $380,000 for an asset with Blinkin. Blinkin paid $20,000 cash in addition to surrendering its machine (which cost $300,000 and had accumulated depreciation of $168,000). The Blinkin machine has a fair value of $160,000.

Required: a. Write the journal entries on both companies' books assuming the assets exchanged are similar and the companies are in the same line of business.
b. Write the journal entries on both companies' books assuming the assets are dissimilar.

SOLUTIONS TO TEST YOUR UNDERSTANDING

Fill-in-the-Blanks

1. Depreciation
2. Depletion
3. Amortization
4. book value
5. residual (salvage) value
6. useful life
7. straight-line; sum-of-the-years' digits; declining-balance
8. service-hours; productive-output (units of production)
9. impairment
10. gain; loss
11. dissimilar assets
12. similar assets
13. indicated gain
14. indicated loss
15. deferred gain
16. accelerated cost recovery system (ACRS)
17. modified accelerated cost recovery system (MACRS)

Multiple Choice

1. B	7. A	13. C	19. B
2. D	8. B	14. C	20. B
3. A	9. D	15. A	21. C
4. D	10. D	16. B	22. D
5. B	11. D	17. D	
6. C	12. A	18. A	

Exercises and Problems

1. Depreciation methods
   1) Straight-line
      D = (C - R)/n
      $10,250 = (90,000 - 8,000)/ 8
      1994 depreciation $5,125 (half year); net book value $84,875
      1995 depreciation $10,250; net book value $74,625
      1996 depreciation $10,250; net book value $64,375

   2) Double-declining-balance
      D = BV x (straight-line rate x 2)
      1994: [$90,000 x (.25)] x .50 = $11,250; net book value $78,750
      1995: $78,750 x .25 = 19,688; net book value $59,062
      1996: $59,062 x .25 = 14,766; net book value $44,296

3) Units of production (service-hours)
   r (per hour) = (C - R)/n (total hours)
   r = (90,000 - 8,000)/18,000 = $4.56 per hour
   1994: $4.56 x 1100 hours = $5,016; net book value $84,984
   1995: $4.56 x 2300 hours = $10,488; net book value $74,496
   1996: $4.56 x 2400 hours = $10,944; net book value $63,552

2. Impaired assets and subsequent retirement
   Note: keep in mind that special tax and accounting rules exist for livestock and racehorses. Those special rules have been ignored in this problem, and the problem has been designed to illustrate two points (i.e., impairment and retirement) as opposed to proper accounting for racehorses.
   a. 1) Yes, it is quite likely that Lady Gillian could be considered an impaired asset. She is a brood mare, which means she is supposed to foal regularly. Since she has not been in foal for two years, she is not doing the job for which she was acquired, and thus, her value could be considered impaired.
   2) Dayton would need to undertake an impairment analysis as soon as it became apparent that the asset, Lady Gillian, was not performing. Though it is not unusual for brood mares to skip a year in foaling, and thus, the analysis may not have been needed in 1996, by 1997 it would be quite clear that the analysis should be undertaken.
   3) Assessing the point in time when the asset became impaired is one of the greater challenges in dealing with impaired assets. By the end of 1997, it is quite clear that Lady Gillian is impaired, but it's not at all clear in 1995 (it's not unusual for brood mares to not foal every year; in fact, some breeders prefer to let them rest a couple of years between foals). There is some doubt in 1996 as well. While we can assume that Dayton's tried to get Lady Gillian in foal during 1996, it's difficult to assess if Dayton's has enough evidence in 1996 to declare the asset impaired. So, most likely, Dayton's will record the impairment in 1997.
   4) Measurement of the impaired value is another challenge in dealing with impaired assets. In this case, we are not given any salvage value for the horse, such values could be determined rather easily. However, since it is quite unlikely that the horse would be sold for salvage at this point, it is more reasonable to have the horse appraised in her present condition. (In her present condition the horse could be appraised as a beginner horse [horse for beginning riders], a pleasure horse [riding horse], or a show horse.) The value of the asset would depend upon the appraisal, and it's likely that would be the value to which the horse would be written. The difference between the current net book value and the new appraised value would be the loss on impairment.
   b. It is very unlikely that the horse would be sold for salvage. It is also unlikely that Dayton's would want to keep the horse if she is no longer a brood mare. Therefore, the most likely plan is that Dayton's would donate the horse to a charity or to a 4-H horse club.

3. Amortization of goodwill
   $40,000
   Calculation:

Purchase price of complex:	$4,200,000
Fair value of individual assets	3,600,000
Goodwill purchased	$ 600,000

   Estimated useful life of tangible asset purchased: 15 years
   Amortization = $600,000/15 years or $40,000 per year
   Note: in this case, goodwill could be amortized over a shorter period of time on the theory that the renovation of the complex might change the nature of the complex and hence, change the nature of the goodwill associated with it as well.

Chapter 13

4. Depletion
   $1,090,400
   Calculation:
Cost of land	$ 8,400,000
Less: Salvage	840,000
Add: Development costs	4,824,000
Depletion basis	$12,384,000

   Depletion per unit = Depletion basis / estimated units of production
   $1.88 per ton = $12,384,000/6,570,000 tons

   Depletion charged to cost of goods sold = units sold x depletion per unit
   $1,090,400 = 580,000 tons x $1.88 per ton

5. Exchange of assets
   a. Blinkin:
Asset	152,000	
Accumulated Depreciation	168,000	
Asset		300,000
Cash		20,000

   Winkin:
Asset	106,667	
Accumulated Depreciation	380,000	
Cash	20,000	
Asset		500,000
Gain on Exchange		6,667 *

   * [20,000/ (20,000 + 160,000)] x (180,000 – 120,000) = $6,667

   b. Blinkin:
Asset	160,000	
Accumulated Depreciation	168,000	
Asset		300,000
Cash		20,000
Gain on Exchange		8,000

   Winkin:
Asset	160,000	
Cash	20,000	
Accumulated Depreciation	380,000	
Asset		500,000
Gain on Exchange		60,000

CHAPTER 14

INVESTMENTS IN DEBT AND EQUITY SECURITIES

KEY POINTS

I. Why Companies Invest in Other Companies
   A. Ownership: equity securities
   B. Creditor: debt securities
   C. Variety of objectives:
      1. Earn return on excess cash
      2. Diversify products or services
      3. Control or significantly influence operations of investee
      4. Buy the competition
   C. Authoritative literature regarding investments in debt and equity securities of other companies
      1. FASB Statement No. 115 (1993), "Accounting for Certain Investments in Debt and Equity Securities"
      2. APB Opinion No. 18 (1971), "The Equity Method of Accounting for Investments in Common Stock"

II. Classification of Securities
   A. Debt securities: financial instruments issued by a company with the following characteristics:
      1. Maturity value represents amount to be paid to investor at maturity date
      2. Interest (either fixed or variable rate, either explicitly or implicitly stated)
      3. Specified maturity or due date
   B. Equity securities: financial instruments representing ownership interest in the company
   C. Debt and equity securities investments can be classified into four categories:
      1. Held-to-maturity
      2. Available-for-sale
      3. Trading
      4. Equity method
   D. FASB Statement No. 115 establishes accounting and financial reporting guidelines for investments in equity securities with readily determinable fair market values and for all investments in debt securities.
   E. FASB Statement No. 115 does not apply to:
      1. Investments accounted for under the equity method
      2. Investments in consolidated subsidiaries
      3. Certain other special cases (such as not-for-profit entities and certain special industries).
   F. FASB Statement No. 115 requires classification of debt and equity securities at the time of purchase:
      1. Held-to-maturity
      2. Trading
      3. Available-for-sale
   G. Held-to-maturity securities
      1. To classify a security as "held-to-maturity" the purchaser must not only *intend* to hold the security until it matures, but also must demonstrate that it *can* hold the security that long.
      2. Securities can be considered as "held-to-maturity" if their sale occurs at or near maturity.
      3. This category includes only debt securities. **Thinking question:** Why? [Answer: equity securities do not mature, thus, the concept of holding until maturity makes no sense for equity investments.]
      4. In general, report at amortized cost (i.e., no marking to market).
   H. Available-for-sale securities
      1. Equity securities with readily determinable fair market values that are not trading securities and certain debt instruments that are neither held-to-maturity nor trading (i.e., this is the category for everything that doesn't fit somewhere else).
      2. Reported at fair market value, but unrealized gains and losses are reported in a separate section of the equity section of the balance sheet and NOT on the income statement.

234 **Chapter 14**

- I. Trading securities
    1. Includes debt securities that are not "held-to-maturity," and certain equity securities with readily determinable market values.
    2. These securities are bought and sold frequently.
    3. Securities are revalued at each balance sheet date and are reported at fair market value, with unrealized gains and losses reported on the income statement.
- J. Equity method securities
    1. Equity securities purchased with the intent to control or significantly influence the operations of the investee.
    2. Typically, for significant influence to exist, the investor must hold a large block of voting stock, usually between 20 and 50 percent.
    3. Not reported at fair value on balance sheet; rather investment account (an asset) increases or decreases as the net assets of the investee increase or decrease.
- K. Why the different categories?
    1. Different management objectives imply different economic consequences of investment, thus necessitating different accounting treatments.

III. Purchase of Securities
- A. Record at cost, including price, brokers' fees, taxes, and other acquisition costs.
- B. When debt securities are acquired between interest payment dates, the amount paid will also include interest accrued to date.
    1. Two different methods can be used:
        a. Asset approach
        b. Revenue approach
    2. Asset approach
        a. Treats the security and the right to the interest earned on it as two separate assets. So interest receivable is accrued at the time of purchase if purchase occurs between interest dates. (Remember the price of the debt security will include a component for the interest "accrued" to it at the point of sale.)
    3. Revenue approach
        a. Treats the purchase of the security and its related interest as one transaction and one asset.
    4. Be sure to classify investment as either held-to-maturity, trading, or available-for-sale.
- C. Purchase of equity securities
    1. Cost includes price, brokerage fees, taxes, and other acquisition fees.
    2. Even when part of the purchase price is deferred, the full cost should be recorded as "investment in stock," with liability for remaining amount yet to be paid.
    3. Classify as trading, available-for-sale, or equity method.

IV. Recognition of Revenue from Investments
- A. Recognition of revenue from debt securities (interest revenue)
    1. Debt classified as held-to-maturity
        a. Typically, record investment net of premium or discount, without special account for the amount of discount or premium.
        b. Amortize discount or premium, thus increasing or decreasing amount of interest revenue recognized (effective-interest method).
            1) Premium amortization decreases interest revenue recognized.
            2) Discount amortization increases interest revenue recognized.
    2. Debt classified as trading or available-for-sale
        a. Typically, ignore discount or premium at purchase date, and therefore, record interest revenue as the amount of cash received from interest payments.
- B. Recognition of revenue from equity securities
    1. Accounting for revenue from equity investments is a function of the level of influence the investor has in the company in which the investment is made.
    2. Three possibilities:
        a. Majority voting interest

b. Significant influence, but not majority voting interest
c. No significant influence
3. Majority voting interest
   a. Investor owns 50% or more the voting stock.
   b. Investor is the "parent" corporation.
   c. Investee corporation is the "subsidiary".
   d. FASB Statement No. 115 does not apply in this case.
   e. FASB Statement No. 94 applies and requires consolidation of subsidiary's activities into parent's books.
   f. Accounting nightmare—thankfully for the intermediate accounting student, this topic is covered in advanced accounting.
4. Significant influence, but not majority voting interest
   a. Generally, investor owns more than 20% but less than 50% of the voting stock of the investee (APB Opinion No. 18).
   b. Percentages are just guidelines, though.
   c. Important factor is economic influence.
   d. FASB Statement No. 115 does not apply in this case.
   e. APB Opinion No. 18 applies and requires use of the equity method to account for these investments.
5. No significant influence
   a. Less than 20%, in other words, not enough ownership to demand a seat on the board or force votes.
   b. FASB Statement No. 115 applies.
   c. Cost method applies, subject to periodic assessments of market value.
6. Recognize revenue with cost method—see FASB Statement No. 115
   a. Dividends
   b. Recognized when received
7. Recognize revenue with equity method
   a. Investment is initially recorded at cost (just like the cost method).
   b. Investment account is periodically adjusted to reflect proportional changes in underlying assets of the investee.
      1) Therefore, investor will increase investment account by its share of the net income of the investee.
      2) Therefore, investor will decrease investment account by the amount of dividends it receives from the investee.
   c. In other words, the investment account (a noncurrent asset) reflects all activity with respect to the equity investment in the investee.
8. Complexities under the equity method:
   a. When a company is purchased by another company, the purchase price usually differs from the book value of the assets of the acquired company, so an adjustment may have to be made to the carrying value of the net assets in the new entity. (Recall this idea from Chapter 11.)
   b. Same issue arises when a company purchases only a portion of investee's stock.
   c. Adjustment is necessary if purchase price exceeds investor's share of book value of the investee.
      1) Adjustment will NOT be made to asset values.
      2) Rather, adjustment will be made to investor's reported income to reflect:
         a) Depreciation adjustment (if difference is due to changes in operating assets' values).
         b) Goodwill amortization (for non-specific adjustments).
   d. Example: Net assets of Bee Corporation are $200,000. Aaa Corporation purchases 25% of the outstanding stock of Bee for $60,000. Market value of Bee's total stock would then be $240,000 or $60,000/.25. Therefore, purchase price is $40,000 greater than book value ($240,000 less $200,000). Let's assume we cannot allocate any of the difference to specific assets. In this case, then, the entire differential is goodwill. Aaa will amortize its share of the goodwill ($40,000 x .25 or $10,000) over 40 years as follows:
      Income from Bee   250
         Investment in Bee   250
         [calculation: $10,000/ 40 years]
   Note: this adjustment affects not only income recognized from the investment in Bee, but also the carrying value of the investment on Aaa's assets as well.

V. Accounting for the Change in Value of Securities
   A. Accounting for temporary change in value of securities is detailed in the following table. (Study it carefully.)

Classification of Securities	Types of Securities	Disclosed at	Reporting of Changes in Fair Value
Trading	Debt and equity	Fair market value	Income Statement & Balance Sheet
Available-for-Sale	Debt and equity	Fair market value	Stockholder's Equity
Held-to-Maturity	Debt only	Amortized Cost	Not recognized

   B. Accounting for permanent declines in value of securities
      1. Permanent declines in value must be recognized currently.
      2. Loss is recorded in current year income statement.
      3. Market adjustment account is not used.
         a. Rather, credit the investment account.
      4. Applies to all debt and equity securities held for investment, regardless of classification or accounting method.

VI. Sale of Securities
   A. Gain or loss on the transaction is equal to the difference between:
      1. Cash received and
      2. Carrying value (investment balance) of the security.
   B. Market adjustment account associated with the security sold will be adjusted at year-end.
   C. Note: difference between REALIZED and UNREALIZED gains and losses.
      1. Realized gains and losses occur when security is sold or transferred (i.e., transaction occurs).
      2. Unrealized gains and losses occur because market value changes, but investor still owns the security (i.e., no transaction).

VII. Transferring Securities Between Categories
   A. General guideline:
      1. If a company reclassifies a security, the security is accounted for at the fair value at the time of transfer (FASB Statement No. 115, paragraph 15).
         Thinking point: the treatment specified in FASB Statement No. 115 assumes the transfer is, in essence, a transaction.
         a. Since the security is maintained in the investment account (category) at historical cost, it must be removed from that account and reclassified to the new investment account (category) at fair value.
      2. Accounting for the change in value is accounted for differently depending upon the category being transferred to and the category transferred from.
   B. Accounting for transfers of securities between categories. (See FASB Statement No. 115, par. 15.)

Transferred	Treatment of the Change in Value
From "Trading"	Any unrealized change in value not previously recognized will be recognized in net income during the current period. Previously recognized changes in value are not to be reversed.
To "Trading"	Any unrealized change in value not previously recognized will be recognized in net income in the current period.
From "Held-to-Maturity" to "Available-for-Sale"	Recognize any unrealized change in value in a stockholders' equity account.
From "Available-for-Sale" to "Held-to-Maturity"	Any unrealized change in value recorded in a stockholders' equity account is to be amortized over the remaining life of the security using the effective-interest method.

C. What do the table above and Exhibit 14-11 (page 805 in your text) mean in terms of recognition and measurement?
   1. Transfers to or from trading category will likely impact the income statement.
   2. Transfers from "held-to-maturity" to "available-for-sale" will generally not affect the income statement.
   3. Transfers to "held-to-maturity" are REALLY complex! Why?
      a. Must amortize any unrealized change in value over the remaining life of the security while concurrently amortizing the held-to-maturity security to its eventual maturity value (i.e., amortization of the premium or discount).
      b. Can these be netted?
         1) Doing so would be easier.
         2) FASB Statement No. 115 is unclear on this point.

VII. Classification and Disclosure
   A. Cash Flow Statement
      1. Generally, buying and selling investment securities is reported as an investing activity.
      2. Trading securities are now (because of FASB Statement No. 115) reported as operating activities.
   B. Income Statement
      1. Unrealized changes in value of trading securities are reported in current income.
      2. Unrealized changes in value of securities reclassified to or from trading category are also reflected in current income.
   C. Balance Sheet
      1. Noncurrent assets reflect fair value of available-for-sale and trading securities.
      2. Noncurrent assets reflect equity investment in securities accounted for with the equity method.
      3. Noncurrent assets reflect the historical cost of held-to-maturity assets.
      4. Cumulative effect of unrealized changes in value are reflected in stockholders' equity.
   D. Footnotes
      1. Trading securities
         a. Change in net unrealized holding gain or loss that is included in the income statement.
      2. Available-for-sale securities
         a. Aggregate fair value, gross unrealized holding gains and loss, and amortized cost basis. If appropriate maturity information is required as well.
         b. Proceeds from sales, gross realized gains and losses from sales, cost basis for calculating realized gains and losses.
         c. Change in the net unrealized holding gains and losses during year.
      3. Held-to-maturity securities
         a. Aggregate fair value, gross unrealized holding gains and losses, amortized cost basis, and contractual maturities.
      4. Transfers of securities between categories
         a. Gross gains and losses included in earnings as a result of the transfer.
         b. Amount transferred, related realized or unrealized gain or loss, and reason for transfers.

EXPANDED MATERIAL KEY POINTS

IX. Changes in Classification Involving the Equity Method
   A. Changing from equity to cost is no problem.
      1. At the time of the change, the carrying value of the investment becomes the (cost) basis for the investment under the cost method.
   B. Changing from cost to equity is more complex.
      1. Retroactive adjustment required to reflect the amount of income that would have been reported had the investment been accounted for with the equity method all along.
      2. Adjustment is booked to the investment account and to Retained Earnings.

Chapter 14

X. Accounting for the Impairment of a Loan
   A. FASB addressed valuation issues concerning investments in loans receivable in FASB Statement No. 114 (1993).
   B. FASB Statement No. 114 requires loans receivable to be carried at cost unless impaired.
      1. Impairment is indicated if it is probable that the creditor will not be able to collect all amounts due according to the contractual terms of the loan agreement.
   C. Measuring impairment: present value of future cash flows discounted at the loan's effective interest rate. (Note: in measuring impairment for loans receivable discounted cash flows are used, whereas in measuring impairment for noncurrent operating assets, undiscounted cash flows are used.)
   D. Record impairment: create a valuation account (with a credit balance, a contra account to loans receivable) and debit estimated loss to bad debts expense.

TEST YOUR UNDERSTANDING

Fill-in-the-blanks

Required: Fill in the blanks to complete the following sentences.

1. An investment in _____ _____ reflects an ownership interest, while an investment in _____ _____ reflects a creditor relationship.

2. Financial instruments issued by a company with a specific maturity date, a specific maturity value, and specified interest payments are _____ _____.

3. Financial instruments that represent ownership in a company are _____ _____.

4. _____-_____-_____ _____ are debt securities purchased with the intent and ability to hold the securities until the maturity date.

5. Debt and equity securities that do not meet the criteria for either trading or held-to-maturity classification are classified as _____-_____-_____ _____.

6. Debt and equity securities that are purchased with the intent of selling them again in the very near future are _____ _____.

7. _____ _____ _____ are equity securities purchased with the intent of gaining significant influence over the operations of the investee.

8. For held-to-maturity securities, amortization of bond premium _____ the amount of interest revenue recognized while amortization of bond discount _____ the amount of interest revenue recognized.

9. When an investor purchases equity securities of another corporation with the intention of exercising significant influence over the investee, the investor accounts for the investment using the _____ _____. To have significant influence, the investor must generally control at least _____ percent of outstanding voting stock, but usually does not control more than _____ percent of the outstanding voting stock.

10. An investor is said to have significant influence if he/she can impact the _____, _____, and _____ decisions of the investee.

11. An investor is said to have _____ if he/she can decisively influence the _____, _____, and _____ decisions of the investee.

Name: _____ Chapter 14   239

12. The company which exercises control over the investee through majority ownership is the _____ company.

13. The company that is owned or controlled by another company is the _____ company.

14. Financial statements that reflect the combined activities of the parent and its subsidiaries are _____ _____ _____.

Multiple Choice

Required: Circle the best answer.

1. When the fair market value of an investment in debt securities exceeds the amortized cost, at what value should the following be reported at year-end?

	Held-to-Maturity Securities	Trading Securities	Available-for-Sale Securities	
A.	Fair market value	Cost	Cost	
B.	Cost	Fair market value	Fair market value	
C.	Cost	Fair market value	Cost	
D.	Fair market value	Cost	Fair market value	(AICPA adapted)

2. BBB Company purchased 5,000 shares of the common stock of CCC Corporation at $45 per share. Brokerage fees were $1,100. Transaction taxes and other fees totaled $250. BBB paid $50,000 down and all fees, and signed a note for the remainder. The note is due within 60 days. BBB classified the securities as trading. The journal entry to record the purchase of the stock on BBB's books would include a debit to the account, "Investment in Trading Securities—CCC" in the amount of:
    A. $225,000.
    B. $50,000.
    C. $52,350.
    D. $226,350.

3. Which of the following classification tables correctly tabulates the types of securities and their respective classifications under the provision of FASB Statement No. 115?

	Held-to-Maturity Securities	Trading Securities	Available-for-Sale Securities
A.	Debt or equity	Debt or equity	Debt or Equity
B.	Debt only	Debt only	Debt only
C.	Debt only	Debt or equity	Debt or equity
D.	Debt or equity	Equity only	Debt or equity

4. Where will unrealized gains and losses be reported?

	Held-to-Maturity Securities	Trading Securities	Available-for-sale Securities
A.	Not reported	BS & IS*	BS only
B.	Not reported	BS only	BS only
C.	BS only	BS & IS	BS only
D.	BS only	BS & IS	BS & IS

    *BS = balance sheet; IS = income statement

5. An investor uses the cost method to account for its investment in common stock. The investment is classified as a trading security. The investor's books are directly affected by:

	Cash Dividends from Investee	Net Income of Investee	Change in Market Price of Investee's Common Stock
A.	No	No	No
B.	Yes	Yes	Yes
C.	Yes	No	Yes
D.	Yes	No	No

6. An investor uses the equity method to account for its investment in common stock. The investor's books are directly affected by:

	Cash Dividends from Investee	Net Income of Investee	Change in Market Price of Investee's Common Stock
A.	No	No	No
B.	Yes	Yes	Yes
C.	Yes	No	Yes
D.	Yes	Yes	No

7. A review of the balance sheet and income statement for AAA Company as of December 31, 1994 reveals:

   Noncurrent Assets:
      Investments in available-for-sale securities (fair value) $101,450
   Stockholders' Equity:
      Net unrealized gain/loss related to available-for-sale securities   (14,900)

   What is the historical cost of the securities?
   A. $116,350
   B. $86,550
   C. $101,450
   D. $14,900

8. Cash flows from transactions involving investments in securities will be reported on the cash flow statement in which section?

	Trading Securities	Available-for-Sale Securities	Held-to-Maturity Securities
A.	Investing	Investing	Investing
B.	Operating	Investing	Investing
C.	Operating	Operating	Investing
D.	Operating	Operating	Operating

9. New World Dealers entered into the following transactions during 1998:
   - Purchased 40% of the outstanding stock of EEE for $1,000,000 on January 1. New World purchased the stock in EEE to secure a distribution channel for its products. New World plans to maintain the investment indefinitely, but does not plan to significantly increase its investment in EEE. During 1998, EEE earned $200,000. EEE paid $60,000 in dividends on September 30 to shareholders of record on July 15.
   - Purchased 2,000 shares of FFF Company for $100,000. The purchase represents less than 1% of the outstanding stock of FFF Company. New World purchased the stock as an investment of its idle cash. Although it does not plan to sell the stock anytime soon, New World does not intend to increase its ownership in FFF.
   - Purchased $50,000 worth of bonds in GGG Company at 104. New World purchased the bonds as an investment of idle cash. New World plans to sell the bonds when market conditions are favorable.

Assuming the investments discussed represent the total of New World's investment activity, and assuming no accruals for interest, no market value adjustments, and no impairments of assets, what amounts would be reported on New World's year end balance sheet?

	Trading	Held-to-Maturity	Available-for-Sale	Equity Method
A.	$100,000	$50,000	$1,000,000	-0-
B.	$50,000	$1,000,000	$100,000	-0-
C.	$52,000	-0-	$100,000	$1,056,000
D.	$50,000	-0-	$100,000	$1,000,000

10. Which of the following is NOT typically a characteristic of debt securities?
    A. Voting rights
    B. Specified maturity date
    C. Specified maturity value
    D. Interest

11. Arc Welders Inc. began operations on January 1, 1997. As of December 31, 1997, the portfolio of Arc's investments in securities was:

	Trading Securities	Available-for-Sale Securities
Aggregate cost	$360,000	$550,000
Aggregate market value	320,000	450,000
Total market values, analyzing each security in the portfolio individually	304,000	420,000

If the market declines are judged to be temporary, what amounts should Arc Welders report as a loss on these securities in its December 31, 1997 financial income statement?

	Trading Securities	Available-for-Sale Securities
A.	$40,000	-0-
B.	-0-	$100,000
C.	$40,000	$100,000
D.	$56,000	$130,000

(AICPA adapted)

12. On April 1, 1997 Bennet purchased $200,000 face value, 9% U.S. Treasury Notes for $198,500, including accrued interest of $4,500. The notes mature July 1, 1998 and pay interest semiannually on January 1 and July 1. Bennet uses the straight-line method of amortization and intends to hold the notes until maturity. In its October 31, 1997 balance sheet, the carrying amount of this investment should be:
    A. $194,000.
    B. $196,800.
    C. $197,200.
    D. $199,000.

(AICPA adapted)

13. At December 31, 1997, Bank of Commerce had the following marketable equity securities, which were all purchased during 1997, its first year of operation:

	Cost	Market	Unrealized Gain (Loss)
Trading:			
Security A	$ 90,000	$60,000	$(30,000)
Security B	15,000	20,000	5,000
	$105,000	$80,000	$(25,000)
Available-for-Sale:			
Security XX	$ 70,000	$ 80,000	$ 10,000
Security UU	90,000	45,000	(45,000)
	$160,000	$125,000	$(35,000)

All market declines are considered temporary. In the 1997 financial statement, these amounts should be charged against:

	Income	Stockholders' Equity
A.	$60,000	$0
B.	$30,000	$45,000
C.	$25,000	$35,000
D.	$25,000	$0

(AICPA adapted)

14. Bum Steer Enterprises had investments in marketable debt securities costing $650,000 which were classified as available-for-sale. On June 30, 1997, Bum Steer decided to hold the investments until maturity and accordingly reclassified them from the available-for-sale category to the held-to-maturity category as of June 30, 1997. The investments' market value was $575,000 on December 31, 1996; $530,000 on June 30, 1997; and $490,000 on December 31, 1997. What amount of loss from investments should Bum Steer report in its 1997 income statement?
  A. $45,000
  B. $85,000
  C. $120,000
  D. $0

(AICPA adapted)

15. Bum Steer Enterprises had investments in marketable debt securities costing $650,000 which were classified as available-for-sale. On June 30, 1997, Bum Steer decided to hold the investments until maturity and accordingly reclassified them from the available-for-sale category to the held-to-maturity category as of June 30, 1997. The investments' market value was $575,000 on December 31, 1996; $530,000 on June 30, 1997; and $490,000 on December 31, 1997. What amount should Bum Steer report as net unrealized decrease in value on marketable debt securities in the equity section of its 1997 balance sheet?
  A. $40,000
  B. $45,000
  C. $160,000
  D. $120,000

(AICPA adapted)

16. Caribou Enterprises received a cash dividend from a common stock investment. Should Caribou report an increase in the investment account if it has classified the stock as available-for-sale or equity method?

	Available-for-Sale	Equity
A.	No	No
B.	Yes	Yes
C.	Yes	No
D.	No	Yes

(AICPA adapted)

Questions 17 through 19 are based on the following information:
Wyoming Traders acquired 30% of Rhode Island Mercantile's voting stock for $200,000 on January 2, 1996. Wyoming's 30% interest in Rhode Island gave Wyoming the ability to exercise significant influence over Rhode Island's operating activities and financial policies. During 1996, Rhode Island earned $80,000 and paid dividends of $50,000. Rhode Island reported earnings of $100,000 for the first six months of 1997, and $200,000 for the year ended December 31, 1997. On July 1, 1997, Wyoming sold half of its stock in Rhode Island for $150,000 cash. Rhode Island paid dividends of $60,000 on October 1, 1997.

17. Before income taxes, what amount should Wyoming Traders include in its 1996 income statement as a result of the investment?
  A. $15,000
  B. $24,000
  C. $50,000
  D. $80,000

(AICPA adapted)

18. In Wyoming Traders' December 31, 1996 balance sheet, what should be the carrying amount of this investment?
    A. $200,000
    B. $209,000
    C. $224,000
    D. $230,000 (AICPA adapted)

19. In its 1997 income statement, what amount should Wyoming Traders report as a gain from the sale of half of the investment?
    A. $24,500
    B. $30,500
    C. $35,000
    D. $45,500 (AICPA adapted)

20. (Expanded material) When the equity method is used to account for investments in common stock, which of the following affects the investor's reported investment income?

	Goodwill Amortization Related to Purchase	Cash Dividends From Investee
A.	Yes	Yes
B.	No	Yes
C.	No	No
D.	Yes	Yes

    (AICPA adapted)

21. (Expanded material) Northerland Company uses the equity method to account for its January 1, 1997 purchase of General Excavating's common stock. On January 1, 1997, the fair values of General Excavating's FIFO inventory and land exceeded their carrying amounts. How do these excesses of fair values over carrying amounts affect Northerland's reported equity in General Excavating's 1997 earnings?

	Inventory Excess	Land Excess
A.	Decrease	Decrease
B.	Decrease	No effect
C.	Increase	Increase
D.	Increase	No effect

    (AICPA adapted)

22. (Expanded material) On January 1, 1997, Sheridan purchased a 30% interest in Buffalo Company for $250,000. On this date, Buffalo's stockholders' equity was $500,000. The carrying amounts of Buffalo's identifiable net assets approximated their fair values, except for land whose fair value exceeded its carrying value by $200,000. Buffalo reported net income of $100,000 for 1997, and paid no dividends. Sheridan accounts for this investment using the equity method and amortizes goodwill over ten years. In its December 31, 1997 balance sheet, what amount should Sheridan report as an investment in Buffalo Company?
    A. $210,000
    B. $220,000
    C. $270,000
    D. $276,000 (AICPA adapted)

Exercises and Problems

1. Trading securities
   AAA Company purchased $100,000 of U. S. Treasury 8% bonds at 103.5, plus accrued interest of $2,500. In addition, AAA paid brokerage fees of $750. AAA classified the security as a trading security. One month later, AAA received a $4,000 interest payment from the issuer of the bond.

   Required: Record the purchase and subsequent receipt of the interest on AAA's books, assuming:
   1) AAA uses the revenue approach
   2) AAA uses the asset approach

Chapter 14

2. **Purchase of stock**

   On January 1, 1997, Douglas Company purchased 30% (15,000 shares) of Elmwood Machinery and Implement's common stock for $1,500,000 as a long-term investment. Elmwood's 1997 financial statements indicate:

Net income for 1997	$300,000
Less: dividends paid	160,000
Net increase in retained earnings	$140,000

   The market value of Elmwood's stock on December 31, 1997 was $97 per share.

   Required:
   1) Prepare the journal entries to record Douglas' investment in Elmwood during 1997 under:
      a) cost method
      b) equity method
   2) Compute the carrying value (investment balance) in Elmwood stock to be reported on the December 31, 1997 balance sheet of Douglas under:
      a) cost method
      b) equity method

3. **Purchase and sale of securities**

   ABC Company owns the following securities as of June 30, 1997:

Company	Classification	Cost	Market Value
XXX	Held-to-maturity	$10,000	$12,000
YYY	Trading	$10,000	$8,000
ZZZ	Available-for-sale	$10,000	$11,500

   The held-to-maturity securities are 10-year, 10% bonds. ABC purchased the bonds at par. Interest is accrued and received on June 30 and December 31 each year.

   During the fall of 1997, ABC entered into the following transactions:

August 1	Sold YYY securities for $8,500.
September 1	Sold ZZZ securities for $12,000.
December 1	Sold XXX securities for $12,000, plus accrued interest.
December 15	Purchased $40,000 of equity securities in AAA Company. Classified the securities as trading.
December 31	Fair market value of AAA securities is $40,000.

   Required: Record the transactions.

4. **Classification of securities**

   Connelly Company purchased various securities during 1997 to be classified as held-to-maturity securities, trading securities, or available-for-sale securities. The various securities are described below. Classify each security according to the appropriate category and write the answer in the space provided.

   _____ A. Debt securities bought and held for the purpose of selling in the near future.

   _____ B. U.S. Treasury bonds that Connelly has both the intention and the ability to hold until maturity.

   _____ C. $3 million debt security bought and held for the purpose of selling in three years to finance payment of Connelly's $2 million long-term note payable when it matures.

   _____ D. Convertible preferred stock that Connelly does not intend to sell in the near term.

   _____ E. Corporate bonds purchased with 8 months remaining until maturity. Connelly has the intent and the ability to hold until maturity.

_____ F. Municipal bonds with 5 years remaining until maturity. Connelly has the ability and intent to hold until maturity, but will likely sell the bonds if their tax status changes. (AICPA adapted)

5. Investments in securities
The following information pertains to Chadron Inc.'s portfolio of marketable investments for the year ended December 31, 1997:

	Cost	Fair Value, 12/31/96	1997 Activity Purchase	Sale	Fair value, 12/31/97
Held-to-maturity: Security ABC			$100,000		$95,000
Trading: Security DEF	$150,000	$160,000			$155,000
Available-for-Sale: Security GHI	$190,000	$165,000		$175,000	
Security JKL	$170,000	$175,000			$160,000

Required: Compute each of the following:
   A. Carrying amount of Security ABC at December 31, 1997.
   B. Carrying amount of Security DEF at December 31, 1997.
   C. Carrying amount of Security JKL at December 31, 1997.
   D. Recognized gain or loss on sale of Security GHI.
   E. Unrealized gain or loss to be reported in the 1997 income statement.
   F. Unrealized gain or loss to be reported at December 31, 1997, as a separate component of stockholders' equity. (AICPA adapted)

SOLUTIONS TO TEST YOUR UNDERSTANDING

Fill-in-the-blanks

1. equity securities; debt securities
2. debt securities
3. equity securities
4. Held-to-maturity securities
5. available-for-sale securities
6. trading securities
7. Equity method securities
8. decreases; increases
9. equity method; 20; 50
10. operating, investing, financing
11. control; operating, investing, financing
12. parent
13. subsidiary
14. consolidated financial statements

Multiple Choice

1. B
2. D
3. C
4. A
5. C
6. D
7. A
8. B
9. C
10. A
11. A
12. B
13. C
14. D
15. D
16. A
17. B
18. B
19. B
20. D
21. B
22. D

Exercises and Problems

1. Trading securities
   1) <u>Revenue Approach</u>

Investment in Trading Securities	104,250 *	
Interest Revenue	2,500 **	
Cash		106,750

   [* ($100,000 x 1.035) + $750 = $104,250;
   ** interest accrued at the time of the purchase]

Cash	4,000	
Interest Revenue***		4,000

   [*** note, the balance in interest revenue account is $1,500, which represents the amount of interest AAA has earned by holding this security this amount of time.]

   2) <u>Asset Approach</u>

Investment in Trading Securities	104,250	
Interest Receivable	2,500	
Cash		106,750

Cash	4,000	
Interest Revenue		1,500
Interest Receivable		2,500

2. Purchase of stock
   1) <u>Cost Method</u>

Investment in Available-for-Sale Securities—Elmwood	1,500,000	
Cash		1,500,000

Cash ($160,000 x .30)	48,000	
Dividend Revenue		48,000

Unrealized Decrease in Value of Available-for-Sale Securities (15,000 x $3)*	45,000	
Market Adjustment—Available-for-Sale Securities**		45,000

   [* This account appears in the equity section of the balance sheet.]
   [**This account appears as a contra asset to the Investment account in the noncurrent section of the asset side of the balance sheet.]

Equity Method

Investment in Elmwood Machinery and Implement	1,500,000	
Cash		1,500,000
Cash	48,000	
Investment in Elmwood		48,000
Investment in Elmwood ($300,000 x .30)	90,000	
Income from Investment in Elmwood stock		90,000

2) Carrying Value (Investment Balance)
    Cost Method: $1,500,000 - 45,000 = $1,455,000
    Equity Method: $1,500,000 - 48,000 + 90,000 = $1,542,000

3. Purchase and sale of securities

Aug. 1	Cash		8,500	
	Loss on Sale of Securities		1,500	
	Investment in Trading Securities			10,000
Sept. 1	Cash		12,000	
	Gain on Sales of Securities			2,000
	Investment in Available-for-Sale Securities			10,000
Dec. 1	Cash		12,500	
	Interest Revenue			500
	Investment in Held-to-Maturity Securities			10,000
	Gain on Sale of Securities			2,000
Dec. 15	Investment in Trading Securities		40,000	
	Cash			40,000
Dec. 31	Market Adjustment—Trading		2,000	
	Unrealized Loss on Trading Securities			2,000
	Adjust market adjustment account for YYY.			
	Unrealized Increased in Value of Available-for-Sale Securities		1,500	
	Market Adjustment—Available-for-Sale Securities			1,500
	Adjust market adjustment account for ZZZ.			

4. Classification of securities
    A. Trading
    B. Held-to-maturity
    C. Available-for-sale
    D. Available-for-sale
    E. Held-to-maturity
    F. Held-to-maturity

5. Investments in securities
   A. $100,000
   B. $155,000
   C. $160,000
   D. Loss: $15,000
   E. Loss: $5,000
   F. Loss: $10,000